LAWYER'S
CONCISE GUIDE
TO TRIAL
PROCEDURE

LAWYER'S CONCISE GUIDE TO TRIAL PROCEDURE

MARSHALL J. JOX

Prentice-Hall, Inc.
Englewood Cliffs, N.J.

Library of Congress
Catalog Card Number: 65–19556

Second printing . . . . February, 1969

Printed in the United States of America

B&P 52695

The Purpose of this Book

The trial of a lawsuit is a complicated process; many factors may influence the result. Every trial lawyer is convinced at times that the result of a given trial is not in accord with his conception of the merits of the case. It must be acknowledged that some of these factors may be beyond the control of counsel, and to that extent he is, of course, not responsible for the outcome. Nevertheless it is a fact that usually counsel can, by his skill, affect the final determination of a case. *The basic purpose of this volume is to assist the trial lawyer in the development of such skill.*

First of all, adequate client-representation involves a thorough knowledge of the statutes, rules, and decisions which govern practically every step of the trial. No attempt is made to include all the procedural rules found in all jurisdictions. However, every major problem area in litigation is considered, typical cases are cited, and reference is made to secondary authorities for fuller discussion. Where necessary, a brief statement of the history and purpose of a rule is included.

This volume therefore provides something in the way of a check-list of matters to investigate, and should enable the attorney to find more easily the local material in practice books, digests, statutory compilations, etc. This comprehensive scope and detailed treatment is valuable even to the seasoned and busy trial practitioner.

Reference is made throughout the volume to variations in practice found in the different jurisdictions, rather than to the practice of only one jurisdiction so that the volume may assist the practicing attorney no matter where he practices. The treatment of a problem in other jurisdictions may give direction to its solution in one's own jurisdiction. The bench and bar of no one state have a monopoly on ingenuity and good sense.

Because the law governing trials is in a constant state of flux, the reader is admonished to verify any statement by reference to the latest material from his own jurisdiction. The emphasis here is upon current practice, with only such excursions into the past as are necessary to present the historical development of a particular point.

Second, and equally important, adequate client-representation involves a knowledge of, and sensitivity to, many matters not covered by the rules. It is necessary to know, not only how to avoid making mistakes and how to avoid the harmful consequences of past mistakes, but also whether, how, and when to take advantage of the mistakes of your adversary. Beyond this lies a vast area of permissible activity, and counsel must always be prepared to choose that approach which best furthers the interest of his client.

To alert the trial lawyer to the possibilities inherent in a given situation, *this volume contains suggestions applicable to all stages of the trial.* These suggestions are based on the experience of representative trial lawyers from various sections of the country. Their generous responses to the author's requests are hereby gratefully acknowledged.

Illustrative forms have been omitted as they are usually appropriate only for a particular jurisdiction. However, a detailed table of contents and an index are included.

Marshall J. Jox

Table
of Contents

LAWYER'S CONCISE GUIDE TO TRIAL PROCEDURE

Chapter 1

Pre-Trial Procedures

SECTION 1. STATEMENTS OF CLIENT AND WITNESSES. It is a matter of common knowledge among attorneys that many meritorious cases are lost because of inadequate preparation for trial. This chapter discusses briefly some of the most common steps that should be taken to assure an adequate presentation of a case on its merits.

During the initial interview written statements of the client and witnesses should be obtained. These statements should contain a summary of the interview and should be read and signed by the person being interviewed. The statement may be prepared from notes taken by the attorney or by his stenographer. Ordinarily a copy of the statement is not given to the person interviewed. Because such statements are helpful for refreshing recollection of the witness and the attorney, or for possible impeachment purposes, it is imperative that they be obtained as soon as possible.

Similarly, it is advisable to record the essence of any telephone conversations.

SECTION 2. INVESTIGATION SUBSEQUENT TO INITIAL INTERVIEWS. The attorney should not accept as accurate the client's version of the event. This does not imply that clients will normally knowingly misrepresent the facts. It does imply, however, that, due to an emotional involvement, unfavorable elements may be unwittingly overlooked.

Subsequent investigations of the circumstances should include possible grounds of impeachment of your client or his witnesses. The circumstances of the particular case will usually determine possible sources of information; it may be noted, however, that public records of many kinds contain a wealth of information about individuals. Similarly, if it is known what persons will be called as witnesses by the adverse party, the background of such persons should be investigated with a view to possible impeachment.

SECTION 3. EXPERTS. Where some aspect of a case is beyond the usual lay experience, it is necessary to rely upon a person with specialized training and experience, the expert, to establish a given proposition. Thus, in a personal injury action, medical testimony must be elicited as to the question of causation and permanency of the injury. The role of an expert as a witness is quite common. It is less common, but equally important, to rely upon the expert as an advisor. The expert can assist the attorney in many ways other than that of establishing a proposition; in fact, he may even assist him in developing the theory of the case.

Enlisting the aid of an expert may involve a number of problems. Perhaps the foremost of these problems is that of communication. The expert speaks one language, the attorney, judge and jury another. It thus becomes necessary for the attorney to acquaint himself to the extent possible with the terms, the theories and the approaches of the expert. On the other hand, the expert must be led to translate these matters at the trial so that the triers will understand the expert's testimony.

The testimony of an expert will normally be in the form of an opinion. An opinion is usually admissible only if the court is satisfied that the witness is an expert. Whether the witness is an expert is determined by his training and experience. The attorney must therefore know before trial, and bring out at the trial, the nature of such training and experience. This should be done even where opposing counsel is willing to acknowledge that the witness is an expert, for the judge and jury must be made aware of the witness's qualifications.

The expert's opinion may be based upon the evidence which the expert has heard, or upon facts stated in a hypothetical question. Since the expert normally will not be present in court during the entire presentation of the case, the hypothetical question device is the most common. This question must be carefully prepared, as it must contain all the facts introduced in evidence upon which the opinion is based. At the same time the question should be kept as short as possible, lest it confuse the jury and be open to objection. A rough draft of the question may be prepared, with the cooperation of the expert, in advance of trial, and a notation made of any law supporting the form of the question and answer. If the expert has made any notes during his examination or experimentation, it is well to advise him to bring them to court for purposes of refreshing recollection. Also, the impact of the expert's testimony is greater if it is supported by charts, drawings, etc. Many experts, particularly members of the medical profession are reluctant to appear in court and testify. This problem is aggravated when a case is venued to another county. Frequently this reluctance may be overcome by arranging a fairly precise time for the expert's appearance in court. This may involve calling an expert not in logical sequence. Also, it is usually necessary to compensate experts adequately for court appearances, and to advance such compensation prior to final settlement of the case. If the testimony of a particular expert is desired, and he is unwilling to appear during the trial, it is advisable to take his deposition. This procedure is discussed in a subsequent section.

Occasionally the matter of selecting an expert presents a problem. In the event medical testimony is required, greater latitude is allowed in examining the witness where he is the treating physician and is familiar with the pre-accident condition of the plaintiff. Also, it is usually not necessary to use a hypothetical question where the expert is the treating physician. Further, the treating physician is less subject to attack in final argument. At the same time a treating physician may be a poor witness because of inability to communicate or to stand up under a withering cross-examination. The qualifications of the expert must also be taken into consideration in deciding what expert to call.

SECTION 4. SUBPOENAES. If a prospective witness is within the jurisdiction, it is advisable to serve him with a subpoena as soon as the trial date becomes known. This applies to witnesses that are presumably friendly to the client as well as those known to be unfriendly. It may be necessary under the rules to tender the witness fees and expenses at the time the subpoena is served. Occasionally the service of the subpoena will generate hostility on the part of the witness. In that event it may be necessary to explain that the attorney's duty to the client demands such action; that continuances because of absence of witnesses are generally not granted unless the attorney can show that he did everything possible to secure the attendance of such witnesses.

If a witness is to testify to the contents of a particular document, he may be compelled to produce the document in court by means of a subpoena duces tecum. Where the witness is an employee of a corporation the subpoena should name the person to be served.

Where a witness is not within the jurisdiction, it is advisable to take his deposition, provided the same can be introduced in evidence in the event the witness does not testify in person.

SECTION 5. DISCOVERY DEVICES. In the federal courts and in a number of state courts, it is now possible to take depositions, after an action has been filed, for the purpose of discovery as well as for use as evidence or for impeachment purposes.[1] By means of this device it is frequently possible to ascertain in advance of trial the nature and purport of the opponent's proof. Statutes and rules must be consulted to determine the allowable scope and the procedure to be followed.[2]

Where the rules are broad and liberal, tactical problems remain. For example, while depositions by written interrogatories and answers are much less costly than those involving oral questions and answers, the former are not nearly as searching. The cost of an oral deposition depends in large part upon its length. In some cases, part or all of the cost may be assessed against the other party.[3] Depositions may, under certain conditions, be used by the adverse party. Also since opposing counsel is usually present during the taking of a deposition, this procedure prematurely "tips one's hand." Occasionally the taking of depositions will cause the other side to retaliate in kind. Finally, the taking of a deposition may constitute a waiver of the right to attack the competency or credibility of the witness.

Prior to the taking of depositions of your own client or witness, have a conference with him, along the lines suggested in Section 1. The direct examination of the opposing party or witnesses may be conducted as on the trial proper. The cross-examination probably will be comprehensive only if the witness is unlikely to be available at the trial. Objections as to substance are rarely made, and when made, are usually ruled upon by the court and not by the official before whom the deposition is taken.

Written interrogatories addressed to the adverse party are, where permitted in the jurisdiction, useful if limited to a few key issues.[4] Written interrogatories are less effective than depositions,

---

[1] Fed. R. Civ. P. 26 (a); 94 A.L.R. 2d 1172.

[2] Id. 26 (b); Id. 30 (b), (d), 31 (d); 70 A.L.R. 2d 685.

[3] Hope Basket Co. v. Product Advancement Co., 104 Fed. Supp. 444; 76 A.L.R. 2d 953.

[4] Fed. R. Civ. P. 33; 72 A.L.R. 2d 431; 74 Id. 534; 88 Id. 657; 96 Id. 598.

as the answers thereto are generally framed by counsel for the adverse party. In some jurisdictions answers to interrogatories are admissible in evidence. Each interrogatory should be unambiguous and addressed to but a single issue.

Requests for admissions may be used to obviate proof of matters that cannot be disputed, but which proof would lengthen the trial.[5] Stipulations may often be used for the same purpose. The authenticity of documents is frequently conceded in one of these ways.

In some jurisdictions a physical examination of the plaintiff may be requested by the defendant.[6] Usually counsel for the plaintiff is provided with a copy of the medical report.

In a proper case the right to inspect and copy documents in the possession of the adverse party, or to examine certain premises or chattels, may be requested.[7]

A motion for summary judgment may, to a limited extent, be considered to be a discovery device, in that it compels the adverse party to produce evidence to prevent the granting of the motion. However, the moving party is required to disclose his proof in order to make a prima facie showing.

SECTION 6. PRE-TRIAL CONFERENCES. In a number of jurisdictions, provision is made by statute or rule for a more-or-less formal conference of opposing counsel and a judge. In some jurisdictions such conferences are held as a matter of course,[8] in others only when the court so orders,[9] and in still others when requested by counsel.[10] In some courts all cases are subject to such conference, in other courts the conference is used only in select types of cases.

---

[5] Fed. R. Civ. P. 36 (a); 36 A.L.R. 2d 1192; 93 Id. 757.

[6] Fed. R. Civ. P. 35; 164 A.L.R. 967; 25 A.L.R. 2d 1407; 36 Id. 946; 62 Id. 1291; 64 Id. 497; 70 Id. 384; 71 Id. 973; 89 Id. 1001.

[7] Fed. R. Civ. P. 34; 13 A.L.R. 2d 657; 23 Id. 862; 70 Id. 240; 74 Id. 876; 83 Id. 302; 84 Id. 1261; 95 Id. 1061; 95 Id. 1084.

[8] 2 A.L.R. 2d 1061.

[9] Id. 16.

[10] e.g., Ind. Sup. Ct. R. 1–4.

The primary purpose of such conferences is to shorten the trial time, but a secondary purpose is to encourage settlement. In some courts most conferences lead to a settlement, so that only few cases are actually tried. Various matters designed to accomplish such purposes are to be considered at such conferences, such as ways of simplifying the issues and eliminating the necessity of proof.

Where counsel is to participate in such conference, he should be as fully prepared as to the facts and the law as when going to trial. The specific items involved in such preparation are discussed in several sections of this chapter. He should also know what settlement will be satisfactory to the client. The conference is not likely to accomplish much unless counsel is willing to be frank about the weak elements of his client's cause of action or defense. The same attorneys who are to conduct the trial should participate in the conference.

The timing of such conference depends upon the purposes to be accomplished. Thus, if the primary purpose is to limit discovery, a conference should be held as soon as counsel has become familiar with the facts and the law. In a complicated case it may be necessary to hold several conferences, the last one shortly before trial.

SECTION 7. NOTICE, DEMAND, TENDER. In a limited number of situations, such as in suits against a municipal corporation, statutes require a notice of claim to be filed prior to bringing suit.[11] If such notice is not served the action may be dismissed. Similarly in certain types of cases a demand must be made of the opposing party, as where there has been a good faith conversion.[12] Or, a tender of consideration received may be necessary before rescission of a contract may be had.[13]

---

11 McIntee v. Middletown, 80 App. Div. 434, 81 N.Y.S. 124; 18 McQuillin, Mun. Corp. § 53.151, 3rd ed.

12 Southward v. Joy, 65 Nev. 694, 201 P. 2d 302; Prosser, Torts, 90, 3rd ed.

13 E.T.C. Corp. v. Title Guar. & Trust Co., 271 N.Y. 659, 3 N.E. 2d 471; 5 Corbin, Contracts, § 1103.

SECTION 8. EXHIBITS. If the case involves documentary evidence, the documents should be placed in the order in which they are to be introduced. If the documents are numerous, they should also be summarized and indexed. Wherever possible, stipulations as to authenticity should be entered into. If originals are in the possession of the adverse party, a notice to produce should be served upon him, in order to lay a basis for introduction of copies. If identification is to be by witnesses, the procedure for doing so should be reviewed with those witnesses.

SECTION 9. VISUAL AIDS. Testimony of witnesses may frequently be clarified or supplemented by photographs, slides, moving pictures, X-ray film, charts, maps, or models. Whenever possible, such visual aids should be admissable into evidence. For that reason the use of billboard or drawing paper is preferred over a blackboard. If a blackboard is used, a photograph thereof may be made and offered into evidence. No matter what form of visual aid is used, it must be shown to authentically portray that which it purports to portray.[14] Further, it must be shown that conditions at the time the visual aid was prepared were the same as those prevailing at the legally significant time.[15] Unless the item is large enough to be seen by all in the courtroom, its value is greatly limited.

Each type of visual aid presents a peculiar problem of authentication. Thus, where photographs of any kind are to be used, the person taking the photographs is the most helpful witness. He can explain when and under what conditions the photograph was taken, the type of equipment used, the method used in taking the photograph, how he is able to identify the scene or person shown, and why he is able to state that no distortion exists. It is common practice to include some landmark in the photograph in the accident scene. If the person taking the photograph is not available,

---

[14] Oklahoma City v. Lycan, 193 Okla. 170, 141 P. 2d 1013; McCormick, Evidence, 387.

[15] Edelson v. Higgins, 43 Cal. App. 2d 759, 111 P. 2d 668.

under certain conditions his deposition may be used, and one familiar with the object photographed can be used to vouch for the photograph's authenticity.

Charts and diagrams should ordinarily be drawn to scale by one familiar with the scene or object being portrayed. Occasionally a witness can add to the basic items when testifying. In highway accident cases cut-out models of cars or toy cars may be used to indicate positions of the various vehicles at different intervals.

Attorneys who make extensive use of visual aids in personal injury actions report that their use assists counsel to keep the attention of the jury as evidence is introduced. This seems to be particularly true with reference to the evidence of witnesses who have difficulty in expressing themselves. Also, visual aids may be effectively used during final arguments. Visual aids are of course more effective in those jurisdictions where such aids may be taken into the jury room.[16] Partially as a result of such devices verdicts in excess of anticipated amounts are not uncommon.

Care must be exercised lest the visual aid used contain some unnoticed prejudicial item. Thus, a photograph used to show the nature and extent of damages to a car, may be used by the jury to infer speed or force of impact.

Many attorneys indicate a reluctance to make use of court-room demonstrations, even where permitted by the court, because of the uncertainty as to the result. The court may prohibit a demonstration where it believes it would be prejudicial to the adverse party.

SECTION 10. TRIAL BRIEFS. A rule of court may indicate in what situations a court and opposing counsel should be furnished with a trial brief.[17] Even in the absence of such a requirement, the preparation of such a brief will prove to be of genuine value to counsel. A good brief assists in adequate preparation for trial. The

---

16 Sinz v. Owens, 33 Cal. 2d 749, 205 P. 2d 3 (X-ray Picture); 10 A.L.R. 2d 918.
17 86 A.L.R. 2d 1233.

brief may also facilitate settlement, especially where the case is rather complicated, such as anti-trust or stockholders' suits.

The preparation of a trial brief can begin as soon as the facts have been investigated and the law researched. The form and content of a brief, unless laid down by a rule, will vary somewhat from case to case. The brief may contain some or all of the following elements:

1. A summary of the facts as they will be presented at the trial. What facts will be presented will depend upon the legal theory selected. A summary of this kind will be found helpful in preparing an opening statement.

2. An analysis of the pleadings and a statement of the issues. This section should indicate points which are necessary to prove or disprove.

3. A synopsis of the testimony of each witness, in the order in which the witnesses will be called.

4. Citations of law pertinent to anticipated objections to your evidence. Such citations can reduce the length of recesses to research questions during the trial.

5. A statement of the issues of law with appropriate citations. If the citations are to cases, they should be limited in number and should summarize the facts to show that they are pertinent. This section of the brief can be helpful in preparing instructions.

6. A summary of the documentary and physical evidence to be introduced, indicating when and how this is to be done.

SECTION 11. INSTRUCTIONS. It is usually possible to prepare instructions on the most basic issues in advance of trial at least in skeletal form. Usually adequate time for this step is not presented after the evidence is in and the case is ready for submission to the jury.

SECTION 12. FINAL INTERVIEW WITH CLIENT AND WITNESSES. Many persons have not had the experience of testifying in court. Hence it is important that they be informed as to the procedure usually followed. Timid persons may be advised to visit a court-room prior to trial and observe how a trial is conducted. Since the time element between an occurrence and a trial based thereon is frequently quite lengthy, it is advisable to review the facts, step by step. In fact, some attorneys ask a series of questions just as they would be asked during the trial. By means of such review it may be possible to ascertain when a friendly witness has become hostile, and then to establish the point by some other witness. Statements taken during the initial conference can be used for this purpose. The need for such careful review can be demonstrated by first asking the witness what he recalls of the incident. There will usually be a considerable deviation from the original statement.

It is extremely important that the witness be prepared for a searching cross-examination. This again may be done by asking a series of questions, in as harsh and vicious a manner as possible. The witness can then be informed that in all probability opposing counsel will not engage in such tactics. Among the questions he should be advised to answer truthfully are the following: "Have you discussed the case with anyone?" "Were you subpoenaed to be here or did you come voluntarily?" "Are you being paid for your testimony?" The witness should be informed as to the points the opposition will try to establish on cross-examination.

The background of the witness should be reviewed, and any possible impeachment techniques considered, as well as methods of rehabilitation that could be used.

It is sometimes necessary to advise a witness how to dress and how to conduct himself in court; to answer no question before it is completed, and to volunteer no information; that if a question is not clear, to so state; that if the answer is not known for any reason, to admit that fact. The witness should pause long enough before answering that counsel may interpose an objection. The witness should be advised how to answer leading questions so as not to leave the wrong impression. It may be helpful to point out that counsel conducting the direct examination will object when the cross examination goes beyond the bounds of reasonableness; that when an objection is made, the witness should not answer until the court has ruled thereon. The witness may be informed that counsel sometimes employ baiting tactics to arouse the ire of the witness, and that the witness should not lose his temper when such tactics are used. Also, the witness may be informed that the opposite tactic, namely flattery, may be used to entrap him. These tactics should be illustrated so that the witness recognizes them for what they are.

The above suggestions are not intended to imply that counsel should inform the witnesses to conceal damaging facts or to create facts to fit a certain theory. Such conduct would clearly violate the canons of ethics. To be sure that no impression will be left that counsel has used such techniques, it may be well to remind the witnesses that they will be under oath and that they should answer the questions in their own words.

Some attorneys make it a point not to inform key witnesses that they are such, lest they be unduly concerned about cross-examination and reluctant to testify.

Where testimony is likely to involve considerable detail, witnesses should be reminded to bring to court any notes they may have made, for purpose of refreshing recollection.

SECTION 13. CONTINUANCES. In some courts the procedure for obtaining a continuance, as well as the grounds therefore, is governed by a general or local rule. Where this is not the case, the granting of a continuance is largely within the discretion of the trial court.[18] In some courts continuances are rarely granted, in others the grant is dependent upon a showing of good cause, and in still others requests are granted without such a showing.

Many attorneys indicate that they rarely request a continuance. This is because such a request may be interpreted by the

---

[18] 47 A.L.R. 2d 1058; 48 Id. 1156; 49 Id. 1073; 67 Id. 497; 68 Id. 470; 68 Id. 540.

opposition as a sign of weakness. Also, such request may be unfavorably viewed by the court. Where such request is made, it is usually made as soon as the reason therefore becomes apparent. Some of the more common grounds are: Inability of counsel or a key witness to be present, surprise or newly discovered evidence.

It is customary to notify opposing counsel that such a request will be made, especially if made before the trial date.

If a denial of a request for a continuance is to be made one of the bases for an appeal, usually the request must be made in writing, stating the grounds therefore and that counsel exercised due diligence.[19] If the grounds are that one or more witnesses cannot be present, it is usually necessary to state in essence what his testimony will be.[20] It may also be necessary to affix an affidavit as to the reason why the witnesses cannot be present. If counsel does not know until the trial date that the witnesses will not appear, it is advisable to show that subpoenaes have been issued.

Where the motion is based upon the inability of a witness to be present, opposing counsel may be able to defeat the motion by admitting that the witness would testify as indicated.

In determining whether to request a continuance, counsel must consider not only whether probable grounds exist, but whether the reason for the continuance will have been removed at some future trial date; what the probable result would be, and the procedure to be followed, in the event the request is denied; what the probable effect would be if the request is granted, such as having the case tried by a different jury or assigned to a different judge; and how continuance would affect a favorable settlement. In short, a continuance should be requested only if the best interests of the client would be served by such a request.

SECTION 14. CHANGE OF VENUE OR CHANGE OF JUDGE. In most

---

19 Ladson v. Gaskins, 30 Ga. App. 676, 118 S.E. 765; 67 A.L.R. 2d 504.
20 Gall v. New York & New Brunswick Auto Express Co., 131 N.J. Law 346, 36 A. 2d 403; 17 C.J.S. Continuances § 94 (4).

jurisdictions statutes or rules specify how and when, and under what circumstances a change of venue or change of judge may be obtained.[21] Generally such change is obtained by motion addressed to the judge to whom the case is assigned. An affidavit stating the grounds for the motion is commonly required, as is notice to opposing counsel. The grounds usually specified involve the improbability of a fair and impartial trial due to such matters as improper publicity in the case, local prejudice, and the like.

Generally, verdicts in rural communities are smaller than those in urban centers. As this fact is not a ground for a change of venue, it should be considered in the original selection of a place of trial.

Assuming that proper grounds for a change exist, counsel must still determine whether it is advantageous to his client to request a change. It is possible that a change may involve conditions even more adverse to the client. Some attorneys regularly use this device merely for purposes of delay, but it is questioned whether this tactic can be approved.

SECTION 15. SEPARATION OF WITNESSES. Statutes or rules frequently contain provisions regarding separation of witnesses.[22] Where separation is allowed, the practice varies. Some attorneys regularly request a separation, others rarely do so. Some attorneys request a separation only in certain types of cases, as criminal prosecutions, contested divorce actions, claims against an estate and personal injury actions. Other attorneys use this device only at the time when depositions are taken, and the depositions are then used for impeachment purposes if a witness changes his testimony at the trial.

Parties and officers of corporations are normally not included in any order of separation. As stated earlier, experts are sometimes

---

21 Howard v. Ware, 192 Miss. 36, 3 So. 2d 830; 56 Am. Jur. Venue § 42.

22 Anderson v. Putnam County Beer Board, 184 Tenn. 623, 201 S.W. 2d 994; 88 C.J.S. Trials § 65.

allowed to hear all the testimony.[23] Parties generally remain in court during the entire trial, to confer with counsel, and corporate officers occupy the same position as parties.

Witnesses excluded from the courtroom while another witness is being examined should be placed in the custody of the bailiff, to prevent communication with one another outside the courtroom.

A separation of witnesses may be requested where there is a considerable disparity between the number of witnesses on one side and those on the other side; where collusion between parties is anticipated; when it appears from statements taken that the evidence is likely to be conflicting; when it is anticipated that the adverse party will lead off with a strong witness who will set the stage for the other witnesses; or when it is expected to subject opposing witnesses to a rigorous cross-examination. By the same token, separation may be opposed where it is expected that opposing counsel will exaggerate and dwell upon minor variations in the testimony given by witnesses for the party opposing separation.

SECTION 16. ORDER OF CALLING WITNESSES. There is no uniform rule as to the order in which witnesses are called upon to give testimony. This is due to the almost infinite variety of circumstances. However, certain generalizations may be made. Other things being equal, as an ideal, evidence should be introduced in natural, chronological or logical order. If the pleadings are quite detailed, they may be used as a guide. Also, the rules of evidence specify in what situations it is necessary to lay a foundation before other evidence is admissible. In practice, however, this ideal can rarely be followed.

In the first place, the convenience of witnesses, especially that of experts, must be considered. As suggested above, it is generally an inducement to an expert to testify if he knows precisely when he will be called.

---

[23] 85 A.L.R. 2d 478.

Secondly, not all witnesses are equally effective. Hence some attorneys lead off with a "strong" witness, follow with witnesses not as effective, and close with the "strongest" witness. Other attorneys call all the "weaker" witnesses first and save the "stronger" ones until the last. A witness may be effective because of the convincing manner in which he testifies, or because he obviously has no interest in the outcome of the case.

Thirdly, trials frequently take unexpected turns. Thus, if a witness testifies other than as anticipated, it is frequently advisable to then call a witness to counteract the surprise testimony.

Fourthly, the client's testimony often can be said to serve as a foundation for other testimony, so that he would normally testify first. However, if the client testifies last, he has the benefit of hearing the other testimony. It may thus be possible for him to explain any apparent conflict in the testimony of other witnesses and to relate the occurrence in a more coherent fashion.

Where the practice is allowed by rule or statute some attorneys representing plaintiffs will at the outset call the defendant as an adverse witness.[24] This practice is deemed to be helpful to the plaintiff especially if a case is set for trial upon short notice. The defendant, being poorly prepared, will not present his defense in the most effective manner. Also, this practice allows the plaintiff to rebut the defendant's testimony at an early stage in the trial, when the jurors are presumably more alert. If the plaintiff calls the defendant as an adverse witness, he should be cross-examined at that time, to reduce the effectiveness of the plaintiff's tactic.

SECTION 17. OVERCOMING MAJOR OBSTACLES. Some of the obstacles encountered in the trial of lawsuits are due to the tactics of opposing counsel, and others are inherent in the judicial process. These obstacles vary from jurisdiction to jurisdiction, and even from court to court. Also, what will be considered an obstacle

---

24 Ex parte American Life Ins. Co., 262 Ala. 543, 80 So. 2d 299; 97 C.J.S. Witnesses § 15.

depends upon what party counsel is representing. In this section reference will be made to what are believed to be typical problems encountered in day-to-day trial work.

Many plaintiff's lawyers point out that inordinate delaying tactics of the opposition constitute their major problems. Such tactics may involve requesting continuances or changes of venue, attacks upon the pleadings, taking depositions or submitting interrogatories. These moves can sometimes be met by showing that a fair trial can be had here and now, and that the result would not be different if a deferment or change were granted; by preparing pleadings so carefully that they will be impervious to attack; by pressing for early hearing of motions; and by retaliating in kind where an excessive number of depositions are taken. In any event, tactics designed solely to delay the final disposition of a cause can be exposed as such.

The success of any such counter-moves will be reduced if defendant's attorneys are employed on a per diem basis while plaintiff's attorneys, sole practitioners, are employed on a contingent fee basis, and if only a few large firms usually represent defendants in the community. In the former instance defendant's attorneys stand to gain by frequent court appearances while fees of plaintiff's attorneys remain the same; in the latter instance the fact that defendant's counsel is engaged in another trial may be deemed an adequate cause for postponement.

Other plaintiff's attorneys report that they encounter a general unwillingness of defendants to discuss settlement, despite the merits of the claim, until the trial is under way. Such unwillingness can be countered, however, by use of the discovery devices, and by insisting upon a pre-trial conference.

On the other hand, many attorneys representing defendants state that plaintiffs tend to exaggerate their injuries or the facts surrounding an accident. Accordingly, such attorneys rely heavily upon discovery techniques, particularly physical examinations of plaintiffs and upon medical testimony. In such cases plaintiff's attorneys corroborate the plaintiff's testimony by the testimony of disinterested witnesses.

The plaintiff's attorney may be expected to introduce an excessive amount of detailed medical testimony and medical devices such as traction apparatus and cervical collars, to show the "horrifying" nature of the injury and thus to capitalize upon the sympathy of the jury. If so, a proper conditioning of the jury on voir dire, plus an effective cross examination and summation will go far to avoid a verdict based solely upon sympathy. Where possible, counsel for defendant should, in such cases, emphasize the liability aspect throughout the trial.

In smaller communities, where parties or witnesses are frequently known to the members of the jury, it is possible to discredit such parties or witnesses by mere innuendo. While such tactics are admittedly difficult to counteract, every effort should be made to select those witnesses least subject to attack, and to suggest that the witnesses called have testified truthfully, regardless of reputation in unrelated areas.

The mobility of our population may create problems for either side. The whereabouts of key witnesses may be unknown at the time of the trial. Where it is anticipated that such a situation may be presented, depositions may be taken to perpetuate testimony.

Quite frequently a case may involve so many technicalities that the jury is likely to overlook some of the important elements. For example, early in the case the plaintiff may testify only briefly as to his injuries. No objection is made by defendant for fear of emphasizing this testimony. The case does not go to the jury until several days after this testimony has been given. In such a situation counsel for plaintiff should in his closing argument stress the important facts which were presented very rapidly during the trial.

Chapter 2

Trial by Jury
or to the Court?

SECTION 18. RIGHT TO JURY TRIAL. At common law, issues of fact in equity cases were determined by the chancellor, while issues of fact in law cases were determined by the jury. All state constitutions, as well as the federal constitution, make some reference to the right of trial by jury, and in most states there is further statutory supplementation.[1] There is considerable variation as to the approach used in specifying when such right exists. In some jurisdictions the right is preserved in those cases in which the right existed at a particular time,[2] while in others the types of cases triable by jury are spelled out.[3] Regardless of the approach used, the cases generally hold that the right of trial by jury is preserved in those cases in which the right existed at common law —that is, reference is made to the situation as it was at the time the constitution was adopted.[4] In a doubtful case, therefore, it is necessary to go back to such early cases.

---

1 Blume, American Civil Procedure, § 9—01.
2 Matter of Leary, 175 Misc. 254, 23 N.Y.S. 2d 13.
3 Hamilton v. Hamilton, 59 Mo. 232.
4 Note, "The Right to Jury Trial under Merged Procedures," 65 Harv. L. Rev. 453; 33 A.L.R. 2d 1145.

In equity cases a chancellor occasionally directed that a jury be impaneled to decide a vexing issue of fact, but the verdict in such cases was advisory only.[5] Hence no further reference is made in this section to this practice.

A statute may usually confer a right of trial by jury in cases where none existed at common law, as in will contests[6] or workmen's compensation cases.[7] However, a statute generally may not take away a right of trial by jury where such right existed at common law unless the statute abolishes the cause of action completely.[8]

SECTION 19. WAIVER OF JURY TRIAL. Constitutional and statutory provisions preserving the right of trial by jury have not been considered as compelling the parties to try their case with a jury if they do not wish to. Consequently there are early nineteenth century cases in which the parties agreed to have fact issues in law cases determined by the court. However, in the absence of statutory authorization for such practice, serious questions arose as to its validity. In addition to the problem involving the jurisdiction of the court to try fact issues, there were these questions: Should the rules of evidence, which were developed in jury cases, be applied to non-jury cases? What would be the scope of appellate review—would findings of fact, or only rulings of law be reviewable? How would questions of law be raised and preserved?

In the middle of the nineteenth century, legislation began to appear which provided for a legal trial by expressly permitting the judge to try fact questions when a jury was waived, or conferring such power by implication from the fact of waiver. Other problems were either expressly referred to by such legislation, or it was assumed that the techniques of the jury trial would be carried over to the trial by court to the extent possible.

---

5 Norris v. Moody, 120 Me. 151, 113 A. 24.

6 Simes, "The Function of Will Contests," 44 Mich. L.R. 503.

7 Busch, Trial Procedure Materials, § 23; L.R.A. 1917 D 51, 56.

8 Application of Smith, 381 Pa. 223, 112 A. 2d 625.

Early legislation provided that a jury trial could be waived by expressly consenting to a trial by court, either orally or in writing.[9] In some jurisdictions such provisions are still applicable, but there is a conflict as to whether the methods set out are exclusive. In those jurisdictions where the statutory modes of waiver are deemed to be exclusive,[10] and an express consent is required, a defendant has an opportunity to obtain a reversal and a new trial where no such express consent was given. On the other hand, it may be fairer to the trial court to require such consent as it does simplify the drawing up of the calendar.

In those jurisdictions where the statutory modes of waiver are not deemed to be exclusive, and where such consent may be implied,[11] difficult questions arise as to what constitutes such waiver; as for example, where both sides move for a directed verdict, or where there was a waiver in a first trial but not in the second, or where there has been a failure to appear at the trial. It is generally held that a court may order a jury trial despite a waiver thereof by the parties.[12]

More recent legislation and rules provide that trials of law cases shall be by court unless proper and timely demand for a jury trial is made.[13] In some jurisdictions such demand must be accompanied by the payment of a jury fee. The change thus affected is quite drastic; under the older legislation if counsel did nothing, he was, at least in theory, entitled to a jury trial, whereas under more recent provisions such inaction will be considered as a waiver of right of jury trial.

One further trend is clearly discernible: The period within which one may make an effective demand for a jury trial has been

---

9 R.L. Okla., 1910, § 5016; Blume, supra. n. 1.
10 Pancoast v. Eldridge, 157 Okla. 195, 11 P. 2d 918; 73 A.L.R. 2d 1332 (contractual waiver).
11 Mackellar v. Rogers, 109 N.Y. 468, 17 N.E. 350.
12 Kornblau v. McDermant, 90 Conn. 624, 98 A. 587.
13 Fed. R. Civ. P. 38 (d).

shortened very considerably; thus, such demand must be made before the introduction of any evidence, in some jurisdictions,[14] or not later than ten days after service of the last pleading raising the issue, in other jurisdictions.[15] Generally the time for making a demand may be extended by the court upon a showing of excusable neglect.

In those jurisdictions requiring a demand for jury trial, it is generally sufficient, if the case is one properly triable by jury, that the demand be made by either party.[16] Normally the non-demanding party cannot object to a granting of the motion. But where a demand is refused, there is some difference of opinion as to whether the non-demanding party can object to such refusal.[17] Where such refusal may be objected to, the objection must be made in apt time, generally before the hearing begins. Usually, courts have allowed a demand for a jury to be withdrawn, although conditions may be attached to such withdrawal.[18]

SECTION 20. TRIAL BY COURT OR JURY. Where the case is such that fact issues may be tried by either court or jury, many factors enter into the decision as to the preferable mode of trial. Some of these factors will now be considered.

1. The need for an early settlement of the dispute. In some courts the jury calendar may be quite congested but the court may hear non-jury cases in a relatively short time. On the other hand, the court is less likely to adjourn the hearings from time to time in jury cases than in cases tried to the court. Generally the time consumed in a non-jury case is less than if the case is tried with a jury. Almost every step of the trial is shortened in a non-jury case, and several steps are eliminated altogether. A trial by jury

---

[14] Rhoades v. State, 27 Ohio N.P. N.S. 252.

[15] Fed. R. Civ. P. 38 (b).

[16] Stukey v. Stephens, 37 Ariz. 514, 295 P. 973.

[17] Dunham v. Reichlin, 217 Cal. 289, 18 P. 2d 664.

[18] Bass v. Hoagland, 172 F. 2d 205 (consent of opposing party required); 90 A.L.R. 2d 1162.

is more formal than a trial to the court, and this necessitates proceeding more slowly.

2. The nature of the case. If the case to be tried is a rather complex one and involves a large number of technical points, many lawyers prefer to have the case tried to the court. Formerly it was standard procedure to have cases tried by the jury where the plaintiff relied upon making an appeal to sympathy, and where a large verdict was being requested. In recent years, however, many of those cases have been tried to the court, the verdicts frequently being comparable to those which juries had returned in similar cases. In short, many lawyers use court trials except where there is a genuine question as to liability.

3. The possibility of appealing an adverse judgment. Due to the greater complexity of a jury trial, the possibilities of reversible error are greater, usually, than in a non-jury case. Many more rulings on objections to evidence, to instructions, and on miscellaneous motions, will occur in jury trials than in trials to the court. Further, the appellate court is frequently more inclined to view errors in non-jury trials as non-prejudicial.

4. The personal characteristics of the judge who will preside. If the court in which the case is filed has a number of judges to whom the case may be assigned, the question of whether to request a jury trial becomes more complex, as frequently an assignment is not made a sufficient time before trial to assess the judge's characteristics. If the judge is known to counsel, the situation is similar to that where only one judge presides in a given court.

In either situation it is probably advisable to request a jury trial if among other things (a) the court is known to be disposed to be impatient with prosecution of certain types of claims, of which the case at bar is one; (b) the court has formerly evidenced animosity toward counsel to the extent that a fair court trial seems impossible; (c) the court is required to handle many administrative matters and thus is not able to devote full time and attention to the case being tried; (d) decisions are taken under advisement and no judgments are forthcoming for an inordinate length of time; (e) the case involves close questions of credibility and the court is not noted for his ability to distinguish between truth and falsity. The above points are, it will be noted, merely illustrative and not all-inclusive.

5. The relative qualities of counsel. It is generally conceded that juries seem to favor the underdog. Hence if counsel is a novice, he frequently will fare better at the hands of the jury than the judge. But if the judge is patient and kindly disposed toward beginning attorneys the converse may be true.

6. The make-up of the probable jury. While it is true that an attorney has a certain degree of control over the make-up of the jury through the use of peremptory challenges and challenges for cause, there may still remain questions in the mind of counsel as to those remaining on the panel. This is especially possible in communities which rely heavily on the so-called "professional" jurors. In such a case, the doubt should probably be resolved in favor of a trial to the court. As an alternative, the motion for a directed verdict may be used.

7. The desirability of applying a popular and flexible standard. In Section 105 reference is made to the fact that sometimes the conduct of the defendant should be judged by his peers and be measured against a community standard. In such cases, the jury trial is more likely to result in the application of such standard. Again, the standard to be applied should in certain cases be quite flexible in its application, at other times not. A trial by court is more likely to result in a rather rigid application of past precedents, a result which is advantageous in cases involving certain commercial transactions but not so advantageous in cases involving negligent conduct.

SECTION 21. CASES INVOLVING LEGAL AND EQUITABLE ISSUES. Occasionally counsel is presented with a fact-situation in which there exists a choice of remedies, as for example, damages for breach of contract, or specific performance of the contract. If either type of relief is acceptable to the client, counsel may construct his theory in such a way that the case may be triable by court or jury, as he desires. Such cases present no unusual difficulties.

However, cases arise in which both legal and equitable relief may be required in order to do complete justice, and under modern statutes may, and sometimes must, be sought in the same action. How should the case then be tried? There are authorities holding that it must be tried in its entirety as an equity case, or as a law case,[19] while others hold that it may be tried by both court and jury.[20]

Various theories have been adduced to reach the different results. In some jurisdictions it is held that the plaintiff, by joining actions in which there are legal and equitable issues, is deemed to waive a right of trial by jury. Or, if a defendant files an equitable counter-claim in a legal action, he may be deemed to have waived a right of trial by jury. Under such a view, a demand, though made properly and in due time, is ineffectual. On the other hand, in some jurisdictions, the court attempts to determine whether the action is "in its essence" a law action or a suit in equity and settles the question of the right of trial by jury accordingly. The courts following such view consider one type of relief as preliminary to, or supplementary to, the principal relief sought. Thus, where the plaintiff seeks reformation of a contract and to recover damages on the contract as reformed, the entire action may be deemed legal in essence. In still other jurisdictions, reliance is had on the historical position of equity that once a chancellor properly assumed jurisdiction, he could and would grant legal relief if necessary.

---

[19] Fraser v. Geist, 1 F.R.D. 267.
[20] Union Central Life Ins. Co. v. Burger, 27 F. Supp. 554.

Where both the judge and jury act simultaneously as triers of fact, that arm of the court renders a decision first on that aspect of the case which may be determinative of the entire action. Thus, if in the case above supposed the plaintiff is not entitled to reformation, there may be no cause of action for damages. While theoretically, issues of fact in equity cases should be tried by the court, and issues of fact in law cases should be tried by the jury, it is easier administratively to have the entire case tried in one way or the other.

Thus far it has been assumed that the parties are able by their proofs to show that they are entitled to the relief demanded. But if at the trial it develops that this is not the case, further problems arise. If equitable relief is demanded but the right to such relief is not proven, should the trial court dismiss the action, or render such legal relief as is warranted under the facts proven? There is respectable authority for either position. Dismissal is supported by the doctrine of failure of proof,[21] and the rendering of legal relief by the doctrine of waiver by failure to demand a jury trial.[22]

The above discussion suggests that the decision as to trial by court or jury, if it be deemed important, should be made as soon as possible. If a jury trial is desired, not only will a demand be made at the earliest possible time, but the pleadings themselves will be drafted with that type of trial in mind.

---

[21] Jackson v. Strong, 222 N.Y. 149, 118 N.E. 512; Clark, Code Pleading, § 17 (2d ed.).

[22] McLennan v. Church, 163 Wis. 411, 158 N.W. 73.

Chapter 3

Selection of the Jury

A. Challenge to the Entire Panel

SECTION 22. NATURE OF THE CHALLENGE. At common law, the clerk of the court issued a writ to the sheriff to summon a specified *number* of qualified persons to serve as jurors for a particular trial. Since the writ did not direct the sheriff to summon any specified *persons,* it was possible for that official to summon persons who were, on general principles, more favorably inclined to one side than to the other. Where it could be shown that the sheriff was himself interested in the outcome of the trial, or for some reason could not act impartially, counsel for either side could challenge the array or the entire panel of jurors summoned. From the fact that the sheriff was interested it was presumed that the jury could not try the case fairly.

Modern statutes have taken this power out of the hands of the sheriff and have placed it instead in the hands of designated officials, sometimes called jury commissioners. While the statutory procedure varies somewhat in different jurisdictions,[1] the general pattern is somewhat as follows: The designated officials make out

---

[1] 50 C.J.S. Juries, § 155 b; Vanderbilt, Minimum Standards of Judicial Administration, pp. 181–185.

a large list of persons from designated sources, such as voters' registers, tax records, directories, etc. The names of the persons so selected are placed in a container and shuffled. A certain number of the names are then drawn out, and these names, which constitute the panel, are then given to the sheriff so that he may summon the specified persons for jury service for a particular period.

While then the common law grounds for challenge to the array have been abolished by statute, there are created thereby new grounds,[2] namely: 1. that some of the persons involved in the selection process were not qualified under the law, 2. that some of the necessary statutory steps were not taken as prescribed, 3. that there was a systematic exclusion of whole classes of eligible juror prospects. The classes may be based upon sex, political, economic, racial, or religious lines, and if the litigant belongs to such class, such exclusion may violate the due process and equal protection clauses.[3] However, the mere fact that on a particular panel no person of a specified group is drawn is not of itself a sufficient ground for challenge. Counsel must show that such a situation could not occur by mere operation of the laws of probability.[4] Also, it is generally no ground for a challenge that certain occupational groups, which would be entitled to exemptions from service, are consistently omitted from jury lists.

Statutes frequently specify the grounds for a challenge to the array, and these grounds may be deemed exclusive. In the absence of statutory grounds, the courts distinguish between mandatory and directory provisions of the statutes governing the selection of the jury. Only deviations from those provisions considered to be mandatory may be relied upon in a challenge to the array.[5]

---

2 50 C.J.S. Juries, § 262.
3 Thiel v. Southern Pac. Co., 328 U.S. 217; 166 A.L.R. 1422.
4 Patton v. Mississippi, 332 U.S. 463.
5 L.H. & St. L. Ry. v. Schwab, 127 Ky. 82, 105 S.W. 110.

Usually these deviations involve flagrant violations of those provisions which directly affect the impartiality of the jury. Local authorities should be consulted to determine which deviations have been so classified.

SECTION 23. ASCERTAINING WHETHER GROUNDS FOR CHALLENGE EXIST. Generally, the grounds, if any, of a challenge to the array can be ascertained prior to trial. Local practices should therefore be checked from time to time, and compared with the statutory scheme of selection. There may be more frequent instances where a showing can be made that the panel is not truly representative of the community than instances of other deviations. This information may be obtained from court attachés.

Even if an investigation discloses no substantial deviation from statutory requirements, the information obtained thereby may prove to be helpful in the voir dire examination.

SECTION 24. HOW THE CHALLENGE SHOULD BE MADE. Statutes should be consulted to see if there is some procedure prescribed for the making of the challenge. If there is no statute on the subject, the challenge may be made by a motion to quash the venire or panel.[6] It may be necessary, and in all cases it is advisable, to make the motion in writing, specifying in what respect the statutory scheme has not been followed. If the court sustains the motion, he will sign an order that the panel be quashed.

SECTION 25. WHEN THE CHALLENGE SHOULD BE MADE. The challenge to the array should be made at the commencement of the trial, and in any event before attempting to exercise a challenge to the individual juror.[7] In rare instances, the court may sustain a challenge to the array at a later stage of the trial, if a satisfactory showing can be made that the ground was not known prior to that time.

---

[6] Rawes v. State, 93 Okla. Crim. 219, 226 P. 2d 984; 50 C.J.S. Juries § 261.
[7] Ullman v. State, 124 Wis. 602, 103 N.W. 6; 50 C.J.S. Juries § 763.

B. Challenge to the Individual Juror

a. For cause

SECTION 26. NATURE OF THE CHALLENGE. Challenges of the individual juror are sometimes referred to as challenges to the polls, to distinguish them from challenges to the array. The former are usually divided into challenges for cause and peremptory challenges, for which no ground need be shown. Further, there is no limit as to the number of times jurors may be challenged for cause, while statutes limit peremptory challenges to a specific number per side.

There are two basic grounds upon which a juror may be challenged for cause: 1. That he does not possess the statutory qualifications to serve as a juror at that time *in any case*. 2. That he possesses some special disqualification to act as a juror *in the particular case on trial*.[8] The former is illustrated by the juror who is not a citizen, the latter by a juror who is prejudiced against one of the parties. As may be expected the latter type of situation is much more common than the former.

It is customary to refer to the practice of challenging a member of the panel, either for cause, or peremptorily, as "selecting" or "picking" a jury. Some judges take this to mean that certain attorneys try to win their cases on the voir dire. But the theory behind the challenge is that it is the right to reject and not the right to select. It is not the right to have a jury biased in favor of your point of view, but rather the right to have a jury without bias for or against your point of view. However, if one side attempts to retain jurors biased in its favor, under the adversary system the other side has the power to reject, and if counsel on both sides are skilled in the art of examination and challenge, the resulting jury is apt to be as impartial as it is humanly possible to be.

---

[8] State v. Weidlich, Mo., 269 S.W. 2d 69; 72 A.L.R. 2d 673; Id. 905; 76 Id. 678.

Quite obviously only the side against which prejudice or bias would operate may challenge for cause. But as in any aspect of advocacy, a client's cause can suffer because of the lack of skill on the part of the advocate. Hence, it is strongly urged that counsel engaged in trial work become as proficient as possible in the interrogating and challenging of panel members. Also, it is suggested that the right to examine should not be waived.

SECTION 27. ASCERTAINING WHETHER GROUNDS FOR CHALLENGE EXIST—THE VOIR DIRE. There are a number of ways in which counsel may obtain information pertaining to the qualifications of prospective jurors; among such methods are the following:

1. In some courts, information obtained by means of questionnaires sent out by the clerk's office is available.[9] Where this practice does not obtain, it is usually possible to see the names and addresses of persons summoned to attend upon a term of court at which a case stands for trial. Sometimes a list of such persons may be had upon the payment of a nominal fee.

In a small community, the jury list can be checked as soon as it is published, to see whether it contains names of your own clients or those of opposing counsel. An alphabetical card file of the names so published may be prepared, indicating such matters as marital status, religious and political affiliation, occupation and general community reputation.

2. Where counsel may obtain only the names and addresses of those summoned, he may, where this is permitted and feasible, conduct an independent investigation of his own. Obviously, great care must be exercised in this type of activity, which should be conducted in an indirect, unobtrusive manner. In this connection it is advisable, especially in a smaller community to consult your client to determine what, if anything, he knows about certain members of the panel.

3. Information as to the prior jury service of any members

---

[9] Vanderbilt, Minimum Standards of Judicial Administration 181.

of the panel may usually be obtained in the clerk's office. Specific instances so discovered may be investigated by conferring with counsel who tried such cases. In this way it may be possible to learn about any untoward events which occurred during the trial, and possibly the voting record of the jurors involved in such cases and currently on the panel.

4. In some larger cities, jury information services are available for a fee.[10] There is considerable variation as to the information thus made available.

5. Much data may be obtained by closely observing the members of the panel, noting especially the manner in which they answer questions put to them during the voir dire by counsel for both sides. Physical characteristics may be observed, as well as the behavior of the members toward each other. In general, conduct in and out of the courtroom is an important key to the personality of the panel members. However, counsel, as well as the parties, should assiduously refrain from engaging in conversation with any members of the panel, even before they formally become the jury, as such conduct may be grounds for a mistrial.

6. The voir dire examination was originally used to prove a ground of challenge already known.[11] But in the course of time its purpose was changed to become a chief means of determining whether a ground for challenge existed. Trial lawyers generally conduct the voir dire even though they were able to gain considerable information about the panel by one of the other means suggested. However, occasionally an attorney will accept a panel without asking any questions, perhaps for the purpose of placing opposing counsel in an embarrassing position. In such an event, it is generally advisable to interrogate the panel despite the fact that your adversary did not do so, as you may bring out some

---

10 Dow v. Carnegie–Illinois Steel Corp., 224 F. 2d 414.
11 Blume, American Civil Procedure, 403.

ground for challenge so apparent that the panel will not hold it against the challenging counsel.

It should be noted that information elicited on the voir dire examination is equally available to opposing counsel, but this is not the case as to information elicited by some preliminary investigation. Further, counsel is not "bound" by an answer of the panel member if an independent investigation is made. Finally, there are some characteristics of a prospective juror, as for example, his religion, which good taste precludes discovering by means of the voir dire.

Many attorneys trying a case away from "home base" will retain local counsel to assist them especially in conducting the voir dire examination, under the assumption that such counsel may know something about the panel members and also any possible local prejudices. Other attorneys prefer to do the entire job themselves.

There is some variation among courts as to how the voir dire examination is conducted. In the federal courts, the judge may conduct the examination himself, and allow counsel to frame supplementary questions which the judge then submits to the jury, or, he may allow counsel to address additional questions directly to the members of the panel.[12] Quite naturally the questions from the bench will relate mostly to general qualifications, while counsel is in a better position to frame questions concerning possible prejudices in the particular case. The practice in state courts will usually follow the federal practice, or the court will permit counsel to conduct the entire voir dire themselves.

The practice in the federal courts does have the advantage of speeding up the process of selecting the jury, but it also limits the use of the voir dire by counsel as a means of conveying to the jury the theory relied upon. But the opportunity to make good first impressions remains.

---

12 Fed. R. Civ. P. 47 (a).

Generally, a plaintiff in a civil case and a defendant in a criminal case have the first opportunity to examine the members of the panel.

SECTION 28. OTHER PURPOSES OF THE VOIR DIRE. It is generally conceded that the voir dire examination, in addition to disclosing possible grounds for a challenge, either for cause or peremptorily can, if properly conducted, serve some or all of the following purposes:

1. If the members of the panel have not served as jurors in other cases (and there are usually some who have not), the voir dire may be employed to explain to them the function of the jury in the trial of a lawsuit.

2. Since the members of the panel should ordinarily not have personal knowledge of the facts of the case, a brief statement of the pertinent facts which may be referred to in subsequent questions is not only possible but also necessary. Care must be exercised not to attempt to make at this point what in reality amounts to an opening statement. It is, however, quite proper to inject a brief reference to the theory upon which counsel intends to proceed. Further, it is appropriate at this time to explain any technical terms that may be involved. If counsel is aware of the theory relied upon by the adversary, it is often possible, by means of inquiring into the state of mind of a juror, to begin the attack upon that theory.

3. Occasionally it may be deemed wise to bring out into the open any unfavorable aspects of one's case, if it is suspected that the opposing attorney will attempt to make capital of such weakness at a later stage in the trial.

4. The voir dire provides an opportunity for counsel to explain some steps that may be taken during the course of the trial, such as a vigorous cross-examination or the making of frequent objections, and why this is done.

5. Information obtained by counsel can be of genuine value in suggesting how the case should be presented, even if no cause

for challenge should appear. Such examination usually discloses, for example, whether any one juror stands out, and to some extent, what his possible leanings may be.

6. The voir dire presents the first opportunity to acquaint the members of the panel with the characteristics of counsel and the client. It is important that the impressions left with the jury be as favorable as possible, as this may have a bearing on the jury's interpretation of the evidence.

7. Many trial lawyers consider a prime objective of the voir dire to be the obtaining of a promise or an assurance from the respective members of the panel that a given circumstance will not influence them adversely in the rendition of the verdict. These lawyers believe that such assurances are seriously considered by the jurors when they are faced with doubt.

SECTION 29. SCOPE OF THE VOIR DIRE. The scope of the voir dire will be governed obviously by the type of case, the extent to which screening was done by the selecting officials, and by the ends which counsel has in mind. Assuming that counsel will attempt to use the voir dire to accomplish all the objectives which are set out in Section 28, the following hypothetical case may serve to illustrate the breadth of inquiry possible:

Suppose that your client, an attractive married woman, formerly holding a responsible position as private secretary, is bringing suit to recover damages for permanent injuries from the operator and owner of the car in which she was riding and the driver and owner of a truck, the injury having occurred as a result of a collision between the car and truck. Assume that you are trying to establish negligence on the part of the truck driver and owner in operating a truck with defective brakes, and on the part of the car operator and owner in that the operator was operating his vehicle at a speed that was unsafe under the conditions present at the time of the accident. Assume further that these contentions have been placed in issue by the defendant's answer.

1. As counsel for the plaintiff you ordinarily have the first

opportunity to speak. It may be advisable to call the attention of the panel to the difference between the measure of persuasion in a civil case as compared to a criminal case, and to point out that it is only necessary for the jury to conclude that you have established your propositions by a preponderance of the evidence rather than beyond a reasonable doubt. An assurance from the panel that they will be governed by the proper standard may then be sought. Similarly, the jury may be informed that it is their function to apply the law, as it will be given to them by the judge, to the facts as they find them, and again an assurance may be solicited.

2. If it is anticipated that some rather technical questions concerning the construction and operation of the braking system on the truck will be involved in the presentation of the case, it may be advisable to make a brief explanation of such matters and direct an inquiry to the panel concerning any special knowledge any juror may have in this area. Whether a juror is to be challenged because he possesses such special knowledge will depend, as will be more fully discussed later, upon all the circumstances, and not merely upon this one item. If such juror seems on the overall not to be hostile to your point of view, he may be a valuable juror in that he can more fully grasp your theory and present it to the other jurors.

3. If it is anticipated that the opposition will bring out the fact that your client, though married, on the night in question was taking a "joy-ride" with someone not her husband it may be advisable to bring this out, explain it if possible, and then inquire of the panel whether this fact would affect their verdict.

4. If it is anticipated that the case will involve an application of the guest statute, or the like, about the wisdom of which there may be a difference of opinion, that statute may well be mentioned and inquiry made as to the juror's feelings with respect thereto.

5. Inquiry may be made of the panel as to their familiarity with the scene of the accident. If such familiarity is admitted by

some of the jurors, this may be a factor operating in favor of or against the defendant.

6. If, as is probable under the assumed facts, a very substantial verdict will be asked for, this fact may properly be called to the attention of the panel, and again, inquiry made as to their reaction to this type of claim. But it is improper to exact a pledge from a prospective juror that he will vote for a particular sum.[13]

7. In addition to an inquiry related specifically to the particular case on trial it is customary to ask a series of rather standardized questions which pertain largely to general qualifications. The scope here will depend partly upon the information available to counsel prior to trial and the statutory qualifications. Thus, for instance, it is proper to ask, in addition to questions pertaining to name, address, age, occupation, voter, freeholder, householder status, marital relationship, those relating to knowledge of the facts of the case and the formation of an opinion concerning it; if the present case is a re-trial, their knowledge of the former trial; acquaintance with the attorneys, parties, witnesses (including experts); questions relating to previous experiences in similar or other litigation, former jury service, and the like.

There is some information which good taste demands be obtained by means other than direct questions, such as religious affiliation, race, financial condition, moral character, national origin, political affiliation, fraternal affiliation, and the like. In fact, such inquiry may not be permitted by the court, when objection is made, unless the group, affiliation with which is the subject of inquiry, is a party to the litigation. Frequently, it is possible to draw inferences from data that can be obtained on the voir dire, such as nationality from name, address and occupation; race from physical appearance; financial condition from address and occupa-

---

[13] Atlanta Joint Terminals v. Knight, 98 Ga. App. 482, 106 S.E. 2d 417; 82 A.L.R. 2d 1420.

tion; ability to understand the English language from response to questions; physical handicaps from observation.

In the discussion so far, reference was made only to the possible areas of inquiry. The extent to which the area should be explored depends of course upon all the circumstances. Frequently, for example, inquiry should be made as to exactly what the prospective juror does in his work; how long he has been so occupied; what his previous work experiences were; if the juror is a housewife, whether she is gainfully employed part time, and what the occupation of her husband may be. With reference to previous experience with litigation, the inquiry may cover not only the juror but also members of his family, and his friends, and may delve into the details of such experience.

SECTION 30. MANNER OF CONDUCTING THE VOIR DIRE. The manner in which the voir dire may be most effectively conducted, like the scope of the examination, will of course depend in large measure, upon the objectives counsel hopes to achieve. There are some matters, however, which are of general significance.

In the first place, counsel should have an overall plan in mind. Questions should not be asked haphazardly, but the form and sequence should clearly indicate a definite purpose. Obviously, the specific line of questioning to be developed will depend partly upon the responses of the juror and cannot be determined precisely in advance. If a statute prescribes the form in which questions may be put, that form should be followed.

In conducting the voir dire, counsel should bear in mind whatever information about the panel he was able to obtain prior to the trial. If, for instance, the practice of having members of the panel return questionnaires prior to being summoned for jury service is followed in that jurisdiction, and such questionnaires are made available to counsel, certain responses may indicate the need for an extensive additional inquiry into particular areas of the member's life.

There is a considerable variation in practice with reference to, on the one hand, the examination of individuals or, on the other, groups consisting of the entire panel or a fraction thereof. Undoubtedly some questions may well be directed to the entire panel, while others should be addressed to the individual jurors. Some information may not be voluntarily given by the individual juror when an inquiry is addressed to the group, either because the juror wishes to remain on the panel or he is embarrassed to speak out. On the other hand, an examination of the entire panel does save time and avoids some boredom. It may be possible to combine a general question to the entire panel with each juror giving his own answer, thus achieving the advantages of both systems.

It may on occasion be advisable to question an individual juror out of the presence of the other members of the panel. Permission of the court, or consent of opposing counsel would ordinarily be necessary for the use of this method of examination.

It should be noted that the number of panel members that may be questioned before it is necessary to exercise one's challenges is a separate but related problem. This aspect of the voir dire is discussed more fully in Section 34. Counsel generally will want to examine as many jurors as possible, either singly or in groups, before exercising especially his peremptory challenges, so that he may make the most effective use of such challenges.

Reference was made earlier to the fact that the voir dire presents the attorney with his first opportunity to create in the minds of the jurors a favorable attitude toward counsel, the client and his cause. Great care must therefore be used during the voir dire to avoid alienation of the jury. The following examples will indicate some techniques generally employed by trial practitioners:

1. Explain the purpose of the voir dire. Point out that it is provided for by law to insure the highest possible degree of im-

partiality of the jury, and that questions are not asked because of the morbid curiosity of counsel. Counsel may properly emphasize that the purpose of the examination is to provide assurance that the impressions the jury receive during the course of the trial will be the first impressions, which is precisely what the law demands.

2. Be considerate of the feelings, not only of the prospective juror being questioned, but also of the other members of the panel. It is sometimes surprising to counsel to note how quickly an esprit de corps can develop in the panel. Either the form of the question or the subject of the inquiry may be offensive. Thus, it is better to phrase a question as if it is assumed that the juror has average knowledge and intelligence than to crudely ask whether he does know a certain fact. Again, many members of a panel would resent an inquiry into certain aspects of their private life, such as religious affiliation, unless they can see the relevance of such inquiry.

3. Whenever possible, impress the jury with your sense of fairness. This can be accomplished by refusing to take undue advantage of opposing counsel when the opportunity to do so presents itself. Thus, a juror who seems to be biased in your favor may be excused by you.

4. Avoid boring the jury with a constant repetition of the same statement or question. If repetition is necessary, change the form or refer to the statement or question made or asked earlier. In general, the voir dire should be conducted in as short a space of time as possible. Keep in mind the fact that most jurors are losing money while serving and hence do not generally condone a long, drawn-out trial.

5. Do not try to impress the jury with your importance or your brilliance. Hence, avoid language or mannerisms that may be so interpreted by the panel. At times, even the matter of proper dress should be considered. Questions should be in simple direct form, and technical terms should be avoided whenever possible. In general, be warm but not overly solicitous in your approach.

6. While an occasional bit of humor, if spontaneous and genuine, is usually not offensive, jurors may be irked by cutting satire or ridicule. At times the patience of counsel may be sorely tried, either by evasive or apparently stupid answers of the jurors, by the tactics of opposing counsel, or by the rulings of the court, and the impulse to lash back must be curbed as much as possible. Thus, if a juror should, as rarely happens, admit to a bias, it is generally considered wise for counsel to state that such "feelings" are not unnatural, but under the rules are not proper bases for a verdict, rather than to scoff at the admission or be critical of the juror.

On many occasions, the question may be so phrased that the juror is required to make a statement concerning his attitude rather than merely answering "yes" or "no." This is particularly true with reference to bias or prejudice. As stated above, a panel member will rarely admit that he is biased. But if he is required to make a statement, counsel will have a sounder basis for deciding whether the juror should be challenged. On other occasions, a statement from the juror may serve to unduly influence other members of the panel, in which event a direct "yes" or "no" is preferable. As stated earlier, some attorneys phrase a question so as to elicit a promise from the jurors not to allow a particular fact to influence them adversely in the rendition of the verdict. Such response would normally be in a simple affirmative or negative form.

Some attorneys make it a regular practice to ask the entire panel, after the individual jurors have been interrogated, whether there are any reasons why they cannot objectively try the case. This may bring to light some matter not known to counsel, and in any event serves to emphasize to the jury what its true function is.

It is also a fairly common practice to ask a juror, at the conclusion of the examination, whether he, if a litigant, would be willing to have his case tried by a jury that possesses the same predilections and feelings that he possesses. This must be done, however, in a very careful manner, or it may result in antagonizing the juror or the other members of the panel.

The suggestions made above are of course conditioned always by circumstances. Thus, the time allotted to the voir dire is determined by the condition of the docket; if this is current, the court is more willing to grant counsel adequate time for the voir dire. The seriousness of the crime or the amount of money involved in the litigation will also influence the time allowed, and also the time counsel will devote to preparation for the voir dire. In some communities, the long, drawn-out voir dire is a thing of the past.

SECTION 31. INTERROGATING JURORS RELATIVE TO INSURANCE. In a few jurisdictions there are statutory provisions concerning the extent to which inquiry may be made of the prospective jurors as to their relationship to an insurance company. In addition the courts in practically all jurisdictions have laid down some rules on the subject.[14] While the cases are not in complete agreement, it seems to be generally held that prospective jurors may be asked whether they are interested as stockholders, employees or agents, provided that such examination is conducted in good faith. Apparently this means that the court must be satisfied that the purpose of the inquiry is to discover whether any members of the panel may be biased, and that the purpose is not to implant in the minds of the jurors the fact that the defendant is insured. There is no agreement as to what conduct on the part of counsel indicates the one or the other purpose. If, however, the matter of insurance is injected into a case in an unlawful manner, it is generally grounds for a mistrial.

Where a plaintiff's counsel is permitted to make such an inquiry, and a member of the panel admits a connection with an insurance company, it is inadvisable for plaintiff to challenge him

---

14 Dowd–Feder, Inc. v. Truesdell, 130 Ohio State 530, 200 N.E. 762; 31 Am. Jur. Jury §§ 207–211.

at that time, as this may be considered leaving an improper inference with the jury.

Where inquiry by the plaintiff is permitted, it may on occasion be advisable for defendant to state that he is insured, and then to proceed to inquire of the jury as to how this would affect their decision. Or, defendant could acknowledge that the plaintiff had the right to make such an inquiry, regardless of whether the defendant was insured or not. Or, it may be advisable for defendant to simply let the matter drop and not direct the jury's attention to this facet of the case.

SECTION 32. MAKING A CHART, SHOWING WHERE JURORS ARE SEATED. It will be found helpful to counsel, during the voir dire and later during the trial, to prepare a blank sheet of paper divided into twelve rectangles representing the jury box. The names of the members of the panel are then written in the appropriate squares in accordance with the seating arrangement. Pertinent data learned during the voir dire may then be inserted under the names. As any juror is excused and replaced, the name of the new panel member is then inserted and the process is continued in this fashion.

Counsel may wish to note probable challenges, and certainly peremptory challenges, as they are made. In this fashion, the total number of peremptory challenges used is easily determined at any time.

If any juror who is retained seems to be a probable leader, or perhaps even the foreman, this fact can be noted and remarks can be directed especially to him.

During final argument it may thus be possible to allude to some characteristics of some of the jurors, with considerable telling effect. Jurors cannot but help be favorably impressed by the fact that counsel has remembered this or that item, provided, of course, that it is not embarrassing to the jurors.

SECTION 33. HOW THE CHALLENGE SHOULD BE MADE. Since

a challenge for cause is ordinarily made in the presence of the entire panel, care must be exercised so as not to antagonize the others, some of whom may sit as jurors in the case. Several techniques may here be employed. For one, it is often advisable to delay challenging the juror as soon as some ground becomes apparent. Later, when a challenge is made, the other members of the panel may have forgotten the portion of the interrogation relied upon by counsel. Again, the manner in which a challenge is made is important. In addition to explaining to the jury that it is a duty upon counsel to do his best to be certain that the jury is impartial, he should politely ask that Mr. X be "excused." This does not have a harsh ring, and de-emphasizes the lack of qualification.

In a few instances, a challenge may be made out of the presence of the jury, after the interrogation by both sides has been completed. Leave of court must be obtained before this procedure is followed. This system is used more frequently in courts where the judge conducts the voir dire examination himself.

SECTION 34. WHEN THE CHALLENGE SHOULD BE MADE. The proper timing for a challenge for cause is partially determined by the rules of the particular court. On the one hand, it is usually possible to challenge a particular member of the panel immediately after the close of the examination, or as soon as a ground for challenge becomes apparent. On the other hand, the deadline for challenging varies.[15] If blocks of jurors, say four in number, must be accepted before going on to the examination of the rest of the panel, then a challenge must be ordinarily made before the block is tendered to opposing counsel.[16] If the entire panel may be examined before challenging, and if each side has the benefit of the voir dire conducted by opposing counsel, challenges are apt

---

[15] 50 C.J.S. Juries, §§ 250–254.
[16] Missouri Pac. R. Co. v. Fikes, 211 Ark. 256, 200 S.W. 2d 97.

to be more effective than if they must be exercised at an earlier time.

It is ordinarily to the advantage of counsel to postpone the challenge until required to exercise it. There are several reasons for this suggestion: 1. If a challenge is made immediately after learning of a probable cause, the challenge may be deemed to be offensive by the other members of the panel, whereas if questioning is continued, the panel is not as acutely aware of the grounds for a challenge made later. 2. When counsel makes a challenge for cause, opposing counsel generally has the right to ask further questions himself. If the juror seems to be favorably inclined to the opposite side, that side no doubt will attempt to rehabilitate the juror. The counsel making the challenge does not have another opportunity to ask further questions before the court rules on the challenge.

Before making the challenge, counsel should lead the juror into a repetition, in as many different forms as possible, of the basis for making the challenge. In this way, opposing counsel is limited in what he may accomplish in the way of rehabilitation by phrasing a question in a slightly different manner.

In any event, it is usually too late to exercise a challenge for cause on a member of a panel who has been peremptorily challenged. However, a court has discretion to allow a challenge for cause to be used after a juror is accepted, and under special circumstances even after the jurors are sworn in to try the issues in the case.

It is often advisable to consult with the client and co-counsel before accepting a panel. These persons may have noted something about one or two of the panel members that escaped the attention of counsel who conducted the voir dire. In the case of the client, such consultation may prove to be more satisfying in the event that the jury returns a verdict adverse to him, and the relationship with counsel is thus less likely to be strained.

In the process of deciding whether to challenge a particular member of the panel for cause, attorneys generally keep in mind the factors referred to earlier, such as the type of case, the parties, the characteristics of those members of the panel already accepted, any special procedures to be used during the trial, the number of peremptory challenges still available, which side is being represented, etc. With reference to the last factor, it should be noted that if the jurisdiction requires the verdict to be unanimous, a defendant need convince only one juror of the soundness of his defense, but the plaintiff must win all jurors over to his point of view.

Some attorneys believe that it is best to think positively about the members of the panel when determining whether to exercise a challenge. Under this approach, the attorney looks for reasons why a panel member would be a good juror rather than reasons why he should be challenged.

In general, it is well to challenge only when absolutely necessary.

SECTION 35. PRINCIPAL CHALLENGES AND CHALLENGES TO THE FAVOR—MODERN SIGNIFICANCE.[17] Statutes frequently provide that a certain close blood relationship between a prospective juror and a party or attorney, or certain specified situations involving possible interest in the outcome of the litigation, serve to automatically disqualify a juror as a matter of law; a conclusive presumption of bias is raised from the fact shown.[18] In such cases, the challenge is referred to as a principal challenge.[19]

On the other hand, where there are no distinct legal rules on the subject, a situation may be discovered on voir dire from which the inference of bias may be made. For example, the prospective juror may admit that he read newspaper accounts of an accident which is the subject of the lawsuit.[20] The problem then presented

---

17 50 C.J.S. Juries § 278c.
18 Jewell v. Jewell, 84 Me. 304, 24 A. 858.
19 Coughlin v. People, 144 Ill. 140, 33 N.E. 1.
20 Kumli v. Southern Pacific Co., 21 Ore. 505, 28 P. 637; 73 A.L.R. 2d 1312.

is whether the juror is in the light of all the circumstances, reasonably impartial. In such case a challenge is said to be to the favor, and to be based on a question of fact.

Originally, the "fact" involved in a challenge to the favor was decided by triers, but today the trial judge decides both principal challenges and challenges to the favor.[21] However, the distinction between the two types of challenges may have modern significance in appellate review. If the appellate court may review both fact and law, there is no problem. But if that court may only review law, a further distinction must be made between answers of a juror that would *require* a finding of bias and those that would merely *warrant* such a finding. If a challenge based upon answers of the first type is overruled, the appellate court may then review such ruling, as it would be considered to be an error of law. But if the answers are of the second type, there is no review of the overruling of the challenge, as the ruling is considered to be in effect a finding of fact. Hence it becomes important to note how the matter is presented to an appellate court. If the review is on a ruling of a motion for new trial, both matters of fact and law are reviewed by the appellate court.

This distinction is frequently expressed today in this form: The ruling on a challenge to the favor is a matter within the discretion of the trial court, and, according to the standard approach, is not reviewable unless there has been an abuse of discretion. The ruling on a principal challenge is, on the other hand, ipso facto reviewable.

b. Peremptory

SECTION 36. NATURE OF THE CHALLENGE. As stated earlier, statutes generally allow each side a limited number of peremptory challenges.[22] No cause need be shown, and hence the court is re-

---

21 1 Thompson on Trials 112 (2d ed.).
22 31 Am. Jur. Jury § 231; 95 A.L.R. 2d 957.

quired to excuse a juror so challenged, provided that the number of allowable challenges has not been exhausted. Although there were no peremptory challenges at common law in civil cases,[23] statutes today allow such challenges in civil as well as criminal cases. The allowance of such challenges is a recognition of the fact that counsel may, for some unexplainable reason, sense hostility in a prospective juror. Attorneys generally are of the opinion that if they have a feeling of dislike for a juror, that feeling is apt to be mutual.

SECTION 37. DETERMINING WHETHER TO CHALLENGE PEREMPTORILY. As in the case of a challenge for cause, all available information should be considered in determining whether to exercise a peremptory challenge to a particular panel member. Thus, interrogatories to prospective jurors, reports of private investigators, conduct during the voir dire examination, opinions of co-counsel and client, etc., will provide pertinent data. Refer to Section 27 for a discussion of sources of information concerning prospective jurors.

SECTION 38. HOW THE CHALLENGE SHOULD BE MADE. Again, as in the case of a challenge for cause, if counsel, having determined that he does not wish to have a panel member serve on the jury, merely states to the court that he wishes to have the member "excused" rather than using the term "challenge," the procedure will be less offensive to the other members of the panel. Further, if an explanation is made in advance as to why peremptory challenges may be exercised, the remaining members of the panel are less likely to be hostile to the side which later does exercise this right.

If it becomes apparent during the voir dire examination that two panel members are friendly with each other, and if counsel intends to challenge one peremptorily, it is generally advisable either to ask that both be excused, or to pass them both.

---

23 Gordon v. City of Chicago, 201 Ill. 623, 66 N.E. 823.

In general, it is suggested that the challenge be "played down" as much as possible—that is, to refrain from placing undue emphasis upon it. Accordingly, the procedure should be completed as quickly as possible.

In some courts the challenges are made secretly by means of notes of counsel delivered by the bailiff to the court, but more frequently the challenge is made in the presence and hearing of the jury.

Counsel generally determine during the voir dire whom they will challenge. In that case, it may be advisable to propound a series of questions of such a nature that in the minds of the other members of the panel a peremptory challenge is justified.

SECTION 39. WHEN THE CHALLENGE SHOULD BE MADE. The time when a peremptory challenge must be exercised varies from state to state and from court to court.[24] Thus, it may be at the conclusion of the examination of the individual juror, or blocks of jurors, or the entire panel; or, it may be after the entire jury panel has been accepted for cause. The rule followed should therefore be ascertained prior to trial.[25] It should be noted at this point that there is a difference between "passing" a juror to opposing counsel, and "accepting" him. Once a juror has been "accepted," it may be too late to challenge him.[26] Care should therefore be exercised in the use of proper terms.

It is generally to the advantage of counsel to delay the challenge as long as possible, since the number of challenges is limited, and more objectionable panel members may replace those challenged. If the challenges need not be made by either side until both sides have completed the voir dire examination, the plaintiff has the benefit of the information elicited by the defendant. Further, if certain panel members are objectionable to

---

24 31 Am. Jur. Jury § 236.
25 Commonwealth v. Marion, 232 Pa. 413, 81 A. 423.
26 DeCarlo v. Frame, 134 Conn. 530, 58 A. 2d 846; 3 A.L.R. 2d 499.

both sides, the adversary may challenge them peremptorily, thus saving that many challenges for the other side. Where the practice of both sides examining all panel members before challenging obtains, counsel should note on the chart referred to in Section 32 probable challenges to be made later.

There is a similar variance in practice as to the order in which the challenges must be exercised.[27] In some courts plaintiff must exhaust all his peremptory challenges before the defendant is required to exercise any challenge, or even before the defendant conducts the voir dire examination.[28] This is obviously advantageous to the defendant. In other courts the parties alternate in challenging the panel.

It is generally advisable to challenge one prospective juror at a time.

Regardless of the procedure followed, it is usually too late to challenge peremptorily after the panel is sworn to try the issues in the cause. As noted in Section 44, a court may allow a challenge to be exercised after that time in unusual situations, but it may not add to the number of peremptory challenges. Generally the court must be satisfied that the objectionable juror could not have been successfully challenged for cause.

A peremptory challenge is frequently used when a challenge for cause has been overruled because of a fear that the juror would be hostile to the side which challenged him if he remained on the panel. Also, as noted in Section 42, in some jurisdictions this step is necessary to obtain appellate review of the overruling of the challenge for cause.

Similarly, a peremptory challenge is frequently used where counsel anticipates a personality clash, though no challenge for cause was made.

---

27 50 C.J.S. Juries § 256.
28 Pointer v. U.S., 151 U.S. 396.

SECTION 40. GROUNDS FOR CHALLENGE. Since it is usually
difficult, if not impossible, to probe a juror's mind sufficiently to
discover whether he is in fact biased, attorneys usually operate on
the basis of certain fairly well-defined assumptions as to the type
of juror they wish to exclude. As may be expected, there is some
disagreement among attorneys as to these assumptions, but the
following discussion concerns illustrative assumptions quite generally made. Obviously only experience can determine their
validity. Sometimes it is possible to check validity by discussing
the case informally with one or two jurors after they have returned
the verdict and been discharged, but before they have disbanded.
Although counsel frequently believe that a favorable verdict is
evidence of the validity of the assumptions used, and an unfavorable verdict is evidence to the contrary, in fact no such easy generalizations are justified. Much remains to be done in the matter
of ascertaining the factors which influence a jury in their finding
for one side or the other.

Residence. This may indicate to an extent the economic
status of the juror. If a substantial verdict is sought, a juror who
is accustomed to think in large numbers is more likely to favor
such a verdict if the necessary damages can be shown.

Occupation. Sometimes an effort is made to retain persons
who do work like, or similar to, that of the client, anticipating
that the process of identification with the client's cause will operate
in the client's favor. At other times, such persons may be excluded
if deemed hostile because of envy. Aside from this, one's occupation is apt to color one's attitude toward prosecution of certain
types of claims: an employer is more likely to look askance at a
claim filed by an employee against another employer. A laboring
man is considered to have less respect for the opinion of a
psychiatrist than would a professional man.

Age. Younger jurors are assumed to be more liberal, more
attentive and interested, and perhaps more capable of seeing

through a complex situation. Middle aged persons are considered more tolerant than older persons.

Sex. It seems to be generally agreed that women are more likely to be conscientious in their efforts to perform their duties properly, to be more apt than men to follow instructions, more likely to rely on intuition, but also more likely to be conservative in awarding damages. If one's client is a woman, many attorneys exclude women jurors if possible, as men are deemed to be less critical in judging a woman.

Race or nationality. North Europeans are assumed to be less emotional than South Europeans, and hence require strict proof and insist upon law and order. Minority group members are probably more severe on members of their own group than jurors who do not belong to the group.

Previous jury service. Prolonged or repeated service is considered to make a juror more cautious and less subject to suggestions of counsel. This view may be qualified after investigating the voting record in previous cases. Many attorneys avoid using the same jury in the same term of court in similar cases.

Leadership qualities. If one member of the panel demonstrates that he possesses such qualities, some attorneys will attempt to retain him if he does not indicate leanings toward a point of view contrary to that which counsel is attempting to urge.

Marital status. The responsibilities of maintaining a household are assumed to have a mellowing influence upon both men and women and to make then sympathetic toward the juvenile or young adult and the special problems of that group.

Overall experience. This factor is probably of more importance than any other, and frequently overrides any assumption. Thus, one who has been physically disabled in an automobile accident may be hostile or favorably inclined toward automobile drivers who allegedly cause an accident, dependent partly upon whether he feels he has been treated fairly in his efforts to obtain compensation.

SECTION 41. NUMBER OF CHALLENGES AVAILABLE—MULTIPLE PARTIES. Statutes today commonly provide that each side in a civil case may have a limited number of, up to six in some states, peremptory challenges. In the federal courts each side is entitled to three challenges.

In criminal cases, the number of peremptory challenges allowed varies with the severity of the offense. In some states as many as thirty challenges are allowed to a side. In the federal courts the maximum number is twenty.

One of the vexing problems, confronting courts in jurisdictions where there is no specific statute or rule covering the situation, is that of determining the number of challenges available to each party where there are multiple parties on one side.[29] Frequently the courts have insisted that the total number available to a side must be divided among the co-parties as they deem proper.[30] Exceptions however have been made where it is shown that the interests of the co-parties conflict,[31] and a federal statute[32] expressly authorizes the trial court in such cases to allow additional challenges. In criminal cases the courts have often indicated a greater willingness to allow each co-defendant to exercise the maximum number of challenges.

SECTION 42. EXHAUSTING PEREMPTORY CHALLENGES AFTER OVERRULING OF CHALLENGE FOR CAUSE. It is quite generally held that appellate review of the overruling of a challenge for cause is not available unless the party so challenging has also exhausted his peremptory challenges.[33] This is considered necessary to show that the error, if any, was prejudicial.

In some jurisdictions it is required in addition that the party challenging for cause attempt to exercise another peremptory

---

29 31 Am. Jur. Jury § 238.
30 Downey v. Finucane, 205 N.Y. 251, 98 N.E. 391.
31 Curtis v. Lowe, 338 Ill. App. 463, 87 N.E. 2d 865.
32 28 U.S.C.A. § 1870.
33 People v. Schafer, 161 Cal. 573, 119 P. 920.

challenge.[34] In this way the trial court, if in error in overruling the challenge for cause, can be said to have wrongfully deprived the party of a peremptory challenge.

The rule followed in a particular jurisdiction should therefore be determined prior to the trial.

c. In general

SECTION 43. RECORDING CHALLENGE AND RULING. It will be found helpful if counsel will, on the chart described in Section 32, record challenges for cause and peremptory challenges made both by him and opposing counsel, and the rulings of the court on the challenges for cause. This is especially important with reference to peremptory challenges.

If the court reporter is not present during the interrogation of the panel, counsel should request that he record that portion of the interrogation relating to a challenge, even if this means repeating a portion of the proceedings. The reporter should also note the challenges and the ruling, to preserve the record for possible appellate review.

SECTION 44. PROCEDURE WHERE GROUNDS FOR CHALLENGE NOT DISCOVERED UNTIL AFTER JURY IS IMPANELED. If the grounds for a challenge could have been discovered during a voir dire examination, but the examination was not searching enough to accomplish this, courts generally will not afford relief.[35] This is true even if such examination would have disclosed that a juror lacked the proper statutory qualifications.

Where, however, a juror falsely answers questions on the voir dire, or fails or refuses to disclose facts that would affect his qualifications, relief is generally afforded. If the trial is still in progress, this matter can be called to the court's attention by a motion to declare a mistrial.

If the trial is completed, and the time within which a motion

---

[34] Frank v. U.S., 59 F. 2d 670.
[35] 50 C.J.S. Juries § 251 a. (2).

for a new trial may be filed has not expired, that is the appropriate remedy. Whether a new trial will be granted depends upon a number of factors: Whether the losing party has been prejudiced by the juror's conduct; whether the offending juror played a decisive role in the deliberation of the jury; whether the question was so worded that its import was readily understandable by the juror; whether counsel interrogating juror had other means of obtaining the requested information, so that his failure to pursue such other means constituted a waiver of the objection.[36]

If it is too late to file a motion for a new trial, counsel may be required to use one of the extraordinary remedies or institute an independent action to set aside the judgment, depending upon the procedures available in a particular jurisdiction.

SECTION 45. EXCUSING JURORS—AGREEMENT OF COUNSEL. Where a juror does not possess the personal qualifications prescribed by statute, he may not serve when challenged, even though he may desire to do so.[37] Such qualification may refer to age, residence, citizenship and the like.

On the other hand, statutes frequently provide that certain classes of persons, largely for occupational reasons, are likewise considered unavailable for jury duty.[38] Such classes usually consist of persons who otherwise possess the necessary personal qualifications to serve, but because of the inconvenience to the public resulting from such jury service are not required to do so. Public officials, clergymen, school teachers, lawyers, doctors, servicemen, and, in some states, women fall into this category. Such persons are ordinarily said to be "exempt" or "privileged" from serving but may do so if they choose. As a matter of practice such persons are rarely called to serve.

---

[36] Pearson v. Gardner Cartage Co., 148 Ohio St. 425, 76 N.E. 2d 67; 38 A.L.R. 2d 624; 63 Id. 1061.

[37] Wassum v. Feeney, 121 Mass. 93, 23 Am. Rep. 258; 31 Am. Jur. Jury §§ 157–170.

[38] 28 U.S.C.A. § 1862; 50 C.J.S. Juries § 213.

Lastly, courts are vested with considerable discretion to relieve individuals or groups from the burdens of jury duty if the performance would work a hardship upon them.[39] It is customary to say that such persons are "excused" from service at a particular time. However, they may be required to serve at a later time when their conditions have changed. Thus, in a rural community, farmers are generally excused during critical periods, providing a sufficient number of potential jurors are available in the jurisdiction. Or, illness may postpone service.

It will be recalled that reference was made in previous sections to the use of the term "excuse" in place of "challenge." This use then is to be distinguished from an "excuse" where the choice is left to the juror. When counsel, either singly, or jointly by stipulation, "excuse" a juror, it may be therefore in effect a challenge or not a challenge. If the juror is unacceptable to one side or to both sides, an offer to "excuse" is in reality the exercise of a challenge; if the juror is otherwise acceptable to both sides, but for personal reasons would prefer not to serve, the offer to "excuse" is not truly a challenge. This distinction may be important where counsel on one side "excuses" a juror and the court should refuse to remove him from the panel.

Where a prospective juror is unacceptable to one side, counsel representing that side may request opposing counsel to join in excusing the juror. If the request is refused, counsel may then insist on removal.

A joint request to excuse a juror may be used where a ground for challenge did not appear until the trial is in progress. In such event, the request is usually granted as a matter of course. In fact, the court may deem a ruling to be unnecessary whenever counsel join in a request, regardless of the reasons.

---

[39] 28 U.S.C.A. § 1863; 31 Am. Jur. Jury §§ 70, 71.

Chapter 4

Opening Statement

SECTION 46. ORDER IN WHICH MADE—WAIVER. Statutes or rules of court frequently specify the order in which the opening statements are to be made.[1] As a general proposition, the party having the burden of proof has the right to make the first statement. Ordinarily this party is the plaintiff. Frequently the plaintiff has this right if he has the burden on any issue.[2]

Some statutes provide that the prosecutor is required to make an opening statement,[3] but there is no such requirement for the plaintiff in civil cases. However, it is quite generally agreed that a plaintiff should never waive the opportunity to make an opening statement, as this is one of the devices developed by the law to partially offset the disadvantage imposed upon him by the burden-of-proof doctrine.

Although the interest of the jury in the case has already been stimulated by an effective voir dire examination, this interest must be sustained during the time the evidence is presented. This period may be days or even weeks. Further, evidence must at times be presented in a disconnected sequence. The jury is then expected

---

[1] Throckmorton's Ohio Code Ann. § 11420–1 (1940); 53 Am. Jur. Trial § 69.

[2] Johnson v. Josephs, 75 Me. 544.

[3] Busch, Trial Procedure Materials, § 146; Mendelson, Criminal Cases, 32 (Practising Law Institutes Series).

to piece these fragments together into a meaningful whole. In order to do this reasonably well, it is necessary for the jury to learn as soon as possible what the lawsuit is all about. A good opening statement will enable the jury to follow the testimony more intelligently, and to fill gaps in the testimony itself.

If the trial is by court, counsel for both sides may prefer not to make an opening statement if the facts are relatively simple, lest the court consider this an effrontery. If the facts are complicated, an opening statement should generally be made.

There is considerable variation in practice as to the sequence of events after the plaintiff has made his opening statement. In some jurisdictions the defendant has one of several choices available to him: 1. He may make his opening statement immediately after that of the plaintiff, before the introduction of any evidence.[4] 2. He may defer making his opening statement until the plaintiff has completed with his evidence in chief, and just prior to the introduction of his own evidence.[5]

Some attorneys favor the practice of waiving the opening statement under certain circumstances, to be discussed below. While each technique has certain advantages and disadvantages, depending upon the circumstances, it is considered by many attorneys to be unwise for a defendant to make no opening statement. For no matter what the circumstances, defendant can create a good personal impression by tailoring his remarks to fit the situation. The suggested choices then are narrowed to the question: *When* should defendant make his opening statement? It should be noted that a defendant may be required expressly to reserve the right to defer making his statement until the plaintiff has completed the presentation of his evidence.

Where the defendant is confident that the evidence of the plaintiff is insufficient to make a prima facie case, or if the defend-

---

4 Supra, n. 1.
5 Mason's Minn. Stat. § 9295 (1927).

ant intends to rely chiefly upon impeachment of the plaintiff's witnesses, it may be advisable to defer the opening statement.

On the other hand, if reliance will be placed chiefly upon an affirmative defense, it is well to make the statement immediately after that of the plaintiff. And in any event, if the latter course is followed, the defendant has the opportunity to present his point of view while the plaintiff's theory is still fresh in the minds of the jury. In this way the main issues are presented before the jury accepts the plaintiff's version as the correct one. Further, any necessary corrections in the plaintiff's statement are most effectively made at this time.

Prior to the time when widespread use was made of discovery devices, it was a common practice for a defendant, who was confident that he had a defense not known by the plaintiff, to defer his opening statement, or to waive his right. With the advent of such devices little is gained by such deferment or waiver. However, if counsel still wishes to rely on surprise, it is still possible to call the jury's attention to the fact that the plaintiff's statement is not evidence, that there are two sides to every lawsuit, and that the jury should not form any conclusions until all of the evidence has been introduced.

Where the plaintiff anticipates that a defendant may choose to defer making his opening statement, he may, in the concluding portion of his own statement, state that it is customary at that point for the defendant to make his statement (if that is a permissible practice in the jurisdiction). Such a statement places the defendant in the position where he will either have to make a statement or explain why he does not choose to do so at that time.

SECTION 47. SCOPE. Because of its importance, an opening statement should be carefully prepared in advance of trial. This will prevent counsel from overlooking some important point. While the scope of an opening statement obviously will vary from case to case, certain points are quite generally included.

Plaintiff in his statement should begin by stating the purpose thereof. He should then introduce himself, opposing counsel and the parties, identifying the latter by name and their relationship to the case. Thereafter, the attorney's client should be referred to by name. This should be followed by a brief description of the nature of the action.

The jury should then be informed as to the issues. In order to accomplish this, counsel may summarize the pleadings. Generally pleadings should not be read. It is generally not advisable to go beyond the pleadings when stating the claim or defense. Rarely will a court consider such a statement equivalent to the pleadings, when a question of the sufficiency of the latter arises. Ordinarily, the law in the case is not referred to at this point. However, if the cause of action or defense is based upon a specific statute, it is generally considered appropriate to call this to the jury's attention when the issues are explained to them.

At this point, it is advisable to make a statement of the facts, in chronological order, and in narrative form. It is well to point out that counsel investigated the facts and this is what he believes happened. It is customary to state that the jury is, however, not to accept the statement as proof, but instead to look to the evidence to determine what actually occurred. If the liability of defendant is doubtful, some attorneys emphasize damages at this point, whereas if the plaintiff has a strong case as to liability, this element is underscored.

It may be deemed advisable to indicate in a general way how the proof will sustain the allegations. But it is usually not considered wise to become too specific as to who will testify as to what, for counsel may discover to his chagrin that the anticipated proof is not forthcoming. Such discrepancy will very likely be called to the jury's attention by opposing counsel. Further, if counsel should not call witnesses who have been previously identified, he will again be placed in an embarrassing position. Care should also be exercised that the summary does not include proof that will be subject to an objection of incompetency, immateriality or irrelevancy. Counsel may, however, give the testimony of certain witnesses in greater detail if it is anticipated that their testimony will be difficult to comprehend.

There is some difference of opinion as to whether the plaintiff should remind the jury that he is seeking a large verdict, if that be the fact. Some attorneys believe that it is psychologically preferable merely to state the nature and extent of the damage, and reserve the matter of compensation for the closing argument. Other attorneys feel that it may be necessary to condition the jury to think in terms of large amounts, before the evidence is introduced.

The defendant's opening statement is normally shorter than that of the plaintiff. In the event the defendant accepts as accurate the plaintiff's statement of the nature of the action and the issues, he will rely chiefly on a different version of the facts. Also, his statement of the evidence to be introduced will vary from that of the plaintiff. It is much more effective to show how there is a conflict in the evidence rather than merely to refer to such conflict. If a defense is doubtful, counsel may question the credibility of plaintiff's witnesses, or attempt to reduce the amount of recovery.

Both sides generally conclude a statement with the assertion that counsel is confident that the evidence will support his contentions. A favorable verdict may be requested, although this is more appropriate in the closing argument.

During the course of the statement any technical terms, including legal terms, should be explained. In this connection it may be well to state that certain experts will be called, and in a general way what they will testify to. For such experts are likely to use certain technical terms. If this has not been done during the voir dire, mention may be made of vulnerable parts of one's case which are, or may be, known to the adversary, and an attempt made to show that, despite this fact, there is a good claim or defense. Where it is anticipated that portions of the opponent's case are vulnerable, the jury may be alerted to pay particular attention to such portions of the testimony. One must be quite sure of one's ground, however, before proceeding in this direction.

Ordinarily the plaintiff should not anticipate a defense, unless it is a matter of record. Even then it should be referred to only where the plaintiff is quite certain that he may successfully rebut it. This may at times be accomplished by referring to certain elements in the factual situation, rather than by a specific reference to the defense as such. In brief, the defense should not be emphasized by the plaintiff. The same principles governing a reference to insurance during the voir dire are applicable to the opening statement. Generally, no reference is made to any attempts that will be made to impeach the opponent's witnesses.

SECTION 48. HOW MADE. As stated in the previous section, an opening statement, to be effective, requires careful preparation. This includes especially that portion of the statement in which the facts or events are presented to the jury. These events should normally be referred to in the sequence in which they have taken place, and only those facts should be selected which are necessary to state a claim or defense. Hence the statement should be made as short as possible, depending upon the complexity of the case. Repetition should be held to a minimum. Counsel are expected, as partisans, to state the case favorably to the client. But it is well to remember that a jury will be more impressed if the evidence indicates a stronger claim or defense than as stated by counsel.

It is good practice to make a brief memorandum of the most important points to be included, to serve as a reminder when the statement is made. Some attorneys test the effectiveness of an opening statement in a rehearsal before some critical layman. If counsel is successful in recreating the events as they occurred in such fashion that the hearer receives the impression that he was present at the time, then, as in the effective telling of a story, he will have accomplished his purpose. This implies that counsel refrain from using such stilted phrases as "we propose to show" more than once. It also implies that personalities should be dwelt upon more than occurrences, if the case lends itself to that type of treatment.

Jurors are most favorably impressed with a direct statement, made with sincerity and conviction and in a friendly fashion. It is important to keep in mind the information about the jury gained by the voir dire examination and other sources. Remarks may be directed especially to any "key" juror thus discovered. The intelligence of the jury should not be underestimated, and their respect must be earned and maintained. This does not imply that only unconversational language should be employed. If it is doubtful whether the jurors are familiar with some fact, principle, condition or situation, a knowledge of which is necessary to properly understand a claim or defense, it is preferable to preface a statement of the fact or other matter with a statement assuming such knowledge, as "Of course, you know that Main Street runs north and south."

It should always be kept in mind that the purposes of the opening statement and closing argument are not the same. Hence, it is improper in the former to suggest what inferences should be drawn from the evidence. Further, inflammatory or highly emotional remarks have no place in an opening statement, nor do appeals to prejudice or sympathy.

Thus, persistent references in personal injury actions to the fact that the plaintiff is a married man with X number of children,[6] or remarks reflecting on the character or integrity of opposing counsel, party or witnesses[7] should be avoided. In general, the opening statement should be limited to matters which could be introduced into evidence.

---

[6] C. & N.W. R. Co. v. Kelly, 74 F. 2d 31; 68 A.L.R. 2d 990.

[7] Raucci v. Connelly, 340 Ill. App. 280, 91 N.E. 2d 735; 68 A.L.R. 2d 999.

By the same token, counsel should object at once when opposing counsel engages in argument, reads extensively from exhibits or refers to immaterial or irrelevant matter. If a question arises as to the propriety of some portion of the opening statement, the matter should be settled out of the presence of the jury. In an extreme case, improper remarks may be grounds for a mistrial. In any event the jury should be instructed to disregard them.

SECTION 49. AS BASIS FOR DISMISSAL OR DIRECTED VERDICT. The rule in some jurisdictions permits a dismissal where the opening statement of the plaintiff fails to show a prima facie case.[8] In other jurisdictions an action may be dismissed only where the plaintiff's statement affirmatively shows that he has no cause of action.[9] The former is illustrated by a statement in an action for breach of contract which narrates the facts in such a way that indicates a lack of consideration; the latter by a statement which refers to a contract unenforceable because against public policy. In the former situation, a dismissal will not be ordered where the statement is ambiguous, or where the omission is inadvertent. Further, the motion must specifically point out the omission so that the plaintiff may supply it if he can.

Furthermore, an admission made in an opening statement obviates proof of the admitted point, though it is not sufficient to take the entire case away from the jury.[10] This applies to the statement of the defendant as well as to that of the plaintiff. Where counsel wishes to take advantage of an admission by his adversary, he should call in the reporter to make note of the admission, in the event the reporter is not taking down the entire statement.

---

8 Oscanyan v. Arms Co., 103 U.S. 261; 53 Am. Jur. Trials, §§ 373–381.

9 Kelly v. Bergen County Gas Co., 74 N.J.L. 604, 67 A. 21.

10 Redding v. Puget Sound Iron & Steel Works, 36 Wash. 642, 79 P. 308; McCormick, Evidence 520.

Chapter 5

Examination
of Witnesses

SECTION 50. PROVING A CAUSE OF ACTION OR DEFENSE. The elements necessary to establish a cause of action or defense are ascertainable by research into standard legal materials and specialized texts relating to various types of cases. In determining the elements upon which evidence must be introduced, consideration should be given to the role of judicial notice and presumptions, as well as any express or implied admissions deducible from the pleadings. Also, it may be necessary to ascertain the scope of any general denials in the particular jurisdiction.

Ideally each element to be proven should be proven as a unit. If several witnesses are to testify to the same element, this could mean that a particular witness is called to the stand a number of times. While this technique is used occasionally, more often the appearances of each witness are limited as much as possible. Since the facts are thus unfolded in a fragmentary fashion, reliance is placed upon the opening statement and closing argument to present the case as a unified whole.

SECTION 51. MANNER OF CONDUCTING EXAMINATION. (a) There

are two ways in which a witness may testify,[1] namely, a narration of legally significant events in the order of their occurrence,[2] or by answering specific and limiting questions.[3] Frequently both methods are used with reference to the same witness.

Each method has certain advantages and disadvantages. When the narrative form is used, the jury is apt to receive a clearer picture of what occurred than if information is elicited bit by bit. On the other hand, the narrative form allows the witness to wander into inconsequential or even needlessly harmful areas. In the case of hostile witnesses, a general form of question may produce no results.

When a narrative answer is solicited, the question should be so phrased that the witness begins his narration at the proper point. If the witness begins to wander, he can be stopped or brought back to the subject by interposing a statement or question.

(b) If a specific question is so framed that the answer is suggested thereby, it may be objectionable as leading.[4] Even if such questions are not objected to, the jury may infer that the witness is being coached. Furthermore, such tactics may be exposed on the cross-examination.

There are occasions, however, where the use of a leading question may not only be permissible but advisable. Thus, where the particular testimony desired cannot be elicited otherwise, as where the witness does not recall or understand what is expected;[5] or, where it is not important that the answer is suggested, as where it concerns preliminary matters;[6] or, where it is assumed that the witness is not likely to be moved by the suggestion because of hostility.[7]

---

[1] McCormick, Evidence, § 5.
[2] Northern P.R. Co. v. Charless, 51 Fed. 562.
[3] State v. Allemand, 153 La. 741, 96 So. 552.
[4] Straub v. Reading Co., 220 F. 2d 177; McCormick, Evidence, § 6.
[5] Moody v. Rowell, 17 Pick. (Mass.) 490.
[6] Southern Ry. Co. v. Hall, 209 Ala. 237, 96 So. 73.
[7] People v. Gallery, 336 Ill. 580, 168 N.E. 650.

If an objection to a question is sustained on the ground that it is leading, the question may usually be rephrased to meet the objection.

(c) It is customary to ask each witness a number of preliminary questions, for the purpose of identifying him and to put him at ease.

(d) Each question asked of a witness should be as simple, specific and unambiguous as possible. Such questions will not only aid the witness to understand the question but his answers will convey his impressions in a sharper, clearer fashion.

(e) Questions should be asked slowly enough to give the witness time to collect his thoughts and the jury an opportunity to get the full import of the question. Never begin a question until the witness has answered the former question. It is sometimes difficult for the attorney, who has lived with the case for several years or more, to keep in mind that this is the jury's (or court's) first opportunity to know the facts.

(f) A previous answer should rarely be repeated by counsel and then only for emphasis. Repetition occurs usually only in cross-examination. Similarly, it is generally inadvisable to have the witness repeat a previous answer, lest the jury lose interest in the testimony.

(g) Have a specific objective in mind when interrogating a witness. This is especially necessary during the direct examination.

(h) Normally it is disadvantageous for counsel to argue with the witness. Where a witness gives an unexpected answer, and one known or suspected to be contrary to the fact, counsel will accomplish more by concealing his surprise or anger, dropping the point momentarily, and returning to it later.

(i) It is generally inadvisable to ask witnesses on direct examination to explain their answers. If the explanation supports the answer it is more effective to bolster the case of the direct examiner if brought out on cross-examination.

(j) Where dates, size, speed, distance, etc., are significant, and it is anticipated that they may not be recalled by the witness, questions should be directed at events from which an inference as to the desired information may be drawn. Recollection may also be aided by memoranda of items easily forgotten.[8] If it is doubtful whether recall actually results from a reference to the memoranda, the memoranda should meet the requirements of admissibility in the particular jurisdiction.[9]

SECTION 52. INTRODUCING EXHIBITS INTO EVIDENCE. Documents which are the basis of a cause of action or defense should be introduced into evidence as soon as they are referred to by witnesses.

Quite frequently the admissibility of documents is acknowledged by means of stipulations, entered into during a pre-trial conference or at the trial itself. Where such stipulation is not entered into, the following steps should be taken: Have the court reporter mark the document "Plaintiff's exhibit No. 1 for identification." The witness is then asked what the document is. This question is not subject to an objection that the document speaks for itself, as that objection refers only to its contents.[10] If the exhibit is a tangible object, it may be necessary to ask whether it is in the same condition now as it was at the time of the event, or who had possession thereof since that time.[11] If the exhibit is a photograph or diagram it is necessary to show that it constitutes a true and accurate portrayal of the item it purports to represent.[12] In the case of business records, special legal requirements for admissibility may exist.[13] In brief, a proper foundation must be laid.

The document is then shown to opposing counsel so that he may determine whether to object to its admission. If there are

---

[8] McWilliams v. Lewis, 125 F. 2d 200; McCormick, Evidence, § 9.

[9] U.S. v. Riccardi, 174 F. 2d 883; 82 A.L.R. 2d 473.

[10] McCormick, Evidence, § 195.

[11] Gutman v. Industrial Comm., 71 Ohio App. 383, 50 N.E. 2d 187; 69 A.L.R. 2d 424.

[12] Edelson v. Higgins, 43 Cal. App. 2d 759, 111 P. 2d 668; 72 A.L.R. 2d 308.

[13] Missouri Forged Tool Co. v. St. Louis Oar Co. (Mo. App.) 205 S.W. 2d 298.

several copies of the document, one may be handed to opposing counsel and one to the court. The document is then formally offered into evidence. This is the proper time for an objection to be made if one is to be made. Before proceeding further, counsel should await, and press for if necessary, a formal ruling on the offer. After admission, the words "for identification" are stricken from the reporter's mark.

The witness then may be asked to read the document in whole or in part, or he may be asked a series of questions concerning the contents, or the document may be given to the jury to examine. Often a combination of these methods is used. Further questioning of the witness should be held in abeyance until the jury has completed its examination. Where a deposition is to be read, co-counsel may read the answers while counsel reads the questions; in this way the attention of the jury can be retained. If only the favorable parts of a document are read during the direct examination, unfavorable parts may be read by opposing counsel during cross-examination or as part of his examination in chief.

Once a document has been admitted into evidence, it should be referred to by its exhibit number.

SECTION 53. MAKING A RECORD. Counsel should attempt to determine, prior to trial, whether an adverse decision may possibly be appealed. If an appeal is likely, care must be exercised to be certain that the appellate court is presented with a proper record. Otherwise the appellate court may not determine the case on the merits, but will dismiss the appeal.

To insure the making of a proper record, counsel should see to it that a court reporter makes notes of any proceedings which may form the basis for an appeal. Any stage of the proceedings, from the selection of the jury to instructions or final arguments, may be significant. It is particularly important that stipulations be included in the record. A transcript of the record need not, however, be ordered until it has been decided to appeal.

Appellate courts will generally not reverse for alleged errors that have not been called to the attention of the trial court. The trial court must be given the opportunity to avoid or correct error.[14]

Thus, proferred evidence deemed to be inadmissible must be objected to.[15] An objection should be made, if at all possible, before a question is answered. If this is not possible, the objection should be accompanied by a motion to strike the question and answer, and by a motion that the jury be instructed to disregard the same.[16] If counsel has fore-knowledge that a specific item of evidence will be introduced at the trial, an objection may be made during the pre-trial conference. If the opposing counsel appears to be asking a series of questions, all of which are deemed objectionable, a blanket objection may be interposed.

In some jurisdictions, by rule, every adverse ruling is deemed excepted to;[17] in the absence of such a rule, an exception must be taken, and noted in the record, to each overruling of an objection.

Unless the reason for the objection is apparent, a specific ground must be stated. Sometimes a question may be objected to on several specific grounds; if so, all grounds should be stated. It is not safe to use a general objection of "incompetent, irrelevant and immaterial," for an overruling of such an objection will normally be affirmed on appeal.[18] Instead, counsel should indicate that he is relying on the rule against opinion, hearsay, etc.

The sustaining of an objection to certain evidence can be relied upon as error only if the trial and appellate court is made aware of the nature of the evidence.[19] This is done by means of an "offer of proof," which is simply a statement by counsel made out-

---

[14] 4 C.J.S. Appeal and Error, § 228.

[15] Faden v. Estate of Midcap, 112 Colo. 573, 152 P. 2d 682; McCormick, Evidence, § 52.

[16] Wightman v. Campbell, 217 N.Y. 479, 112 N.E. 184.

[17] Ind. Sup. Ct. Rule 1–5; McCormick, Evidence 121, n. 50.

[18] U.S. v. Sessin, 84 F. 2d 667.

[19] Petition of Mackintosh, 268 Mass. 138, 167 N.E. 273; 88 C.J.S. Trial §§ 73–83.

side the presence of the jury, of what the evidence would be and the purpose to be accomplished thereby.

Occasionally counsel may need to press for a ruling on his objection, for if there is no ruling, the objection may be deemed to have been waived.

Many attorneys do not object to evidence which is damaging even though grounds for an objection are apparently present. It is believed that an objection will fix the evidence in the minds of the jury. Furthermore, an excessive number of objections may antagonize the court and cause the jury to believe that counsel is unwilling to trust them with all the facts. This is particularly true as to objections made by counsel for the defendant. Lastly, constant interruptions may prevent the jury from understanding what the controversy is about.

On the other hand, an objection to a question on cross-examination will give the witness more time to consider his answer, even though the objection is overruled. An objection is proper when the question is ambiguous or misleading.[20] Also, objections may be interposed solely to disrupt a smooth and orderly presentation of a claim or defense.

A distinction must be made between an objection that goes to the form of the question, and one that goes to its substance.[21] In general, the former type of objection is less frequently made because the objection can usually be obviated by rephrasing the question. Similarly, if foundation facts can be supplied later, it is pointless to object until it is too late for opposing counsel to supply such facts. When this occurs, an objection should be accompanied by a motion to strike the evidence previously given; on occasion, such a situation may call for a motion to direct a verdict.

It is usually preferable to argue an objection out of the pres-

---

20 U.S. v. Riccardi, supra n. 9.
21 1 Wigmore, Evidence § 18.

ence of the jury, as that body is then less likely to draw improper inferences and to pre-judge the case. However, it may be advisable on occasion to call attention in argument to certain objections and to the reasons for making them. If this technique is used, the correctness of the rulings should not be challenged, as these are matters of law.

Where evidence is admissible for one purpose but not for another, or against one party but not another, counsel offering the evidence should, when faced with an objection, specify the purpose for which, or the party against whom, the evidence is being offered.[22] The adverse party would normally be entitled to an instruction directing the jury to consider the evidence only for such purpose.

Objections should be addressed to the court and not to opposing counsel. Do not show anger if the objection is overruled.

SECTION 54. RIGHT OF CROSS-EXAMINATION. The right to cross-examine is considered to be so important a device for ascertaining truth that a deprivation of the right will result in the striking of the testimony given on direct examination.[23] Such deprivation may result from the death or illness of the witness after having testified on direct examination.

The right to cross-examine may, however, be waived.[24] Such waiver may result from a failure to exercise the right at the proper time, unless the court grants permission to defer the cross-examination until a later time.

SECTION 55. SCOPE OF CROSS-EXAMINATION. In theory, there is a considerable difference among the various jurisdictions as to the scope of cross-examination.[25] Under the most liberal rule, sometimes referred to as the English or Massachusetts rule, the

---

[22] Curtin v. Benjamin, 305 Mass. 489, 26 N.E. 2d 354.

[23] L. & N.R. Co. v. Gregory, 284 Ky. 297, 144 S.W. 2d 519; McCormick, Evidence, § 19.

[24] Bradley v. Mirick, 91 N.W. 293.

[25] McCormick, Evidence, § 21.

only requirement is that the subject of inquiry be relevant to the issues in the case.[26] At the other extreme is the so-called federal view, that the cross-examination is restricted to matters brought out on direct examination.[27] Some jurisdictions purport to follow what might be called the compromise view, that the cross-examination is not designed to bring out matters upon which the cross-examiner has the burden of proof.[28] Regardless of the rule followed in a particular jurisdiction, cross-examination may be used for the purpose of impeachment.[29]

With reference to appellate court opinions, the trial attorney is more interested in what the court does than in a statement that a particular rule as to the scope of cross-examination is adopted in a particular jurisdiction. A comparison of cases in the same jurisdiction may thus reveal that several different rules are in fact applied.[30]

If the cross-examiner is deemed to have gone beyond the allowable scope, the witness is considered to have been called by the cross-examiner. The witness may then not be impeached by the party cross-examining.[31]

SECTION 56. WHEN TO CROSS-EXAMINE. Because of the fact that circumstances vary greatly from case to case, and because of differences of opinion among trial attorneys, it is difficult to set down fixed and specific conditions under which counsel ought to cross-examine a witness. Consequently reference will be made only to certain factors which should be considered.

Many attorneys do not cross-examine a witness unless his testimony has been particularly damaging. If, for example, the

---

[26] Moody v. Rowell, 34 Mass. 490.

[27] Philadelphia & Trenton R. Co. v. Stimpson, 14 Pet. 448.

[28] Legg v. Drake, 1 Ohio St. 286.

[29] Chicago City Ry. Co. v. Carroll, 206 Ill. 318, 69 N.E. 523.

[30] Cf. Wheeler & Wilson Mfg. Co. v. Barrett, 172 Ill. 610, 50 N.E. 325 and Crosby v. Deland District, 367 Ill. 362, 11 N.E. 2d 937. Note "The Limiting Effect of Direct Examination upon the scope of Cross-Examination," 37 Col. L. Rev. 1373.

[31] Pollard v. State, 201 Ind. 180, 166 N.E. 654; McCormick, Evidence, § 23.

improbability of the testimony on direct examination is apparent, there is no point in cross-examining. Even where the testimony is damaging, it should be noted that cross-examination tends to fix the testimony in the minds of the jury.

Similarly, many attorneys suggest that the cross-examiner should have some definite purpose in mind. The chief purposes of cross-examination are to obtain an admission from the witness, to elicit further information from him to soften the impact of his testimony as given on direct examination, and to impeach the witness. An admission from an adverse witness is deemed to be more effective than establishing the fact by your own witness. The objectives which counsel hopes to achieve must, of course, be within the permissible scope of cross-examination.

Finally, some attorneys do not cross-examine unless they are reasonably sure that some specific objective will be achieved. An extreme statement of this position is found in the oft-repeated "rule": "Do not cross-examine unless you know what the answer will be." Other attorneys are more willing to risk receiving a response damaging to their cause and hence do not hesitate to engage in a "fishing expedition." If this approach is used, counsel should have some plan in mind as to how to counteract an unfavorable response.

In any case the manner of cross-examination is related to the decision as to whether to cross-examine. Thus, some attorneys ask all witnesses at least a few innocuous questions, while other attorneys do not cross-examine unless they can get at the heart of the case. The former device is used to draw attention away from material facts.

Occasionally an attorney is confronted with a situation in which a cross-examination is likely to alienate the jury, and thus any advantage gained by such examination would be eliminated. Illustrative of such situation is the case of the bereaved mother testifying in a wrongful death action.

In determining whether to cross-examine, counsel should also consider the possibility that a failure to so examine may be referred to by opposing counsel in his closing argument as an admission of the truth of the testimony given on direct examination.[32]

SECTION 57. PREPARATION FOR CROSS-EXAMINATION. In some jurisdictions it is possible by means of discovery devices to ascertain what persons the adverse party will call as witnesses.[33] Where this rule prevails, a pre-trial investigation of such persons will frequently determine whether grounds for possible impeachment exist. In many jurisdictions it is at least possible to ascertain by such means the names of any witnesses not discovered by the usual investigative procedures.[34]

If depositions of the most important witnesses are taken, counsel can ascertain rather specifically how each witness may testify at the trial. The same information may be obtained from any statement which may have been taken, or from answers to interrogatories. The basic areas of agreement and disagreement should thus become apparent. Any documents likely to be introduced into evidence should be carefully scrutinized before trial.

By the use of such advance information, a general plan regarding cross-examination can be formulated before trial. In this way the likelihood that the cross-examination will backfire can be reduced to a minimum. Additional notes and modifications can be made at the trial, but such note-taking should not be so extensive as to prevent observation of the witnesses and the jury. If there is likely to be a question as to the propriety of any portion of the cross-examination, the notes should contain references to any authorities to be relied upon in argument of objections.

[32] Santiemmo v. Days Transfer, Inc., 9 Ill. App. 2d 487, 133 N.E. 539; 68 A.L.R. 2d 1072.

[33] Texas and Pacific Ry. v. Buckles, 232 F. 2d 257. Note "Discovery Practice in States Adopting the Federal Rules of Civil Procedure," 68 Harv. L. Rev. 673, 683. 4 Moore, Federal Practice, ¶ 26.19 [4], note 3. (2d ed. 1963).

[34] U.S. v. Matles, 19 F.R.D. 319. Vestal, "New Iowa Discovery Rules," 43 Iowa L. Rev. 8, 31.

SECTION 58. IMPEACHMENT. Probably the most effective impeachment device is proof that the witness made a prior inconsistent statement.[35] This statement may be oral or written, but the latter is obviously easier to prove. Frequently the statement is in the form of a deposition or a document signed by the witness and obtained by an investigator. Even if the inconsistency seems to be trivial, its effect upon the jury is deemed to be significant. The impact is the greater if the witness will on cross-examination admit making the statement. Furthermore, it is usually necessary to ask the witness about the statement, even if it is intended to prove such statement by other means.[36] This requirement gives the witness an opportunity to explain the statement.

If it is known in advance that a reasonable explanation can be given, it may be inadvisable to bring out the inconsistency. Again, if the statement includes elements unfavorable to the cross-examiner, the possible benefit derived from use of the statement may be nullified, especially if the statement is to be offered into evidence.

If an inconsistent statement is to be used, the witness should first be asked to repeat what he testified to on direct examination. The two statements will thus be presented to the jury closer in point of time and the inconsistency will be more apparent.

A second common impeachment technique is that of eliciting the fact, where possible, that the witness lacked the ability to perceive that which he has testified to on direct examination; or, that in fact he does not recall an event; or that the witness is not accurately communicating his knowledge in his direct testimony.[37] This technique is frequently used where the witness testifies to the identity of certain persons or things. It will be noted that the effort

---

35 McCormick, Evidence, § 34.
36 Robinson v. U.S., 144 F. 2d 392.
37 McCormick, Evidence, § 45.

here is merely to show that the witness is mistaken, not that he is guilty of perjury. The latter is difficult to prove.[38]

Finally, it is sometimes possible to bring out on cross-examination facts which tend to show the witness is biased or prejudiced.[39] Thus, if the witness has a personal interest in the outcome of the action, he may be likely to exaggerate. On occasion it is proper to ask the witness why he is testifying voluntarily, if that be the case. Bias can best be approached indirectly and by requiring the witness to be specific. Attention may then be directed in closing argument to facts showing bias or prejudice.

In determining whether to attempt impeachment by any of the above methods, counsel should consider whether the adverse party may be able to rehabilitate the witness, and thus give to his direct testimony a greater than usual significance.[40] For example, opposing counsel may be able to show that any bias which does exist operates in favor of the cross-examiner.

SECTION 59. HOW TO CROSS-EXAMINE. It has often been stated that the ability to cross-examine a witness properly is an art and not a science; or, that a good cross-examiner is born and not made. The implication of such statements is that it is difficult if not impossible to develop that ability. However, many seasoned trial lawyers challenge such a generalization.

As stated earlier, it is difficult to list a number of specific "rules" that are applicable under any and all circumstances. Among the variables that must be considered are the nature of the case, the kind of testimony given, the personalities of the witness, the judge and counsel, and the character of the jury. Each attorney must proceed in a manner natural for him and he must vary his approach depending upon the circumstances. The follow-

---

[38] Clark and Marshall, Crimes, § 446 (5th ed.).
[39] McCormick, Evidence, § 40.
[40] Id. § 49.

ing suggestions, made by experienced trial attorneys, should be considered in light of the above.

Testimony given on direct examination should not be repeated on cross-examination unless such testimony is to be emphasized, as where a prior inconsistent statement is to be used. Again, if it is concluded by counsel that the witness falsified a part of his testimony, a step by step recital of the same testimony given on direct examination, in minute detail, may disclose a deviation which can be used as an opening wedge. This device is particularly effective where the witness seems to be sure of a mass of details, and gives "pat" answers in his direct examination. If this technique is used, the cross-examiner must be able effectively to counteract damaging testimony.

Similarly, there is usually no occasion for counsel to repeat every answer given by the witness.

Material parts of suspected false testimony should not be attacked directly. Rather, counsel should go into the surrounding circumstances to show the improbability or impossibility of the fact as testified. It is rarely advisable to accuse a witness of deliberate falsehood, for the jury's sympathies may be with him.

Surprise is the element that makes cross-examination an effective device for detecting falsehood. Hence a witness suspected of deviating from the truth should not be made aware of the purpose of the cross-examiner. Some attorneys accomplish this by attacking parts of the direct examination in disconnected sequence, so that the witness cannot surmise what the next question will be. Frequently, the witness can be lulled into a false sense of security by a few innocuous questions preceding the really significant ones. The most important point should normally be reserved until the end of the cross-examination.

If a witness has been driven into a contradiction, or into a position that is logically improbable, he should not be asked for an explanation, unless counsel is assured that a satisfactory one cannot be given. Instead, a reference to such testimony in the closing argument is more effective. Once a point has been made, it is best to start a new line of questions.

As noted earlier, it is generally permissible to ask leading questions on cross-examination. The questions should, however, not be misleading nor ambiguous. Such questions are ethically questionable and can serve to alienate the jury.

Usually no advantage is gained by arguing with a hostile or evasive witness. It is sufficient to bring out the fact of hostility or evasion. If a witness refuses to answer, he can be ordered to do so. If this step produces an answer that the witness does not remember, he can be asked whether he remembers other specified events occurring at the same time and place. If instead of stating that he does not remember, the witness continues in his refusal to answer, the direct examination may be stricken.

While it is probably true that no two witnesses should be cross-examined in the same way, in general an inquiry conducted in a quiet, courteous manner is more likely to elicit favorable responses than is a rude, harsh, sarcastic approach. It is well to remember that most witnesses do not intentionally falsify, though they may be mistaken. Harassment of witnesses by means of violent cross-examination can frequently be stopped by calling attention to the fact that the witness is not on trial.

Cross-examination of one witness is more effective if it can be completed during a single session of court.

Cross-examination of experts presents special problems if counsel is not familiar with the subject matter involved or the standards used to qualify the expert. Adequate preparation should, however, enable counsel to cross-examine experts with confidence. A fairly common approach is to inquire whether the same opinion would be given if one of the facts upon which the opinion is based were changed. There must, however, be a conflict in the evidence as to such fact.[41]

If there is reason to doubt the qualifications of the alleged expert, he can be asked to give his definition of certain key terms, and this can be compared with the definition given by acknowledged experts.

Interest in the outcome of the suit can sometimes be shown by bringing out the fact that the witness has appeared frequently as a witness in other lawsuits, and has in a sense become a "professional" witness; or, that his fee is out of proportion to the value of his services, or is payable only in the event of a successful termination of the action.

If the witness has published any material on the subject matter involved in the lawsuit, and opinions therein expressed are contrary to those now testified to, an inquiry may be made as to such contradictions. Likewise, a conflict of opinions of several experts may be brought out, provided that the experts relied upon by the cross-examiner are as well qualified as the expert being cross-examined.

SECTION 60. RE-DIRECT EXAMINATION. When a witness has been cross-examined, the party calling him may conduct a re-direct examination at the close of the cross-examination.[42] The purpose of the re-direct examination is to rehabilitate a witness who has been impeached, or to explain any inconsistencies in his testimony. The scope of the re-direct examination is therefore normally limited to matters which have been brought out on cross-examination, although the judge in his discretion may allow an interrogation into matters which should have been brought out on direct examination.[43]

The need for re-direct examination can thus be determined

---

41 Ulm v. Moore–McCormack Lines, Inc., 115 F. 2d 492; 71 A.L.R. 2d 6.

42 McCormick, Evidence, § 32.

43 State v. Conner, 97 N.J.L. 423, 118 A. 211.

only by carefully noting the damage done by cross-examination. The advisability of conducting a re-direct examination can be determined by evaluating its probable success. If, for example, counsel is uncertain whether an inconsistency can be adequately explained, it is usually a better tactic not to make the effort. Counsel should also take into consideration the fact that a re-direct examination enables opposing counsel to conduct a re-cross examination. If the cross-examiner is allowed by the law of the jurisdiction to bring out matters of defense, and does so, it is usually imperative to conduct a re-direct examination to prevent a directed verdict.

SECTION 61. REBUTTAL TESTIMONY. This term is normally limited to the testimony offered by the party having the burden of proof, after both sides have rested their case.[44] The purpose of such testimony is to counteract that which was introduced by the opposing party's own witnesses. This purpose may be accomplished by introducing contradictory evidence or evidence which raises questions of credibility. Less confusion will occur if the proper order of presenting evidence is observed. A defense should therefore not normally be anticipated in the proof of the prima facie case.

In some jurisdictions it is permissible to bring out rebuttal testimony by means of cross-examination.[45]

---

[44] McCormick, Evidence, § 4.
[45] See § 55 herein.

Chapter 6

Withdrawing a Case from the Jury

A. Voluntary Nonsuit

SECTION 62. NATURE AND EFFECT. Originally a nonsuit was a judgment of dismissal for the failure of the plaintiff to be present in court at the time the jury returned its verdict. Since such judgment would not bar the plaintiff from maintaining a subsequent action on the same claim, it was soon perceived that this practice provided a way for a plaintiff to escape the conclusive effect of an adverse verdict. Hence we find plaintiffs absenting themselves from the courtroom when such a verdict was anticipated. Later, instead of absenting themselves, plaintiffs merely remained in the courtroom and asked to be nonsuited.

Apparently there was no limit as to the number of times a plaintiff could ask to be nonsuited, but this has been changed by rule or statute in some jurisdictions. In the federal courts, for example, a second dismissal operates as an adjudication upon the merits, whether the first dismissal was in a state or federal court.[1]

This practice, known variously by the terms "voluntary nonsuit," "dismissal," or "discontinuance" prevails today in all juris-

---

[1] Fed. R. Civ. P. 41 (a) (1); 65 A.L.R. 2d 643.

dictions and has the same effect, unless changed by rule or statute. It does not operate as res adjudicata.[2] To be distinguished from this practice is that of "withdrawing a juror," which in effect is the declaration of a mistrial, and which merely postpones the trial, the case being kept on the trial calendar. Mistrials may be declared for a variety of reasons, such as misconduct of counsel or some members of the jury, which in the judgment of the court precludes the parties from having a fair trial.

SECTION 63. CIRCUMSTANCES UNDER WHICH ADVISABLE. Perhaps the most common situation in which a nonsuit should be requested is this: If a key witness who has agreed to testify and for that reason was not served with a subpoena, fails to appear at the trial, a continuance very probably would not be granted. However, a nonsuit should not be requested even in this situation if the essence of the witness's testimony can be given by another witness, by exhibits, etc. The nonsuit, in this as well as in other situations where it is appropriate, is based on the assumption that the proof will be available at a later date.

Again, a case may be set for trial before counsel for the plaintiff has had time to prepare his case, and the court may refuse to grant a continuance. A nonsuit is here suggested as a last-ditch device to keep a claim alive for future litigation.

If the practice in the jurisdiction permits, a nonsuit may be advisable where the court indicates that it will rule adversely to the plaintiff on a motion for a directed verdict. Such adverse ruling may be due to the court's determination that the proof submitted would be insufficient to send the case to the jury, or it may be due to a refusal to accept the plaintiff's theory as the appropriate one. Counsel for the plaintiff may believe that he can supply the deficiency of proof at a later time; or, that he may be able to present another and acceptable theory before the same

---

[2] Southern Ry. Co. v. Miller, 217 U.S. 209; 53 Am. Jur. Trial § 304; 11 A.L.R. 2d 1407.

court; or, that he can present the same theory to another court which may deem it to be acceptable.

Before asking for a nonsuit, counsel for the plaintiff should be reasonably certain that he can present a stronger case, given another opportunity; he should be certain that the dismissal is without prejudice; he must consider whether the statute of limitations would have run against the claim; and, finally, he should weigh other alternatives, such as an appeal from an adverse judgment.

SECTION 64. MUST BE TAKEN AT PROPER TIME. Two very significant developments may be discerned when tracing the history of the voluntary nonsuit. These are: 1. The period within which the nonsuit may be taken is being reduced. 2. A distinction is being made between a nonsuit as a matter of right and one as a matter within the discretion of the court.

At common law, a plaintiff was entitled as a matter of right to take a nonsuit at any time until the jury returned its verdict.[3] In New England the rule developed without the aid of a statute, that a nonsuit could be taken as a matter of right before the evidence was introduced, and after that point the court could allow the nonsuit as a matter of discretion.[4]

The standard codes either provided that the nonsuit had to be taken prior to the retirement of the jury to consider their verdict[5] or prior to the submission of the case to the jury.[6] No substantial difference in interpretation due to the difference in statutory language can be detected in the decisions applying the statutes. Subsequent amendments fixed a similar period in cases tried by the court without a jury.

More recent practice acts or rules of court frequently provide

---

[3] Washburn v. Allen, 77 Me. 344. Comment, "Developments in the Law—Res Judicata," 65 Harv. L.R. 818, 837.

[4] Carpenter & Sons v. N.Y.N.H. & H.R. Co., 184 Mass. 98, 68 N.E. 28.

[5] Texas Electric Ry. v. Cox, 49 S.W. 2d 725.

[6] Oppenheimer v. Elmore, 109 Ia. 196, 80 N.W. 307.

that a nonsuit may be taken as a matter of right prior to the filing of an answer, and thereafter only as a matter of discretion.[7] In the former instance, it is not material that the defendant has filed a motion to dismiss. Where it is necessary to obtain the approval of the court, plaintiff must submit a motion stating the reasons therefore. A typical situation would be where the plaintiff could convince the court that he had a meritorious claim, but for some reason beyond his control could not now prove it.

Where there are multiple defendants, a plaintiff may avail himself of the nonsuit practice as to one defendant, though other defendants claim a right of contribution, assuming that the nonsuit is regular in other respects.[8] Again, a plaintiff may wish to take a nonsuit as to one of several causes of action against the same defendant.

There is a conflict in the authorities under the standard code provisions as to whether a nonsuit may be taken after the court has indicated how he will rule on a motion for a directed verdict, where the verdict has not yet been signed.[9] The chances of obtaining a nonsuit prior to the ruling on the motion are of course greater than where the court has announced his decision. The conflict results from the fact that the statutory language did not in fact cover the situation presented.

SECTION 65. IMPOSITION OF CONDITIONS. Where the nonsuit or dismissal is a matter for the exercise of discretion by the court, quite generally the statutes or rules provide that the court may specify the conditions under which the nonsuit may be granted.[10] A common condition is the payment of the ordinary costs of the action up to that point. In some instances, the plaintiff may also be

---

[7] Fed. R. Civ. P. 41 (a) (2); 21 A.L.R. 2d 627.

[8] Whitehead v. Williams, 196 Okla. 411, 165 P. 2d 618; 17 Am. Jur. Dismissal, § 42.

[9] Cherniak v. Prudential Ins. Co. of America, 339 Pa. 73, 14 A. 2d 334; Lykens v. Jarrett, 123 W. Va. 631, 17 S.E. 2d 328; 17 Am. Jur. Dismissal, § 37.

[10] Bolten v. General Motors Corp., 180 F. 2d 379; 17 Am. Jur. Dismissal, § 56.

required to pay the defendant's attorney's fees. Again, the court may specify that a counterclaim shall remain pending for independent adjudication. In short, the circumstances of the particular case determine what conditions, if any, are likely to be imposed. Once they are specified by the court, plaintiff may then determine whether to proceed with his original request.

SECTION 66. WHERE DEFENDANT HAS PLEADED A COUNTER-CLAIM. In the absence of a statute or rule covering the matter, there is a conflict in the decisions as to whether a nonsuit may be taken where the defendant has filed a counterclaim.[11] In some cases the plaintiff was denied the right to take a nonsuit; in others he was allowed to take a nonsuit, despite the fact that the defendant's counterclaim as a consequence could not be adjudicated; in still others, a nonsuit was allowed but the counterclaim remained as an independent action.

Modern practice acts or rules frequently provide that a nonsuit may be allowed if the counterclaim can remain in the case for independent adjudication.[12] For example, in an action by a beneficiary to recover the amount allegedly due under a policy of insurance, the insurer may file a counterclaim seeking cancellation of the policy on the grounds of nonpayment of the premiums. The court may determine that there is no need for affirmative relief in this situation, and hence rule that the counterclaim cannot remain pending. A counterclaim may not, of course, be filed solely for the purpose of preventing a nonsuit.

SECTION 67. WHEN PROHIBITED. Where the granting of a nonsuit or dismissal is a matter for the exercise of the court's discretion, there may be situations, other than that presented by the filing of a counterclaim, where the court will decline to grant the plaintiff's request. In general, this refusal is likely where the court

---

[11] Yellowday v. Perkinson, 167 N.C. 144, 83 S.E. 341; Tomasello v. Walton, 100 Fla. 710, 129 So. 840; 17 Am. Jur. Dismissal, § 47.

[12] Code 1935, Iowa, § 11564; 17 Am. Jur. Dismissal, § 47.

believes the question is such that it can and should be decided now, and in the court where the action is pending.

Thus, a class action, involving as it does, interests of persons not parties to the action, may not be dismissed if such interests are not adequately protected by such procedure.[13] In certain actions, such as those in which the validity of an insurance policy or a will are the principal issues, policy may require the determination of those issues as soon as possible, especially when balanced with the reasons assigned for requesting the nonsuit.[14] A like situation is presented by a creditor's suit to distribute the assets of an insolvent corporation, or where a third party files a petition for intervention.[15]

B. Involuntary Nonsuit; Directed Verdict

SECTION 68. ORIGINS. The involuntary or compulsory nonsuit, and the directed verdict, were developed for the same purpose, namely as a means of controlling the action of the jury. Various features of each procedure will be discussed in the following sections, to indicate which procedure is appropriate in given situations.

As long as the jury acted on its own knowledge, the judge did not interfere with the verdict. Later, as the jury acted more and more on evidence introduced in open court, and less on personal knowledge of the facts involved in the dispute, the courts began to advise how the case ought to be decided. Still later, courts began to set aside verdicts and to grant new trials where it was felt that the evidence did not support the verdict. Finally, courts began to direct juries to return specific verdicts in particular cases.

It will be noted that the power to control the actions of the

---

13 Commonwealth use of Fleming County v. Plummer, 235 Ky. 506, 31 S.W. 2d 897; 17 Am. Jur. Dismissal, § 16.

14 Benoist v. Murrin, 48 Mo. 48.

15 Auburn Button Works v. Perryman Electrical Co., 109 N.J. Eq. 554, 154 A. 1.

jury by means of the directed verdict was only gradually recognized and exercised. But the power to grant an involuntary nonsuit was never recognized at early common law.[16] This procedure has been, however, adopted in a number of American jurisdictions, either by specific statutory provision, or by court decision.[17] This type of nonsuit was designed as a substitute for the archaic demurrer to the evidence. In those jurisdictions which use both the nonsuit (or dismissal) and the directed verdict, a problem of selection is presented. As stated earlier, the following sections deal with this problem.

When courts began to direct a verdict against a proponent we find the beginnings of the doctrine of burden of proof. This doctrine has two phases: 1. The burden of producing sufficient evidence to convince the judge that the jury may find in favor of the proponent (or, to escape a directed verdict). 2. The burden of producing sufficient evidence to persuade the jury to find in favor of proponent (or, to establish the proposition). It is only the first phase which concerns us at this point.

The adoption of the concept of burden of proof represents a milestone in the development of trial by jury as we know it today. The application of the concept is found in the various mechanics used in different jurisdictions.

SECTION 69. RES ADJUDICATA. A directed verdict has always barred the bringing of another action based upon the same cause of action.[18] Thus, the only recourse open to a losing party is to appeal the decision on the motion and its concomitant judgment. But the rule with respect to the involuntary nonsuit or dismissal is not that clear. Generally speaking, however, if there is no rule

---

16 Doe ex dem. Elmore v. Grimes, 1 Pet. 471.

17 Stickney v. Stickney, 21 N.H. 61; 88 C.J.S. Trial § 238 a.

18 Morgan v. C.M. & St. P. Ry. Co., 83 Wis. 348, 53 N.W. 741. Smith, "The Power of the Judge to Direct a Verdict," 24 Col. L.R. 111.

or statute to the contrary, a nonsuit does not operate as res adjudicata.[19]

In some jurisdictions, if the proponent's evidence is merely deficient, and the court is of the opinion that this deficiency can be cured by another trial, the appropriate motion is for a nonsuit; but if the proponent's own proof shows affirmatively that he has no cause of action, the opponent may move for a direction of the verdict.[20] If the motion is for a nonsuit, the court may treat it as one for a directed verdict and apply the rule in finality.

SECTION 70. WAIVER OF JURY; RIGHT TO INTRODUCE EVIDENCE WHEN MOTION IS OVERRULED. Two of the objectionable features of the demurrer to the evidence were the rules that a demurrant waived both his right to a jury trial regardless of the ruling, and his right to introduce further evidence when his demurrer was overruled. Final judgment followed the ruling, just as was the case originally when a pleading was demurred to.

Both of these features have, in most jurisdictions, been eliminated by the introduction of the involuntary nonsuit and the directed verdict.[21] In a few jurisdictions it seems to be necessary for the party moving for a directed verdict to specifically request a jury trial in the event his motion is overruled. This request should be noted in the record.

The situation where both parties move for a directed verdict will be considered in a later section.

SECTION 71. WHO MAY MOVE. The motion, whether for a nonsuit or directed verdict, is normally made by the party who does not have the burden of proof on the issue involved. Rarely will a court sustain a motion made by the party who has the burden

---

[19] Oscanyan v. Winchester Repeating Arms Co., 103 U.S. 261; 17 Am. Jur. Dismissal, § 87.

[20] Dennison v. Musgrave, 20 Misc. 678, 46 N.Y. S. 530.

[21] St. Louis, I.M. & S.R. Co. v. Ingram, 118 Ark. 377, 176 S.W. 692; 38 C.J S. Trial § 256 a.

of proof.[22] This result follows from the view that a question of credibility is involved, even though there is proof on all issues and there is no contradictory proof; the testimony must be believed in order to sustain the motion. But where the motion is made by the party who does not have the burden of proof, the standard approach is that no question of credibility is involved, for the problem before the court is: assuming the evidence to be believable, is the evidence sufficient to send the case to the jury?

Even in jurisdictions where the party having the burden of proof may move, he should seriously consider the fact that, to be successful on the motion, he must satisfy the court on *all* points which are in issue, whereas his opponent may obtain a favorable ruling by satisfying the court on merely *one* such point.

Where both procedures are available, there is some variation as to the stage of the the trial when each is appropriate. Thus, where a nonsuit is generally available only at the close of the plaintiff's case, it will of course be used only by the defendant, whereas the directed verdict may be sought by either party at the close of the whole case.[23]

In determining whether to file a motion for nonsuit or directed verdict, the following additional factors should be considered:

1. Most motions are overruled.[24] Nevertheless many attorneys representing defendants follow a policy of filing a motion regularly. They contend that there is always the chance that the motion will be sustained. With the abolition of the "scintilla test" (as to which, see Section 76), it is more likely to have a motion sustained than it was when that test was followed. Also, it is true that there is no longer any question about going to the jury in the event of an unfavorable ruling. Finally, the overruling presents

---

22 Giles v. Giles, 204 Mass. 383, 90 N.E. 595; 53 Am. Jur. Trial § 386.

23 McCown v. Muldrow, 91 S.C. 523, 74 S.E. 386.

24 13th Ann. Rep. Jud. Council 76 (N.Y. 1947).

another appealable point in the event of an unfavorable verdict and judgment.

2. In those jurisdictions which follow the rule that a jury trial is waived where both parties move,[25] counsel must consider the possibility that his adversary may join in the motion. This rule may not dissuade a party from moving if the case involves ultimately only a question of law, as, for instance, the interpretation of documents. Further, it is usually possible to reserve the right to go to the jury if one's motion is overruled. Finally, it may be possible to withdraw a motion when the adversary also moves. No hard and fast suggestion may therefore be made.

3. Some attorneys consider the possible effect which an adverse ruling may have on the minds of the jury. The jury may resent efforts to take a case away from them and allow such resentment to influence them in arriving at a verdict. Or, the jury may misinterpret the move as an admission by the moving party of the weakness of his case. Lastly, the ruling may be considered as an indication of the judge's feelings as to the merits of the case, and hence influence the jury in the rendition of a verdict. This possibility may be partially countered by an instruction to the effect that the ruling carries with it no such implication. Also, it may be possible to have the argument and ruling take place out of the hearing of the jury.

SECTION 72. THE MOTION—HOW MADE. In some jurisdictions, the motion is made orally in open court, the jury being excused.[26] In such instances the motion should be recorded in the minutes, and the record should include all reasons specified.

In other jurisdictions the motion must be in writing.[27] While at first glance this requirement may seem harsh, it is usually

---

[25] Beuttell v. Magone, 157 U.S. 154; 53 Am. Jur. Trial, § 354; 68 A.L.R. 2d 300.
[26] Southern Ice Co. v. Black, 136 Tenn. 391, 189 S.W. 861; 53 Am. Jur. Trial, § 337.
[27] Ross v. Kohler, 163 Ky. 583, 174 S.W. 36; 53 Am. Jur. Trial, § 337.

possible to anticipate some of the grounds before trial, by the use of the various discovery devices available today. Also one can generally add further grounds at the time the motion is presented.

In still other jurisdictions the motion may be orally made but a written instruction must be tendered at the time the motion is made.[28]

Under any of the above procedures, the record should show the motion, the reasons therefore, the ruling, and, if necessary, the exception thereto if the ruling is adverse.[29]

Likewise, the motion, whether oral or in writing, must state the reasons with particularity. Thus, if the grounds are failure of proof, counsel should point out what proof was not forthcoming. Fairness to the court and the adverse party demands such specification. The court is not required to recall the evidence without a reminder from the moving party. Further, the adverse party is given an opportunity to supply the missing proof, in the discretion of the court, when notice is given. Also, it is difficult for the appellate court to determine whether the trial court committed error if the reasons for the motion are unknown.

If there are multiple counts, or several causes of action, it may be possible to have the verdict directed as to one or more counts or causes, allowing the balance to go to the jury.[30] Or, if several issues are involved in the same count or cause of action, a verdict may, in some jurisdictions, be directed on one or more such issues. The same is true where the case involves multiple parties.[31] In each instance care must be exercised to point out specifically what count, cause of action, issue or party is involved, or the court may overrule the motion if any count, etc. is supported by proof. Where certain counts, etc. are singled out for attack,

---

28 See § 94, herein; 53 Am. Jur. Trial, § 337.

29 Hoose v. Prescott Ins. Co., 84 Mich. 309, 47 N.W. 587; 53 Am. Jur. Trial, § 337.

30 Houlihan v. McCall, 197 Md. 130, 78 A. 2d 661; 88 C.J.S. Trial, § 257 a.

31 Bingham v. National Bank, 105 Mont. 159, 72 P. 2d 90; 88 C.J.S. Trial, § 257 h.

the motion should make clear that it is not intended as an admission of liability as to the part of the case not reached by the motion.

SECTION 73. TIME WHEN MOTION SHOULD BE MADE. In those jurisdictions which sanction the use of a motion for a compulsory nonsuit as well as a motion for a directed verdict, the former is usually deemed appropriate only when the plaintiff has completed his examination in chief and indicates that by stating that he rests.[32] Where, however, the defendant has brought out elements of his defense by means of cross-examination, some courts require the defendant to defer making his motion for nonsuit until after the plaintiff has been given the opportunity to offer rebuttal testimony.[33]

The motion for a directed verdict is properly made at the conclusion of all the evidence, including the plaintiff's rebuttal and the defendant's rejoinder.[34] If the motion to direct the verdict is made at the conclusion of all the evidence, it should normally be made before the jury has retired to deliberate; in special situations, however, the court may grant leave to move to direct after such retirement, but before the return of the verdict.

If the jurisdiction sanctions only the use of the directed verdict, it is appropriately used at the conclusion of either of the above stages.

SECTION 74. RENEWAL OF THE MOTION. At times defendant's counsel may be faced with the problem, whether to move at the conclusion of the plaintiff's case or to wait until all the evidence is in. On the one hand, if counsel chooses the latter course, he runs the risk that the plaintiff may be able to supply the deficiency during rebuttal or cross-examination. On the other hand, it should be noted that the court has the power to allow the plaintiff to

---

[32] Fed. R. Civ. P. 41 (b); 88 C.J.S. Trial, § 240.
[33] Bunnell v. Rosenberg, 126 Ill. App. 196.
[34] McCown v. Muldrow, 91 S.C. 523, 74 S.E. 386; 53 Am. Jur. Trial, § 338.

reopen his case and introduce more evidence, if the motion is made at the close of the plaintiff's case. Obviously the decision must be based upon the nature of the evidence at the conclusion of the various stages.

Where the defendant has moved at the conclusion of the plaintiff's case, he is also required, in most jurisdictions, to move again at the conclusion of the entire case, if he wishes to obtain appellate review of the overruling of his original motion.[35] Various explanations for this requirement have been advanced. If the defendant's evidence, or the plaintiff's rebuttal has supplied the omission in the presentation of the evidence in chief, obviously no prejudicial error has been committed by the court in ruling upon the first motion. Even where no such omission is supplied, it has been suggested as a reason for the rule, that the appellate court should not be required to examine the whole record where the defendant's failure to renew his motion may indicate a waiver of the orginal contention.

In those jurisdictions which provide for a post-verdict motion for judgment (as to which, see Sections 79–82) along with a motion for a new trial, the motion for judgment is deemed to be a renewal of the contention made at the conclusion of all the evidence.

Despite the fact that it may be difficult at times to discover a rational basis for the rule, and that hence it may be labeled purely technical, it is suggested that the rule be followed. A failure to do so may prove costly and compliance does not work a hardship upon the moving party.

SECTION 75. ARGUMENT ON THE MOTION. Counsel should be prepared to argue the motion at the time it is filed, for the court may require argument at that time. Hence it is suggested that notes of the evidence be made during the progress of the trial.

---

[35] Hopkins v. Clark, 158 N.Y. 299, 53 N.E. 27; 53 Am. Jur. Trial, § 339.

The court should be requested to excuse the jury during the argument. Otherwise that body may draw erroneous impressions from any admissions as to the inferences that might legitimately be drawn from the evidence, which admissions are made only for purposes of the motion.

The content of the argument will depend upon the test applied in the particular jurisdiction as to when the motion may be sustained (as to which, see Section 76). In any event, reference should be made to applicable law in the course of the argument.

As in any argument before a court, the presentation should be brief, forceful and orderly. This is no time for emphasis upon emotion or prejudice. On the other hand, since the ruling may terminate the trial, no effort should be spared, and counsel should especially avoid the impression that the motion is being presented in a routine, perfunctory fashion with little or no hope for success.

SECTION 76. TESTS APPLIED IN RULING ON THE MOTION. Jurisdictions vary as to the test to be applied in ruling on the motion. These tests are:

1. The scintilla rule, which is the earliest in point of time.[36] Under this rule, if there is any evidence, however slight, in support of the elements of the proponent's case, the motion would be overruled. The rule still allows the court, of course, to set aside a verdict and grant a new trial, if, in its opinion, the evidence is not deemed sufficient to support the verdict. At that later stage, however, the court is governed by different considerations. While the scintilla rule is followed in only a few jurisdictions today, its early popularity during a period when, as stated earlier, the courts were uncertain as to their power to interfere in the jury's actions is understandable.

Under the scintilla rule the court examines only the evidence offered by the proponent.

---

36 Hamden Lodge No. 517, I.O.O.F. v. Ohio Fuel Gas Co., 127 Ohio St. 469, 189 N.E. 246; 53 Am. Jur. Trial, § 356.

2. The reasonable man test.[37] Under this view, the trial judge is required to make a decision as to how reasonable men (the jurors) would consider the evidence. If such persons would infer that the essential elements of the proponent's case had been shown, the motion would be overruled. If in the court's judgment reasonable men would differ as to the inferences to be drawn from undisputed evidence, or if conflicts in the evidence involved problems of credibility, the motion would again be overruled. And, as noted earlier, in some jurisdictions, a case will not be taken from the jury even if there is no conflict in the testimony, where the proponent is the moving party, on the grounds that credibility is involved here also. If the reasonable man test is applied, the court again looks only to the evidence introduced by the proponent.

The reasonable man test is today recognized as law in a majority of the jurisdictions. In theory it requires a greater quantum of proof by proponent to escape a directed verdict than does the scintilla rule. Also, where this test is applied, it is said that there are no questions of fact to leave to the jury.

3. The contrary verdict rule.[38] Under this rule a verdict will be directed against a party whenever a verdict in favor of that party would be set aside. This view is adopted in a minority of jurisdictions. Under it, the court examines the evidence introduced by both sides.

This third approach has been criticized on the following grounds: (a) It does not furnish a standard as to when a verdict will be set aside and a new trial granted. (b) The setting aside of a verdict involves merely procedure, while the direction of a verdict involves substantive law. (c) The granting of a new trial does not result in a final judgment, while that result follows automatically from the direction of a verdict. Nevertheless, the use of this test

---

[37] Smith v. Morgan, 214 Iowa 555, 240 N.W. 257; 53 Am. Jur. Trial, § 355.
[38] Loewinthan v. LeVine, 299 N.Y. 372, 87 N.E. 2d 303; 53 Am. Jur. Trial, § 360.

seems to be growing, undoubtedly because it is designed to cut off a trial at any early stage where the proponent cannot produce enough evidence to warrant a jury trial, or where counsel has not been diligent in gathering prior to trial what proof is available.

It will be noted that under any of the three tests, the court does not exercise discretion in ruling upon the motion, whereas in some instances of ruling on a motion for a voluntary nonsuit such discretion is exercised.

Also, it will be seen that in acting on a motion for a new trial, the court does determine where the weight of the evidence lies, and under the contrary verdict test this approach is also taken in ruling on a motion for a directed verdict. This is not true, however, when the court follows the scintilla rule or the reasonable man test.

The same test will be applied to motions for involuntary nonsuit or directed verdict in jurisdictions where both procedures are employed.

In order to determine which test is applied in a given jurisdiction, it is necessary to examine what a court does as well as what it says. Thus, while the court may purport to follow the scintilla rule, that term may be broadly construed; on the other hand, the substance of that test may be applied although the court purportedly follows the reasonable man test. And of course, in a given case, the result may be the same regardless of the test applied.

Under the old demurrer to the evidence, as it was applied in later English and in some American cases, it was necessary for the demurrant to expressly admit in writing all inferences, which might properly be drawn from the evidence no matter how damaging to the demurrant. As a result, most courts adopt the rule that in passing upon a motion for an involuntary nonsuit or a directed verdict they must draw like inferences in favor of the party against whom the motion is made. While the cases do not specifically relate this rule to either of the three tests specified above, it would seem that the "proper inference" rule is adopted in all jurisdictions. The difference seems to lie in the matter of credibility.

Under the second or "reasonable man" test, the proponent's evidence is assumed to be true, arguendo; questions of credibility are resolved in favor of the party against whom the motion is made.

But under the "contrary verdict" test, the court rejects evidence which is "inherently incredible," or which no jury could reasonably find to be true. This approach has been subject to the attack that the judge is, thereby, invading the province of the jury, and that he is in reality deciding questions of fact. The theory behind this approach is, however, that the judge is only deciding what reasonable men could find, and that there is no right to a jury trial on any but "substantial" issues raised by the evidence.

Where no objection is made to the introduction of certain evidence, which would be excluded had a proper objection been made, the court considers such evidence on a motion for a nonsuit or the direction of the verdict. This seems to be true no matter what test is applied.

A motion for dismissal is similar to an involuntary nonsuit, and is governed largely by statute or rule of court.[39] It may be appropriate where the plaintiff does not bring the case on for trial within a reasonable time,[40] where he does not appear at the time of the trial,[41] or where there is no jurisdiction, of the subject matter[42] or of the parties.[43]

A dismissal may also be appropriate where the plaintiff has failed to show that he is entitled to relief.[44] In this situation, a

---

[39] Fed. R. Civ. P. 41 (b); 88 C.J.S. Trial, § 238 a.
[40] Donovan v. Hollar, 25 Cal. App. 2d 548, 78 P. 2d 240.
[41] Hewitt v. International Shoe Co., 110 Fla. 37, 148 So. 533.
[42] Grandin Farmers Cooperative Elev. Co. v. Langer, 292 U.S. 605.
[43] Thompson v. Butler, 214 Iowa 1123, 243 N.W. 164.
[44] Tintic Standard Min. Co. v. Utah County, 80 Utah 491, 15 P. 2d 633.

dismissal is somewhat analogous to a directed verdict. A dismissal may be with or without prejudice to the bringing of another action. A statute or rule may provide that, unless the court directs otherwise, the dismissal will be with prejudice, thus barring another action. Normally, an action will be dismissed without prejudice if the court is of the opinion that, given another opportunity, the plaintiff could prove a prima facie case.

SECTION 77. WHEN NONSUIT OR DIRECTED VERDICT IS PROPER. Some of the more common situations in which courts have ordered a nonsuit or directed a verdict for the defendant are:

1. Where the plaintiff's evidence, if accepted as true, supports all elements necessary for recovery, but such testimony is not believable because of the physical conditions involved. Thus, if the plaintiff testifies that he stopped, looked and listened for the defendant's train, but saw and heard none, and the layout of the track is such that he must have seen the approaching train if he had done what he testified he did, his testimony need not be accepted as true.[45] This result certainly would follow if the "contrary verdict" test was applied and probably also under the "reasonable man" test.

2. Where the plaintiff proves a cause of action different than that which he pleaded, and the evidence is objected to, leave to amend the pleadings to conform to the proof not being given.[46] Thus, where the plaintiff pleads a cause of action based on false representation but fails to show that the defendant had knowledge of the falsity of the representation (scienter) and recovery is then sought on the theory of breach of warranty. A verdict would probably be directed for defendant no matter which of the three tests is used.

3. Where there is no essential dispute as to the facts, and the case involves a pure question of law, such as the interpretation

---

45 Carroll v. Pennsylvania R.R. Co., 12 Weekly Notes 348 (Pa.).
46 Wilkins v. Commercial Finance Co., 237 N.C. 396, 75 S.E. 2d 118.

of a document.[47] If the document is set out in the pleadings, the question could, of course, be presented by a demurrer or its modern equivalent, the motion to dismiss. The nonsuit or directed verdict would be appropriate under all three views.

4. Where the plaintiff's own evidence supports a defense, such as contributory negligence (if that be a defense in the particular jurisdiction).[48] Here again the same result would follow regardless of the test applied.

5. Where the plaintiff proves a prima facie case, but the defendant overcomes such case and affirmatively shows there is no liability, a directed verdict for defendant would be proper under the "contrary verdict" test but probably not under the "reasonable man" test.[49] However, the result may depend upon the time when the motion is made, as well as the nature of the proof presented by both sides.

SECTION 78. THE DECISION ON THE MOTION. If the court sustains a motion for an involuntary nonsuit, he enters an order to that effect. There is no occasion for findings of fact and conclusions of law as is the case in a trial to the court. If the court sustains a motion for a directed verdict, it is followed either by a direction to the jury to return a specified verdict, or to the clerk to enter a like verdict. The appropriate verdict is then entered. Finally a judgment of nonsuit or on the verdict completes the procedure.

As noted above, in some jurisdictions the court may direct a verdict on some issue, such as liability, and leave another issue, such as damages (if unliquidated) to the jury.

Also, in some jurisdictions the court may reserve its ruling until after the jury has returned its verdict.[50] When this is done, the court has more time to consider the question and also has the

---

47 Bunnell v. Rosenberg, 126 Ill. App. 196.
48 Chaney v. Louisiana & M.R.R. Co., 176 Mo. 598, 75 S.W. 595.
49 Loewinthan v. LeVine, 299 N.Y. 372, 87 N.E. 2d 303.
50 Baltimore & Carolina Line, Inc. v. Redman, 295 U.S. 654.

benefit of the jury's deliberation. If the verdict is not in accordance with law, the court sets it aside and either grants a new trial or enters judgment notwithstanding the verdict (as to which, see Sections 79–82). If a decision is thus reserved, the procedure set out herein is followed even if the jury cannot agree upon a verdict.

Where the decision on the motion results in final judgment, the decision may of course be appealed. As stated above, this is always true in the case of a ruling on a motion for a directed verdict and sometimes in the case of a motion for nonsuit. The trial court's ruling will not be upset on appeal if it can be sustained on any ground stated in the motion, even if the ruling was not made on that ground, according to the cases in some jurisdictions.[51] In others, the propriety of the ruling is tested only by the grounds relied upon by the trial court.[52]

C. Judgment Notwithstanding the Verdict

SECTION 79. DISTINCTION BETWEEN COMMON LAW AND MODERN PRACTICE. The motion for judgment notwithstanding the verdict has undergone a rather drastic change in purpose and practice. At common law it was directed at the record only and not at the evidence introduced at the trial. The record proper consisted of the praecipe, the process and return, the pleadings and any rulings thereon, the verdict and judgment. Technically the bill of exceptions was no part of the record. A typical situation for the use of the motion for judgment was where the defendant attempted to set up a defense by way of a plea in confession and avoidance, which plea was bad in substance because the matter set up in avoidance did not excuse or justify the act admitted. If the defendant obtained a verdict, the plaintiff could move for judgment notwithstanding the verdict.

---

51 Bailey v. London Guarantee & Accident Co., 72 Ind. App. 84, 121 N.E. 128.
52 In re Mixon, 110 S.C. 270, 96 S.E. 403; 5 C.J.S. Appeal and Error, § 1464 e.

The motion was thus a sort of belated general demurrer or a motion for judgment on the pleadings. The theory behind this motion was that a verdict found only facts which were well pleaded, and if a pleading was bad in substance, the verdict did not justify a judgment for the party receiving the verdict. Consequently, the motion could not be used in the rare instances where the verdict was deemed to cure the defect in the pleadings, or where the pleadings could be amended. Usually, however, the failure to demur to a pleading that was defective in substance was not considered as a waiver of such defects.

Similarly a defendant could move in arrest of judgment where the declaration was defective in substance and the plaintiff nevertheless obtained a verdict. This motion could be countered by the plaintiff himself moving for judgment on the verdict.

On the other hand, where a party against whom a verdict had been returned contended that the verdict was not justified by the evidence, he had available only the motion to direct the verdict and the motion for a new trial. The ruling on the motion to direct the verdict was of course reviewable on writ of error and bill of exceptions. But if the verdict and judgment were deemed by the reviewing court to be erroneous, that court could only reverse and remand for a new trial. A judgment contrary to the verdict could not be entered. There was one exception to this rule: Where the trial court expressly reserved his ruling on the motion for a directed verdict, and the jury returned a verdict against the party making the motion, the trial court, and on review, the appellate court, could enter judgment contrary to the verdict.

By statute or rule today in many jurisdictions the trial court is deemed to have reserved his ruling even when in fact he has ruled adversely to the movant or has simply not acted on the motion.[53] Then, by further provision, if the movant whether

----

[53] Fed. R. Civ. P. 50 (b).

plaintiff or defendant, subsequently (after verdict, that is) moves for judgment notwithstanding the verdict, the evidence is re-examined in light of the verdict, and judgment may be entered in accord with this subsequent motion. Also, the appellate court may reverse the trial court and itself enter such judgment or direct the trial court to do so, thus avoiding the necessity of having a new trial.[54] The appellate court may of course enter judgment on the verdict if justified by the evidence.

Since the motion for judgment notwithstanding the verdict has become, in those jurisdictions adopting such statute or rule, in effect a second motion for a directed verdict, the test as to when such judgment should be entered is the same as that used to determine when the motion for a directed verdict should be sustained (as to which, see Section 76). There is accordingly the same difference of opinion as to what evidence should be con-sidered and as to the respective functions of the judge and jury. Also, some courts consider only evidence introduced prior to the motion for a directed verdict, while others consider all evidence introduced because of the obvious injustice where sufficient evi-dence to support the verdict was available but due to an oversight, was not offered until after the motion for a directed verdict was made.

In most jurisdictions the older function of the motion for judgment notwithstanding the verdict (to reach defects in plead-ings) is still retained side by side with its newer function (to reach defects in proof). The latter is however restricted to trials with a jury.

SECTION 80. NECESSITY OF PRIOR MOTION TO DIRECT THE VERDICT. In order that the party against whom a verdict has been returned may take advantage of this new procedure, he must in many jurisdictions have made a motion for a directed verdict,

---

[54] Cone v. W. Va. Pulp & Paper Co., 330 U.S. 212, 97 L. ed. 90.

or its equivalent, at the conclusion of all the evidence.[55] Some jurisdictions recognize a motion for an involuntary nonsuit, or to dismiss for insufficiency of the evidence, as equivalent to a motion to direct the verdict.

If a motion to direct the verdict has been made at the close of the plaintiff's case, it must be renewed at the close of all the evidence as noted earlier. It has been stated that the reason for this requirement exists in the fact that the adverse party may then ask for a new trial, which may be granted in the trial court's discretion, or such party may dismiss the action and start over again. Further, it has been suggested that the seventh amendment requires such action, as the motion for a directed verdict was one of the means whereby, prior to the adoption of that amendment, the issues of fact that had once been tried by a jury could be reexamined by the court.

In those jurisdictions where a prior motion to direct a verdict is not necessary,[56] it is probably better to defer moving until after the verdict has been returned, when it is extremely unlikely that the court will grant the opponent leave to reopen his case and introduce further evidence.

Also, in any event, a new trial may in most jurisdictions be obtained without having previously moved to direct the verdict.[57]

Further, there is a division among the authorities as to whether a prior motion to direct the verdict must be made by the party who now moves for judgment, in cases where the party who obtains the verdict has received the verdict by direction of the trial court.[58] It is necessary therefore to examine the authorities in a particular jurisdiction.

---

[55] Re Caldwell, 216 Cal. 694, 16 P. 2d 139.

[56] Holloway v. DeCrescenzo, 8 N.J. Super. 24, 73 A. 2d 205; 88 C.J.S. Trial, § 249 a.

[57] Note: "Appeal and Error: Failure of Proof, Variance, Direction of Judgment by Appellate Courts," 36 Calif. L. Rev. 622.

[58] McCauley v. Steward, 63 Ariz. 524, 164 P. 2d 465; Ross v. Arrow Mfg. Co., 134 Colo. 530, 307 P. 2d 196; 69 A.L.R. 2d 449, 483.

SECTION 81. THE MOTION FOR JUDGMENT. In most jurisdictions, a judgment contrary to the verdict cannot be obtained in either the trial or appellate court, unless the party against whom the verdict has been returned seasonably and properly moves for such a judgment in addition to having made a prior motion to direct the verdict.[59] The same reason is here advanced as is set forth for requiring a prior motion to direct the verdict, namely that such motion may be countered by a motion for new trial, and the lack of such motion for judgment hence deprives the court of the power to exercise its discretion.

However, where the principal issue does not concern the sufficiency of the evidence to support a verdict, it is not necessary, to obtain a judgment contrary to the verdict in the appellate court, that a motion for judgment notwithstanding the verdict is made in the trial court.[60] An illustration of this situation is where the question is primarily one of interpretation of a written contract.

Some jurisdictions insist upon a post-verdict motion for judgment even though both sides had previously moved to direct the verdict;[61] where the jury fails to agree, as well as where a verdict is returned;[62] and also where the trial court expressly reserves a decision on a motion for a directed verdict,[63] as well as where the motion is denied.

Where a post-verdict motion for judgment is deemed necessary, the failure to make such a motion will usually not prevent the party from obtaining a new trial.[64]

It should be noted that the overruling of a previous motion to direct does not preclude a subsequent sustaining of a motion for

---

[59] Johnson v. N.Y., N.H. & H. R. Co., 344 U.S. 48.

[60] Howard University v. Cassell, 126 F. 2d 6.

[61] Globe Liquor Co. v. San Roman, 332 U.S. 571.

[62] Sattler v. Great Atlantic & Pacific Tea Co., 18 F.R.D. 271.

[63] Johnson v. N.Y., N.H. & H.R. Co., supra, n. 59.

[64] Cone v. W. Va. Pulp and Paper Co., supra, n. 54.

judgment notwithstanding the verdict, for the previous ruling is not governed by the "law of the case" doctrine.[65]

The post-verdict motion for judgment should therefore not be overlooked, as it is required in many jurisdictions, and this despite the fact that it may frequently be overruled because the controlling questions of law have been already decided during the trial. At the same time, there is a good possibility that such a post-verdict motion would be successful where the pre-verdict motion has not been successful, as many trial courts overrule the latter motion simply because of doubt; that doubt may be resolved by the jury returning a verdict in favor of the party moving to direct the verdict.

The time limits for filing such post-trial motion for judgment are usually set out in the statute or rule. Frequently the motion must be made within ten days after verdict.[66]

Care should be exercised in the drafting of the motion, which of course would ordinarily be made in writing. This too is usually prescribed by statute or rule.[67] The motion should preferably follow the language of such provisions. A motion to set aside a verdict is not the equivalent, even though the trial court reserved a decision on a prior motion to direct.

The reasons should be stated as precisely as they are given in the motion to direct the verdict, or that motion should be specifically referred to. Grounds not specified in the motion for judgment, although stated in the motion for a directed verdict, may be deemed waived.

As is true with reference to the motion to direct, co-parties must all join in the motion for judgment, or it may be overruled as to those not joining.

SECTION 82. THE MOTION FOR A NEW TRIAL. Most statutes or

---

[65] Willis v. Pennsylvania R. Co., 35 F. Supp. 941.

[66] Fed. R. Civ. P. 50 (b).

[67] Johnson v. N.Y., N.H. & H.R. Co., supra, n. 59.

rules which provide for the judgment notwithstanding the verdict also provide that the party so moving for judgment may also ask, in the alternative, for a new trial.[68] This means that the appellate court may grant a new trial in the event that the favorable action of the trial court on the motion for judgment is reversed on appeal. Hence in many jurisdictions the trial court is required to rule on both motions, regardless of the ruling on the motion for judgment.[69] Counsel should be sure that such action is taken. In this manner, the case may often be finally disposed of on one appeal, and without the necessity of having a new trial; and even if a new trial is required, one additional appeal may be obviated.

For the above reasons it is advisable to ask for a new trial in the alternative, though by statute or rule it is optional. In some jurisdictions, to be sure, a new trial may be ordered though it was not requested. In others, the appellate court may remand the case to the trial court so that the motion for new trial may be made, and passed upon in the trial court.

The alternative motion for a new trial must be filed within the same period as is required for the motion for judgment.[70]

The trial court, in ruling on both motions, may do one of four things: 1. He may overrule both motions and enter judgment on the verdict. 2. He may sustain the motion for judgment and overrule the motion for a new trial. 3. He may overrule the motion for judgment and sustain the motion for a new trial. 4. He may sustain both motions.[71]

Situation 1 presents no new problems.

In situation 2, if an appeal is taken, the moving party becomes the appellee. If the appellee wishes to have reviewed certain rulings made during the course of the trial, he must either file a cross-appeal, or cross-assign error, depending upon the local prac-

---

68 Fed. R. Civ. P. 50 (b).
69 Montgomery Ward & Co. v. Duncan, 311 U.S. 243.
70 Ross v. Arrow Mfg. Co., 134 Colo. 530, 307 P. 2d 196.
71 Montgomery Ward v. Duncan, supra, n. 69.

tice. Then if the appellate court determines that the motion for judgment was erroneously sustained, the ruling on the motion for a new trial may be considered. Thus, for example, if the trial court sustained an objection to certain evidence offered by the appellee, and this ruling was included in his motion for a new trial (where local rules so require), the question may be presented to the appellate court without the necessity of a second appeal.

In situation 3 local statutes or rules frequently specify whether it is possible to appeal the overruling of a motion for judgment. If there is no provision covering this situation, the appeal may fail on the grounds that, because of the grant of a new trial, any error in denying the judgment, if error there was, has not resulted in prejudice.

While the action of the trial court in situation 4 may appear at first glance to be inconsistent, it must be remembered that by such action, the court means to say that in the event the appellate court reverses his action on the motion for judgment, the movant is to be awarded a new trial. If this be the intention of the trial court, the order should clearly so state.

It should be noted that the doctrine still prevails that the ruling of the trial court on the motion for a new trial may be upset on appeal only if he has failed to exercise discretion or has abused his discretion. The ruling on the motion for judgment, on the other hand, is either correct or incorrect as a matter of law.

Chapter 7

Closing Argument

SECTION 83. THE RIGHT TO OPEN AND CLOSE—WAIVER.
The terms "opening" and "closing" refer to the sequence in which
counsel present final arguments to the jury. Most frequently, the
party having the burden of proof or the affirmative of the issue has
the right to argue first; then the adverse party presents his argument; this is followed by the second argument of the party having
the burden.[1]

In some jurisdictions there is only one argument by each
side.[2] The party having the burden of proof argues last. Under this
practice, the party who does not have the burden of proof must
determine whether to include any rebuttal material by way of
anticipation. If he does not, he may find that his adversary has
relied heavily upon the unanswered argument; if he does, he may
"awaken sleeping giants."

Under either practice, the disadvantage of having the burden
of proof is partially offset, as the last argument is deemed to have
the greater influence on the jury.

Usually the plaintiff has the burden of proof and thus the
right to open and close. But this is not the case where the de-

---

[1] Johnson v. Josephs, 75 Me. 544; 93 A.L.R. 2d 273; 53 Am. Jur. Trial, § 462.
[2] Joiner, Trials and Appeals, § 533.

fendant has filed only an affirmative defense.[3] Rules of the particular jurisdiction must be consulted to determine who has the
right to open and close in cases of multiple issues or multiple
parties. If there are no specific rules governing the situation, the
matter is usually one for the exercise of the trial court's discretion.[4] Also, the trial court may, in exceptional cases, allow argument in addition to those specified above, as where unfair or unexpected matter is injected into the case by counsel for the adverse
party.

Although there is some difference of opinion among attorneys
as to the effectiveness of the argument to the jury, it is treated by
some courts as a valuable right—so valuable in fact that it may be
reversible error to refuse to allow any argument.[5] This view is
based on the premise that the right to argue is part and parcel of
the right to be represented by counsel. Especially is this so if
counsel can show that such refusal was prejudicial to his client's
cause. Prejudice can be shown if the case was not, in the opinion
of the appellate court, correctly decided. It should be noted that
there is a right of argument only if the case is to be submitted to
the jury, and hence it does not exist where the case was taken
from the jury by means of a nonsuit or directed verdict.

Attorneys generally agree that it is unwise to waive this right,
no matter how strong you believe your case to be and despite the
fact that the entire presentation of the case is designed to achieve
the same goal as is the argument, namely the persuasion of the jury
in the justice of your client's cause. For the argument presents
one last opportunity to present your case in a connected fashion
so that the jury may understand the case as thoroughly as possible.

Although some attorneys prefer to waive the opening argument and reserve all their points for the closing, this procedure is

---

[3] Huntington v. Conkey, 33 Barb. 218.

[4] Lancaster v. Collins, 115 U.S. 222.

[5] Ely Walker Dry Goods Co. v. Blake, 59 Okla. 103, 158 P. 381; 38 A.L.R. 2d
1396; 88 C.J.S. Trial, § 164.

inadvisable. Opposing counsel may waive his argument, and the court then probably would refuse to permit a closing argument, since its purpose is to give an opportunity for rebuttal.[6] Of course, if opposing counsel does argue, the party having the burden of proof has the right to close.

If there has been an opening argument, there should be an answering argument or the lack thereof may be interpreted by the jury as an acknowledgment of weakness of one's case. It should be noted that this is the only opportunity to speak given to the party who does not have the burden of proof.

SECTION 84. LENGTH OF ARGUMENT—APPORTIONMENT OF TIME. The length of the argument is usually set by counsel, and approved by the court. While the court may not refuse to permit any argument, he may limit the time allowed.[7] More time may be allowed one side than the other. In some jurisdictions a refusal to allow as much time as requested must be objected to at once, and an exception noted, or the alleged error will be deemed waived.[8] In other jurisdictions counsel must make a request for additional time when he has used up the allotted time.[9] Where there are multiple parties, either one attorney may argue for all co-parties or several attorneys may argue for their respective parties, depending upon whether their interests coincide or are in conflict. Generally each of several attorneys representing a single party may argue.

The time set by counsel should be governed by such factors as the length of the trial, the complexity of the case, the composition of the jury, the personality of counsel and the time of day. Many attorneys believe that an effective argument may be made in the average case in less than an hour. This belief is based on the following facts: Juries of today are generally more sophisti-

---

[6] Hettinger v. Beiler, 54 Ill. App. 320.
[7] Price v. Laclede Gaslight Co., 219 S.W. 706 (Mo. App.); 88 C.J.S. Trial, § 168.
[8] Jerrell v. Norfolk & P. Belt Line R. Co., 166 Va. 70, 184 S.E. 196.
[9] American Surety Co. v. U.S., 77 Ill. App. 106.

cated and busy than they were in prior times, and hence not impressed by long, flowery speeches; a short summation requires more preparation than does a lengthy one, with the result that it is more apt to influence the jury than a lengthy, unorganized discourse. In any event, it is not necessary to use all the time allowed, and the summation should be tapered off as soon as it becomes apparent that the interest of the jury is waning.

It is generally better to allow more time for opening than for closing. As indicated in the previous section, the opening should be a complete statement of one's position, leaving the closing for rebuttal; also, the jury's attention is more easily held at the beginning. If the major portion of the argument is reserved until the closing, opposing counsel, anticipating such move, may call the jury's attention to the fact that he will not have an opportunity to answer new points thus raised, and in extreme cases may label such conduct as unfair.

SECTION 85. IMPORTANCE OF GOOD ORGANIZATION. As suggested earlier, the ultimate objective of an argument is the persuasion of the jury. It is generally agreed today that this objective can best be attained by a clear, concise and logical presentation. Such a presentation in turn demands an adequate organization of ideas into a meaningful pattern. If counsel has prepared his case thoroughly, an outline of the principal points of his summation will of necessity gradually take shape. Such an outline should be fairly complete before the trial begins, and may be modified from time to time during the course of the trial.

Until one has gained experience by practice, it may be advisable also to write out the argument in full. In no event, however, should the argument be read to the jury, but reference may be made to the outline, to be sure that no salient points are overlooked.

SECTION 86. TAILOR THE ARGUMENT TO FIT THE CASE, THE JURY AND YOURSELF. Each argument to the jury is unique. Hence it is impossible to suggest a perfect model or pattern that will serve adequately in all cases. However, it is possible to set out a number of points that are frequently included in arguments, leaving the particular emphasis and order to the judgment of the attorney. Some of these points will be considered in greater detail in subsequent sections.

1. The introduction. Some attorneys begin an argument by recounting some unusual feature of the case, to gain the undivided attention of the jury. This may be followed by a brief statement of the function of the argument, and that such argument is not evidence.

Although standard instructions usually define such terms as "burden of proof" and "preponderance of the evidence," the introduction may very well include a further explanation. Counsel for the plaintiff should readily admit that he has the burden of proof, if that is the case; he may state the quantum of proof needed to satisfy the burden, at least in negative form. Thus, the jury may be informed that "preponderance of the evidence" requires a lesser quantum of proof than does the standard "beyond a reasonable doubt" which is applied in criminal cases; that hence they may find for the plaintiff even though they may not be convinced to the degree of certainty required in prosecutions for alleged criminal acts. The concept of "preponderance" may be graphically demonstrated by reference to a scale or balance. It may be pointed out that "preponderance" does not mean the greater number of witnesses.

The jury may also be informed that they are the judges of the credibility of the witnesses, and may be told what factors generally affect credibility. Counsel for the defendant may, on the other hand, emphasize that if the evidence is evenly balanced, he is entitled to a verdict.

2. The theory of the case, as initially presented in the opening statement, may now be more fully developed. Thus, the jury

should be informed that the action is brought to recover damages for breach of contract, for fraudulent misrepresentations, for negligent conduct, etc. On the side of the defense the theory may be, respectively, performance of the terms of the contract, lack of knowledge of the falsity of the representation, or contributory negligence of the plaintiff. The theory provides the jury with a background or setting against which the evidence is to be considered, and hence it is essential that it be clearly understood.

Some attorneys believe that it is better practice to rely in argument on one theory, though several may have been set out in the pleadings. This requires careful thought in the selection of the theory to be relied upon. Not only must the attorney consider what evidence he has to support the theory selected, but he must anticipate the possible reaction of the jury, as well as the way in which opposing counsel may turn that theory to his own advantage.

The extent to which several theories may be relied upon is governed, in part, by the rules in a given jurisdiction concerning alternative pleading and election of remedies.

3. The statement of the issues, usually ascertained, as is the theory of the case, by reference to the pleadings and proof. Again, only the principal issues—those which are actually in controversy, as distinguished from the so-called "paper issues"—should be discussed. There is a split in the authorities as to whether the attorney may read from the pleadings.[10] Where such practice is allowed, it is generally preferable to state the substance only, at least at this point in the trial.

4. A statement of the facts, in narrative form, as developed by the testimony (including depositions) and exhibits, to show that the elements of your case have been, and those of the opposition have not been, proven. More time should be spent on the

---

[10] Rasicot v. Royal Neighbors, 18 Idaho 85, 108 P. 1048; Louisville & N.R. Co. v. Hull, 113 Ky. 561, 68 S.W. 433; 53 Am. Jur. Trial, § 487.

former aspect than on the latter, and the fragments tied together as in the opening statement. Although only matters in evidence should be discussed, it is proper to include matters of which the court may take judicial notice.

This portion of the argument may involve a brief discussion of the credibility of the principal witnesses on both sides, referring to them by name and their relationship to the case. A common device used here is to describe their conduct while on the stand. The jury may be reminded that if they are in doubt as to the testimony of a certain witness, they may have the testimony read back to them, or the attorney may himself do so. Also, if the opponent has stated in his opening remarks that a certain element will be proven and this has not been done, the attention of the jury may properly be called to this omission. Again, the jury may be told that the opposition did not produce a witness who could have been called to testify as to a specific point, but was not called, if that be the case.

Occasionally it is necessary to inform the jury as to the significance of a particular bit of evidence which, because of its nature or the manner in which it was brought out, is so obscure that its meaning may have been lost on the jury. Also, any technical terms should be explained, even if this was done while the witnesses were testifying; any disagreement as to meaning should be clarified before the arguments, if possible. Sometimes counsel are very effective in using models to demonstrate their version of an accident or other event.[11] When this is attempted, it is imperative that the model be an accurate and true representation of the original.

It is customary for the plaintiff's attorney to first develop the fact-situation which allegedly gives rise to liability, and then to develop the damage aspect. If counsel for defendant intends to bring out both aspects, he will usually reverse the above order.

---

[11] Robinson v. Kathryn, 23 Ill. App. 2d 5, 161 N.E. 2d 477; 74 A.L.R. 2d 1094.

Where a defendant in a tort case seriously contests liability, he may choose to omit any reference to damages, for fear of lessening the effectiveness of his contentions. However, it is possible to argue convincingly on both aspects by making clear that liability is not conceded. One common error committed by plaintiffs' attorneys is to dwell so long on the liability aspect that but little time remains to consider the damages.

Before beginning the argument, in fact during the presentation of the evidence, the groundwork for any claimed damages must be laid. Especially in tort cases involving unliquidated damages counsel must bring out the various elements of damages. It is generally advisable for the plaintiff to ask for a specific sum for each element, rather than to lump them altogether and ask for a total sum only. In this way the jury can more easily understand how the total requested was arrived at. In some jurisdictions, it is permissible for counsel to use a blackboard to show the various items and how they were arrived at.[12] When using a blackboard, care must be exercised in the computations as the opposing counsel will direct the jury's attention to any discrepancies. If defendant's counsel desires to discuss damages, it is better to do so in general terms.

One of the most difficult items of damage to discuss is that of pain and suffering, especially if it is claimed that the injuries are probably permanent. For here there exists no objective standard to guide the jury as it does for lost earnings and expenses. To begin, the nature of the injury must be accurately described. It is quite common to make an emotional appeal at this point, calling attention to the manner in which the injured person's former activities will be curtailed in the future. In some jurisdictions, where permitted, a specific sum is suggested for a given period, either a day, a month or a year, and then by making use of the person's life expectancy arrive at a total figure for pain and suf-

---

12 Mirabile v. N.Y.C.R. Co., 23 F. 2d 498; 86 A.L.R. 2d 239; 80 A.L.R. 2d 1270.

fering.[13] Sometimes, to impress the jury with the fairness of the figure selected, reference is made to tables of compensation allowed injured persons in special classifications. Or, reference may be made to experiences of the jurors themselves.

From the plaintiff's standpoint the use of the "per diem" method of computing damages has the advantage of showing the jury that the damages claimed are not excessive. For example, suppose a personal injury case in which the medical evidence is to the effect that the plaintiff is permanently injured, and a reference to life expectancy tables shows that he could reasonably anticipate 20 more years of life. If the plaintiff's attorney in argument merely referred to a damage claim of $73,000, at first blush this could be considered to be excessive. But if the plaintiff suggests that $10.00 per day is not unreasonable compensation, this figure, if accepted, would come to $3,650 per year or $73,000 for 20 years. From the defendant's standpoint, the objection goes to the figure of $10.00, which, to him, is "merely pulled out of a hat." This objection can be partially met by using as a standard the wage scale paid to persons in the plaintiff's occupation.

Defendant's counsel must take care not to leave an impression of being niggardly. He may, however, where applicable, call the jury's attention to the fact that the injuries are not as severe as portrayed; that the figure selected need not be used by the jury, but that they are free to use their judgment; that the plaintiff's injury was the result of a pre-existing condition as well as the accident, etc.

Much use is made today of medical testimony. This requires counsel to familiarize himself thoroughly with the technical aspects of the case. If a medical book has been used in the cross-examination of a doctor, passages from it may sometimes be read in argu-

---

[13] Four-County Electric Power Asso. v. Clardy, 221 Miss. 403, 73 So. 2d 144; Botta v. Brunner, 26 N.J. 82, 138 A. 2d 713; 53 Am. Jur. Trial, § 463 (1964 Cum. Supp.); Id. § 480 (1964 Cum. Supp.).

ment. Generally, however, courts frown upon the reading of medical textbooks during argument.[14] If the defendant had his own doctor examine the plaintiff, but the doctor was not called to testify, the jury may be reminded of that failure, provided that the fact of the examination is in the record.

There is currently a conflict among the authorities as to whether it is improper to inform the jury that any recovery of damages as compensation for personal injuries is not subject to taxation as income,[15] or to refer to the decline in purchasing power of the dollar.[16] Where such reference is permitted attorneys are not in agreement as to the wisdom of such tactics. On the other hand, the jury may properly be informed of the fact that a recovery is not to be decreased by any insurance benefits which may be received.

5. Request for a favorable verdict. The plaintiff's request will indicate the amount which he deems is warranted under the evidence and the applicable law. The defendant's request will be for either a flat verdict in his favor, or in the alternative form. In the latter, defendant requests a finding for him or in the event the verdict is for the plaintiff, that it be for a sum substantially less than demanded by the plaintiff. If a special verdict, or answers to interrogatories along with a general verdict, is to be returned, counsel may properly suggest the findings believed warranted under the circumstances. It is improper to inform the jury as to the legal effect of certain findings.[17]

With reference to the manner of delivering the argument, it cannot be emphasized too strongly that there is no one most

---

[14] Phillips v. Roux Laboratories, Inc., 286 App. Div. 549, 145 N.Y.S. 449; 72 A.L.R. 2d 931.

[15] Hall v. C. & N.W.R. Co., 5 Ill. 2d 135, 125 N.E. 2d 77; 53 Am. Jur. Trials, § 463 (1964 Cum. Supp. 46).

[16] Halloran v. New England Tel. & Tel. Co., 95 Vt. 273, 115 A. 143; 53 Am. Jur. Trial, § 481 (1964 Cum. Supp. 50).

[17] Texas & N.O.R. Co. v. McGinnis 130 Tex. 338, 109 S.W. 2d 160; 88 C.J.S. Trial, § 174.

effective method. If counsel does not use a form that is natural for him, the jury will be quick to notice any affectation and to conclude that the attorney is not speaking with sincerity and conviction. This belief on the part of the jury could very well result in an unfavorable verdict. Counsel should therefore use the style most suitable to him, with the strong and weak features of his delivery kept in mind. Thus, some persons are more effective when using gentle persuasion, others when using more forceful techniques.

While an argument is, as suggested, largely an individual matter, there are some generally accepted techniques in use in any style.

For the most part, the argument should be in a conversational manner. Rhetoric and logic are, however, still powerful means of persuasion. At times an emotional appeal is in place, but it will be most effective if not used constantly, and only for special emphasis. An occasional catch phrase or flowery term is proper. On the whole, counsel should be frank, direct and use simple language. Short sentences are more effective than long ones. Speak slowly enough for the jury to follow you, and rapidly enough to avoid boredom.

Repetition should be indulged in only where it is for purposes of emphasis, and not because of lack of orgaization. Mannerisms which distract should be avoided.

While the argument should be addressed to the entire jury, it is well to look directly at various members thereof. It is improper to call individual members by name, or to refer specifically to their personal experiences as discovered during the process of selecting the jury.[18] However, personal experiences of the jury can, and should, be used in formulating the appeal, as long as the appeal is not specifically directed at individuals.

---

[18] Henderson v. Union P.R. Co., 189 Ore. 145, 219 P. 2d 170; 55 A.L.R. 2d 1198.

A common forensic technique, sometimes used in arguments to the jury, is that of propounding questions to the adversary. Most attorneys, however, avoid the practice unless they are certain that opposing counsel has no ready answer.

The overall effectiveness of one's technique may be checked in various ways: discussing a case with a member of the jury after the trial has been completed, by listening to a playback of a recorded argument, by soliciting comments from colleagues familiar with the techniques used, and by observing the behavior of the jury during the course of the argument.

SECTION 87. CONCENTRATE ON A FEW STRONG POINTS. Some attorneys depart considerably in their argument from the scope outlined in the preceding section, making very little reference to the evidence, and discuss instead such broad, philosophical matters as social policy in favor of compensation for injuries, the proposition that in a death action one's station in life is of little significance, or even the desirability of the death penalty. Other attorneys, while referring briefly to the evidence, bring out especially the "human interest" elements whenever possible. Whatever the technique, there is a distinct advantage in the concentration of one's fire.

An interesting technique, sometimes used to good advantage, is that of deliberately refraining from mentioning several major points. Counsel using this technique operate on the assumption that some member of the jury will present these omitted points during the period of deliberation, and with probably more telling effect than if counsel led the jury by the hand.

When dealing with the evidence presented by the opposition, it is likewise advisable to attack only a few points, and these should be the points most vulnerable. It is frequently not safe to disregard a point merely because you do not believe it will be influential with the jury. One can rarely be sure what points will appeal to that body. Sometimes it is necessary to carefully avoid side issues planted deliberately to divert attention from a case that is essentially weak.

SECTION 88. POINT OUT INFERENCES YOU WANT THE JURY TO DRAW FROM THE EVIDENCE OR THE LACK OF IT. Much evidence in the usual lawsuit is circumstantial in nature. Such evidence is introduced for the purpose of pointing to the ultimate facts in issue. Many persons serving on juries find this process of drawing inferences a new experience, at least in the disciplined manner required in the courtroom. Hence the jury often needs guidance as to what inferences may, and may not, be legitimately drawn from the evidence. This is an important function of the argument.

Counsel must be certain that the inferences he draws are reasonable, and based upon logic and common experience. If inferences are not fair, counsel for the adverse party may call that fact to the jury's attention. Even without such assistance, the jury may themselves note the fallacies. Not only must the inferences drawn be logical, but the same rule applies to the order in which the evidence is reviewed for the jury.

If part of one's case depends upon the application of a presumption or the doctrine of judicial notice to supply gaps in the testimony, the effect thereof should be explained to the jury. In some jurisdictions, presumptions are given the effect of evidence and are to be considered therewith, while in other jurisdictions, presumptions merely supply deficiencies of proof.[19] The manner of explanation to the jury will therefore vary depending upon the jurisdiction.

Not only is it proper to call the jury's attention to inferences which might reasonably be drawn from the evidence, but sometimes and more importantly, they may be informed what inferences may be drawn from the fact that no evidence was offered,

---

[19] Wyckoff v. Mutual Life Ins. Co., 173 Ore. 592, 147 P. 2d 227; Mockowik v. Ry. Co., 196 Mo. 550, 94 S.W. 256; McCormick, Evidence, § 314.

though it could have been, on a given point.[20] Thus, the failure
of an employer to call an employee, who is available, competent
and has knowledge of the facts, may be referred to and an inference
drawn that if he had been called, his testimony would have been
adverse to the employer. Care must be exercised, however, not
to state expressly or by implication, that opposing counsel has been
guilty of suppressing evidence, as such remarks may be held to be
prejudicial.

SECTION 89. REFERENCE TO EXHIBITS AND INSTRUCTIONS. In
the majority of jurisdictions arguments to the jury take place immediately after each side has completed the introduction of evidence and has rested. Instructions are given at the close of the
arguments.[21] However in a respectable minority of jurisdictions
this order is reversed. In some jurisdictions of the former group
the court informs counsel what instructions he intends to give.
This procedure enables counsel to refer to certain instructions in
argument.[22]

The purpose of instructions is to inform the jury how to apply
the law to the facts as they shall find them, so that the general
verdict will be the result of such application. In many cases instructions are so worded that a further explanation is needed.
The argument however is not the proper vehicle to take issue
with the instruction as a correct statement of the law. This matter
may be presented to the court out of the presence of the jury, at
a time agreed upon by court and counsel. It is also considered
inappropriate to indicate which side tendered a given instruction.
Since many instructions require a particular finding of facts,
where counsel considers an instruction to be unfavorable to him,
he may properly point out that the instruction does not govern
where such finding cannot be made. This approach assumes of

---

[20] Houston Electric Co. v. Potter, 51 S.W. 2d 754 (Tex. App.); 88 C.J.S. Trial,
§ 184.

[21] Fed. R. Civ. P. 51; Blume, American Civil Procedure, § 9–17.

[22] Louisville Woolen Mills v. Kindgen, 191 Ky. 568; 88 C.J.S. Trial, § 173.

course that your interpretation of the facts would require a finding contrary to that embodied in the instruction.

The extent to which counsel may "read law" or "argue law" to the jury varies among different jurisdictions.[23] In some cases, such practice has been condemned on the ground that it invades the court's prerogative.[24] In others, it is held to be a matter within the discretion of the trial court.[25] Since the fact-situations differ so greatly, it is advisable to become familiar with the rules of the particular jurisdiction before incorporating a discussion of the law in the argument.

It is frequently necessary to explain the nature of exhibits introduced as evidence, and their significance in the case.[26] Such explanation may require a reading of the exhibit. When this is the case, the exhibit should be read in its entirety, including also any portion which does not support one's contentions. In most jurisdictions it is also possible for the jury to examine exhibits in the jury box or in the room where deliberations take place.[27] When counsel reads from an exhibit, this should be done in a manner that will retain the interest and attention of the jury. If there are a number of exhibits, they should be arranged in the sequence in which they will be discussed, to avoid any embarrassing delays while counsel makes a search.

SECTION 90. HOW TO TREAT CONFLICTING TESTIMONY. In many lawsuits the testimony of defendant's witnesses will conflict with that of plaintiff's witnesses. Often the conflict is on points which are crucial to the outcome of the litigation. This situation presents problems so baffling that on first examination no solution is apparent. A closer examination of the testimony, however, will usually indicate several lines of attack. All such efforts are directed

---

23 88 C.J.S. Trial, § 171; 66 A.L.R. 2d 9.
24 Turcick v. Liberty Corp., 217 F. 2d 495.
25 Barber Pure Milk Co. v. Holmes, 264 Ala. 45, 84 So. 2d 345.
26 Com. v. Barrows, 176 Mass. 17, 56 N.E. 830; 88 C.J.S. Trial, § 177.
27 Little v. U.S., 73 F. 2d 861; 53 Am. Jur. Trial, § 924.

toward the same goal, namely, to have the jury accept your witnesses' version of an occurrence or event, and to reject the version of the adversary's witnesses. The jury must be shown why they should come to that conclusion—a mere assertion that they should do so is not alone sufficient.

At times it is possible to call attention to inconsistencies appearing between testimony given by two or more witnesses on the other side, or between various portions of the testimony of the same witness (especially where brought out on cross-examination) or between the pleadings and the evidence.[28]

In general, any successful contradiction or impeachment may be referred to.[29] Most attorneys prefer to use the approach that the adverse witnesses were mistaken, rather than that they were deliberately lying, as this is less offensive to the jury and gives opposing counsel less opportunity for an emotional counterattack. Unless one is certain that a witness was guilty of perjury, it is better to use the approach that the witness, due to human foibles, did not state the facts as they actually were. It can sometimes be pointed out that the witnesses did not have an adequate opportunity to observe, that the event happened so long ago that certain details naturally cannot be clearly recalled. But if there is definite proof of perjury, do not hesitate to come forward with such proof. Similarly, it is proper to make mention of possible bias because of relationship, interest in the outcome of the case, etc.

Occasionally the witnesses for one side testify so much alike as to details that there is strong suspicion of coaching. If that is the case, the jury's attention may be drawn to such unusual similarity of testimony.

Finally, it is often possible to show that the probabilities are

---

28 Vachon v. Todorovich, 256 Mich. 182, 97 N.W. 2d 122; 72 A.L.R. 2d 1304.
    29 Baker v. Market St. Ry. Co., 123 Cal. App. 688, 11 P. 2d 912; 88 C.J.S. Trial, § 924.

against the facts being as testified to by adverse witnesses, and in favor of the version of your own witnesses.

If it is doubtful that the testimony of adverse witnesses can be successfully challenged in some such manner as suggested above, it is preferable to emphasize testimony presented by your own witnesses.

SECTION 91. WHAT SHOULD BE AVOIDED IN ARGUMENT. In the tense and heated situation of a trial, it is quite common for counsel, either inadvertently or by design, to make statements or to use tactics which opposing counsel contend on appeal were improper, and which are relied upon as reversible error. No effort is here made to include all such types of statements or conduct, but the following list may be illustrative.

1. Going beyond the record. This includes a reference to matters known personally to counsel, or even the jury or some members thereof. An example would be to refer to offers of settlement made before trial,[30] or to the evidence or verdict in a former trial of the same cause,[31] or that the defendant has insurance covering his liability.[32]

2. Distorting the evidence, or discussing evidence for a purpose for which it was not, and could not, be admitted. If there is uncertainty as to what the evidence was on a certain point which seems important enough to discuss during argument, check with the reporter before argument, or state that your best recollection is that a certain witness testified thus and so.

3. Appealing to the prejudice of the jury. While courts are quite lenient with respect to appeals to sympathy, if within reason, this is not true with respect to appeals to passion and prejudice. Thus, it is generally improper to refer to the wealth or poverty of a party, or to contrast the financial status of the parties, unless it

---

30 53 Am. Jur. Trial, § 482; Toledo, St. L. & W.R. Co., 82 Ohio St. 129, 92 N.E. 27.

31 Boggs v. Boggs, 138 Md. 422, 114 A. 474; 53 Am. Jur. Trial, § 489.

32 Walsh v. Wilkes-Barre, 215 Pa. 226, 64 A. 407; 53 Am. Jur. Trial, § 480.

is relevant to some issue in the case.[33] The same is true of references to race, religion, etc.[34] Similarly, it is usually improper to state that any judgment recovered will or will not be paid out of taxes,[35] or that if no recovery is allowed the plaintiff will be a public charge.

There is a sharp difference of opinion today as to whether it is a prejudicial error to suggest to the jury that they place themselves in the position of a litigant, or to allow such recovery as they would desire if they were in litigant's position.[36] On the one hand, there is the position that this is an improper standard as the jury is to determine the issue as objectively as possible, and that such standard would have the natural tendency to inflate verdicts.[37] On the other hand, there is the contention that this is what the jury does anyway, and that if this tendency is brought into the open, the jury can be properly guided in its use.[38]

4. Engaging in vituperative attacks upon opposing counsel or party or witnesses.[39] Unless such attacks are material and pertinent to the case, they may not only constitute reversible error, but subject counsel to a suit for slander.[40] Ridicule, if gentle, may be permitted and occasionally is effective. Irony, if not carried to excess is also a potent weapon.

There are many types of conduct which, though not necessarily deemed improper should nevertheless be avoided. Some illustrations of such conduct have been referred to in previous sections.

---

[33] Montgomery Ward & Co. v. Wooley, 121 Ind. App. 60, 94 N.E. 2d 677; 53 Am. Jur. Trial, § 499.

[34] Atlanta Coca-Cola Bottling Co. v. Shipp, 170 Ga. 817, 154 S.E. 243; 53 Am. Jur. Trial, §§ 497, 498.

[35] Williams v. Anniston, 257 Ala. 191, 58 So. 2d 115; 33 A.L.R. 2d 442.

[36] 53 Am. Jur. Trial, § 496.

[37] Russell v. C.R.I. & P.R. Co., 249 Iowa 664, 86 N.W. 2d 843.

[38] Missouri P.R. Co. v. Maxwell, 194 Ark. 938, 109 S.W. 2d 1254.

[39] Georgia Power Co. v. Puckett, 181 Ga. 386, 182 S.E. 384; 96 A.L.R. 2d 9; 29 A.L.R. 2d 996.

[40] Kraushaar v. Lavin, 39 N.Y.S. 2d 880; 61 A.L.R. 2d 1300.

SECTION 92. OBJECTING TO IMPROPER ARGUMENT. There are several methods available to meet an improper argument. One such method is to retaliate in kind, if further argument is permitted.[41] Ordinarily it is inadvisable to engage in such tactics, because of the possibility of alienating the jury and drawing censure from the court. Frequently, however, it is possible to answer the improper argument without stepping outside the bounds of propriety, pointing out that you are not going to engage in an exchange of epithets or the like.

Counsel may also object to improper argument.[42] When this is done, it must be done at the time the improper statement is made, or the objection may be deemed waived. An objection should be made, however, only if the impropriety goes to such extent that a fair trial cannot be had, and should not be made simply for the purpose of interrupting opposing counsel's chain of thought.

When an objection is made, the improper statement, the objection, the ruling, and where necessary, an exception, should be noted by the reporter. Thus, the foundation is laid for appellate review.

It is frequently necessary, in addition to making an objection, to request further relief, such as an instruction to disregard the improper statement, an admonition to offending counsel, or in extreme cases, a mistrial.[43]

Offending counsel may often prevent a reversal by withdrawing the improper statement.[44]

Generally, improper argument is not grounds for reversal unless the appellate court deems the argument to have been pre-

---

41 U.S. v. DeVasto, 52 F. 2d 26; 88 C.J.S. Trial, § 194.
42 Scott v. Times Mirror Co., 181 Cal. 345, 184 P. 672; 88 C.J.S. Trial, § 196.
43 Brooklyn Heights R. Co. v. Ploxin, 294 F. 68.
44 Distin v. Bradley, 83 Conn. 466, 76 A. 991.

judicial.[45] Thus, the judgment is apt to be affirmed if the appellate court is of the opinion that the verdict is sustained by the evidence, wholly apart from the argument.

SECTION 93. IMPORTANCE OF AN EFFECTIVE CONCLUSION. As suggested earlier, a well-constructed argument moves steadily toward a conclusion. The jury should be able to note such progress, and should not get the contrary impression that you do not know when or how to finish.

The conclusion should be carefully prepared, and should be delivered in such a way that the jury is impressed with the sincerity of your belief in the justice of your client's cause. Some emotional appeal at this point is in order. The strongest bit of evidence may again be referred to. It is also quite common to compliment the jury for the time and attention given to the case, providing again that this can be sincerely done.

In short, the conclusion should be designed to create an attitude favorable to your client's cause, with the expectation that such attitude will continue during the process of deliberation.

---

[45] Brungs v. St. Louis Public Service Co., 230 S.W. 2d 181 (Mo. App.); 88 C.J.S. Trial, § 202.

Chapter 8

Instructions

SECTION 94. NECESSITY OF REQUEST. At common law the trial court was under no legal duty[1] but did have the power[2] to instruct the jury, in the absence of a request to do so. In almost all jurisdictions the matter today is governed by statute or rule of court. These statutes and rules vary considerably.[3] In perhaps the majority of jurisdictions the court has the same duty and power as at common law. This view is based upon the proposition that it is unfair to expect the trial judge to know or to research all the fine points of law involved in a case. That obligation is upon counsel, who is certainly more familiar with the applicable legal points than is the court. A failure to charge cannot be assigned as error, under this view, in the absence of a request, properly and timely made.

It should be noted, however, that even in jurisdictions which generally insist upon a request to charge, it has occasionally been held that where the court does charge, the charge must cover all the issues.[4] Also a new trial has been ordered in such jurisdiction where the reviewing court was of the opinion that the record

---

[1] Osgood v. Skinner, 211 Ill. 229, 71 N.E. 869.
[2] Stumps v. Kelley, 22 Ill. 140.
[3] 53 Am. Jur. Trial, § 510.
[4] Judson v. Winsted, 80 Conn. 384, 68 A. 999; 53 Am. Jur. Trial, § 546.

indicated that the jury had taken a wrong view of the law, where no instructions were requested or given.[5] This result has followed also where the trial court has given only general instructions stating what the issues are as raised by the pleadings, who had the burden of proof on these issues, and informing the jury that they were the sole judges of the credibility of the witnesses.[6]

In another group of jurisdictions, the court is required to give substantially correct instructions on all material issues raised by the pleadings and supported by proof, even if there is no request.[7] Sometimes the duty is limited to instructing on "substantial" issues; apparently this means that they must be more than paper issues, and necessary for the jury to arrive at a verdict which will be in accordance with law.

In a final group of jurisdictions, the court is under duty to charge without a request, but the failure to instruct on any particular issue may not be relied upon for reversal in the absence of a request.[8] Similarly no complaint may be made of the failure to give cautionary or definitive instructions unless requested.

Attorneys practicing in a jurisdiction falling within the latter two categories generally do make certain requests despite the fact that the court may be under duty to charge in absence of requests. The chief function of instructions is to advise the jury of the law to be applied to the facts as the jury finds them. Therefore, if counsel is chiefly concerned with obtaining a favorable verdict and one which will stand up on review, it is important that the jury have the tools necessary to do the job. However, it is advisable in this situation to limit the number of requests to the essential issues, to reduce the possibility of reversible error. On the other hand, if counsel does not expect a favorable verdict, he will present numerous requests with the expectation that a number of them

---

5 Sandwich Mfg. Co. v. Shiley, 15 Neb. 109, 17 N.W. 267.

6 York Park Bldg. Ass'n. v. Barnes, 39 Neb. 834, 58 N.W. 440.

7 Jagerisky v. Detroit United Ry., 163 Mich. 631, 128 N.W. 726.

8 Maloy v. Griffith, 125 Colo. 85, 240 P. 2d 923.

will be erroneously denied and thus provide grounds for reversal.

In all but one or two jurisdictions, the court has power to charge even without requests.[9] And, in all jurisdictions a party may complain of an erroneous instruction though he has not made a request involving the point covered by the instruction.[10] Such erroneous instruction may have been tendered by opposing counsel, or it may have been drafted by the court and given of his own volition.

SECTION 95. CORRECTION BY THE COURT. If a request is made in terms which the court deems to be incorrect, he is, in the absence of a statutory prohibition,[11] generally considered as possessing the authority to reject it and either correct it or prepare another substitute instruction.[12] In practice many courts reject tendered instructions, even though substantially correct, and substitute their own, perhaps because they fear undue bias.

There is a division in the authorities as to the duty of the court to correct an instruction.[13] As stated above, counsel is in a better position to know the law to be applied, except for general principles, than is the judge. On the other hand, where the judge is under a duty to correct, such duty is based upon the fact that the point has been called to the court's attention.

A question as to the judge's duty to correct a tendered instruction arises frequently where the request contains two or more propositions. The judge may agree to some of the propositions, and disagree as to others. In some jurisdictions he is at liberty to reject the entire request.[14] Since the request may involve a very important point which would have been given if correctly stated,

---

9 Masonite Corp. v. Lockridge, 163 Miss. 364, 140 So. 223.

10 St. Paul, F. & M. Ins. Co. v. Bachmann, 285 U.S. 112; 53 Am. Jur. Trial, § 515.

11 Thompson v. Alexander City Cotton Mills Co., 190 Ala. 184, 67 So. 407.

12 Sugarman v. U.S., 249 U.S. 182; 53 Am. Jur. Trial, § 531.

13 Barth v. Kansas City El. Ry. Co., 142 Mo. 535, 44 S.W. 778; Broudy-Kantor Co. v. Levin, 135 Va. 283, 116 S.E. 677; 53 Am. Jur. Trial, § 525.

14 Guerini Stone Co. v. P. J. Carlin Constr. Co., 248 U.S. 334; 53 Am. Jur. Trial, § 526.

it is advisable to embody only one proposition in an instruction, whenever possible.

SECTION 96. THE REQUEST—WHEN AND HOW MADE. In determining the number of instructions to be tendered and the form those instructions should take, counsel should bear these questions in mind:

1. Will the trial court accept them, either in the form offered or with a slight modification? Some judges are prone to turn down most requests, preferring to draft their own instructions.

2. How will the requests, if accepted and given, affect the jury? Here counsel must be governed by the difficulty of the case and the make-up of the jury.

3. What will be opposing counsel's reaction? If he is apt to make an objection or take an exception it may be wise to anticipate the possibility of an appeal; if he is spurred on to make counter-requests, the latter may be couched in language quite damaging to your side, and the court, having given your requested instruction, may feel impelled, as a matter of fairness, to grant the request of your adversary. Conversely, in preparing instructions, it is well to anticipate what requests may be made by the opponent, and at least have ready to offer, counter-requests of your own.

4. How will the appellate court view your requested instruction? It is a well-known fact that instructions have provided the largest single ground for reversing.

What weight is to be given to these factors will depend of course upon the nature of the case and the side that you represent.

Statutes or rules frequently specify when requests are to be submitted.[15] In the federal courts and in some states this is to be done not later than at the close of the evidence.[16] The time will vary somewhat depending upon whether the closing argument precedes or follows the giving of instructions. In most courts it is

---

[15] 88 C.J.S. Trial, § 394 a.
[16] Fed. R. Civ. P. 51.

possible to submit at least some requests early in the trial, and it is often advisable to do so.[17] A reference to the pleadings and the use of deposition and other discovery devices will enable counsel to know before trial what most of the major issues will be.

An early and adequate research as to the law insures better preparation by trial counsel, and frequently points up the need for specific information which had previously been overlooked. In this manner the necessity of asking for a continuance or postponement can be avoided. Further, if the court is made aware early in the trial of the precise theory relied upon, he will be able to rule more intelligently on objections to evidence, etc. Also, counsel's arguments will be more readily understood. Preparation on the drafting of instructions can begin, in fact, as soon as a case is accepted, and the requests can be amplified as work progresses. If for some reason formal requests are not deemed desirable early in the trial, the same objective may be attained by submitting a memorandum on the law.

In general, the number of instructions should be kept to a minimum. Thus, the possibility of confusing the jury is reduced, as is the likelihood of error. There seems to be little justification for the giving of 75 instructions in a personal injury case, but such extremes are not at all uncommon. In the average case, it is not necessary to make requests involving general legal principles with which every court is familiar, but assistance is needed for fine points which do not arise frequently. Counsel all too often fail to make this distinction.

Under the common-law system, requests for instructions could be made orally, and this is still the practice in some jurisdictions.[18] In others, as in the federal courts, the requests must be in writing.[19] The requests should be numbered, with only one request to

---

[17] Deering's Cal. Code Proc. 1949, § 607 a.
[18] Hall v. Aiken County, 132 S.C. 420, 129 S.E. 160; 88 C.J.S. Trial, § 397 a.
[19] Fed. R. Civ. P. 51.

a page. This enables the court to arrange those accepted in any sequence he may wish, incorporating those tendered by the opponent and those drafted by the court. In some jurisdictions requests must include supporting citations, in other jurisdictions such practice is optional. It will be found convenient to have such citations readily available should it be necessary to argue the request.

Whenever possible, requests should be submitted to opposing counsel before filed with the court. This enables him to determine whether to object or to submit other instructions on the points covered. Argument is thus expedited.

Argument should be conducted out of the presence of the jury. Not only will counsel feel freer to state his position, but the jury is prevented from drawing unsound inferences from the argument and the rulings of the court.

Subsequent sections will point out some of the more common specific errors of form found in many instructions. At this point a few general suggestions as to form may be in order.

It is possible to state the law accurately and still do so in language which the jury can understand. It is not always necessary to use precise legal terms which may have meaning to the lawyer but not to a lay jury. Also, many requests are so long that even the court has difficulty in comprehending their import. Avoid beginning each instruction with "ladies and gentlemen of the jury." Use names of individuals concerned whenever possible. Instructions in positive form are usually to be preferred over those couched in negative terms, as the jury needs direction, not a series of prohibitions. Requests which relate specifically to certain testimony, along with the inferences which may legitimately be drawn therefrom, will serve such purpose by assisting the jury in the processes of recollection and decision.

If, after tendering a request, counsel has discovered an error in it, or for some reason does not wish it to be given, in most jurisdictions he may obtain leave to withdraw it, at least prior to its acceptance or rejection, and perhaps before it is given to the jury.[20] Likewise, after the charge has been given, it is usually possible to submit additional requests supplying deficiencies or explaining the charge.[21] This is particularly true in those jurisdictions where counsel is not informed as to what instructions will be given before they are in fact given, and the court gives several instructions not requested by either party. This procedure presupposes, of course, careful attention by counsel to the charge, and a check-list of items to be covered by the charge as a whole.

SECTION 97. FURTHER INSTRUCTIONS AFTER RETIREMENT OF THE JURY. The extent to which, and the manner in which the court may instruct the jury after its retirement is frequently regulated by statute.[22] Ordinarily, written supplemental instructions may not be sent to the jury room.[23] If it is necessary to instruct the jury further, either because the jury has indicated such desire or the matter has been called to the court's attention by counsel, the usual practice is to call the jury back into the courtroom. The additional instructions are ordinarily given only in the presence of counsel. If, however, counsel cannot be found, it is proper to proceed in his absence. Hence counsel should be available during the period of deliberation.

The additional instructions normally are explanatory in nature or cover some point omitted in the original charge. Counsel should be aware of the content of the instructions before they are given, so that he may object or request additional instructions.

SECTION 98. SCOPE. The scope of the charge will depend upon the purposes to be achieved. While the overall purpose is to control the actions of the jury and to reduce or eliminate irresponsible behavior, the specific purposes will depend upon a number of

---

20 88 C.J.S. Trial, § 402; Mutual Life Ins. Co. of Baltimore, Md. v. Kelly, 49 Ohio App. 319, 197 N.E. 235.

21 Kimble v. Kiser, 59 F. 2d 626; 88 C.J.S. Trial, § 394 b.

22 88 C.J.S. Trial, § 324.

23 Meinecke v. Fidelity Inv. Co., 62 S.W. 2d 623 (Tex.); 89 C.J.S. Trial, § 478.

factors. Among these factors are the following: The controlling law as to the power of the judge; the complexity of the case; the type of verdict to be returned; the composition of the jury; the nature of the case and the shape of the evidence.

If a general verdict is to be returned, the jury's function is to apply to the facts as they find them the law as given to them by the court. Hence the chief purpose of the instructions would be to acquaint the jury with the applicable legal principles. If, on the other hand, a special verdict is to be returned, the jury's function is merely to find the facts in whatever form they are directed to do so, and the court applies the law to the facts so found. Here there is no occasion to inform the jury what the applicable legal principles are. If the jury is to return answers to special interrogatories along with a general verdict, the function of the jury is a combination of the two first stated.

Regardless of the form of the verdict, it is customary for the charge to state the nature of the action and the contentions of the parties, to give the jury a proper background for the evaluation of the evidence. Thus, it may be pointed out that the plaintiff is relying on the last clear chance doctrine, violation of a statute, etc.

In order that the jury may properly carry out its function, they may be informed as to their role in the judicial process. Thus, they may be instructed that their duty is to find facts, and sometimes also to apply law; that the law must be accepted by them as stated by the court, whether or not it conforms to their notion of what it should be; that the plaintiff (or defendant) has the burden of proof and that a specified degree of conviction is necessary to satisfy that burden; that they are the judges of the weight of the evidence and the credibility of witnesses and in the determination thereof may use such common knowledge and experience as is possessed by men in general as distinguished from special knowledge and experience possessed by one of them.

Technical or legal terms such as ordinary care, recklessness, wanton and willful misconduct, may be defined. In some jurisdictions the judge may comment on the evidence, and specify what the legal effect of a presumption may be.[24] The form of verdict to be returned may be explained. The need for unanimity on each issue may be pointed out. The jury may be instructed that if the plaintiff has shown he is entitled to damages, under the law and the evidence, they may properly consider certain specified elements of damages.

SECTION 99. SOURCE MATERIAL. In a number of jurisdictions standard instructions have been developed by members of the bench and bar working jointly.[25] These instructions generally cover the more common matters included in a charge, and are numbered and bound in book form. Such books are either made available by the organized bar of the particular unit involved, as county, state or city, or copies will be found in the courts of the jurisdictions involved. Sometimes mimeographed copies may be available in the clerk's office. Since these forms have been officially approved, they may be safely used, if applicable. To the extent available, standard instructions eliminate the need to tender written instructions, and may simply be requested by number. However, it is usually necessary to draft several other instructions applicable to the case at bar.

In many instances the files of the court may be examined for instructions which have been approved and given in prior similar cases.

Attorneys doing considerable trial work also develop files of instructions, classifying them as to subject matter. This practice can save time in the preparation of routine instructions.

Instructions given in a particular jurisdiction may be found by use of a digest, either under the heading of "Instructions," or "Trial." In the latter case there is a subdivision labeled "Instruc-

---

24 Texarkana Bus Co., Inc. v. Baker, 142 F. 2d 491; 88 C.J.S. Trial, § 273.
25 E.g., California, Illinois, Minnesota, Missouri, Nebraska, Ohio, Wisconsin.

tions." It is possible in this manner to determine what an appellate court has had to say about a particular instruction. It is not generally advisable to use verbatim a statement by an appellate court on a point of law, as such statement is not designed to guide a jury in its deliberations.

In many jurisdictions there are form books containing instructions given, indexed according to subject matter.

While statutes may be incorporated verbatim in an instruction, it is frequently inadvisable to do so, as the statute may be ineptly worded and hence unclear. In such cases it is probably better to paraphrase the statute.

Whenever an instruction given in a previous case is to be used in pending litigation, the facts and issues of the previous case should be checked to determine the appropriateness of the instruction. Because an instruction was deemed proper in a previous case does not give assurance that it will be so considered in the current litigation.

SECTION 100. HOW GIVEN. The manner in which instructions are to be given is today largely governed by statutes and rules.[26] Such provisions may either require that requests be in writing, or that the instructions as given be in writing. In the absence thereof, the court may, as at common law, instruct orally. This means that the judge gives his charge extemporaneously, perhaps from notes made during the trial, and possibly including requested instructions. The reporter takes down the charge verbatim as given. In about one-fourth of the states the instructions still must be given orally, and in a slightly larger number this manner is permitted. In almost all of these jurisdictions exceptions are provided for, particularly where requests are made in writing.

If the court's duty is limited to the giving of properly requested instructions, the judge merely reads those instructions

---

[26] Vanderbilt, Minimum Standards of Judicial Administration 231.

tendered by counsel and approved by him. If there is no such limitation, the court may instruct on matters not requested.

In the majority of jurisdictions instructions must be in writing.[27] In this situation, the court merely reads the instructions, which are usually numbered, and the instructions may be taken into the jury room.[28] In any event, extemporaneous comments are prohibited. An exception is generally made with reference to admonitions or comments made by the judge during the progress of the trial, such as disregarding certain excluded evidence or inflammatory remarks of counsel, which comments in their very nature must be made orally and at the time the occasion arises. Such reading of instructions, particularly if lengthy and numerous, in many instances serves to confuse rather than enlighten the jury. On the other hand, the requirement of writing does avoid controversy as to the accuracy of the reporter's notes.

As stated earlier, in some jurisdictions the giving of instructions precedes argument, and in others it follows argument.[29] Some courts operating under either system give general instructions, covering such matters as the issues, the contentions of the parties and any applicable statutes or general legal principles, prior to the introduction of any evidence.

Regardless of the above variations in the manner of giving instructions, it is generally agreed that instructions must be given in open court and in the presence of counsel.[30] The latter must have an opportunity to object or except.

SECTION 101. OBJECTIONS AND EXCEPTIONS. Technically, an objection is an indication of counsel's position with reference to a proposed step, such as the giving of certain testimony or the request for an instruction. An exception, on the other hand, is an indication of counsel's dissatisfaction with a ruling of the court

---

[27] People v. Kelly, 347 Ill. 221, 179 N.E. 898; 53 Am. Jur. Trial, § 562.

[28] Cal. Law Revision Comm. Report, Nov. 1956.

[29] 53 Am. Jur. Trial, § 536; 91 A.L.R. 2d 836.

[30] Taulborg v. Andresen, 119 Neb. 273, 228 N.W. 528; 53 Am. Jur. Trial. § 537.

on the proposed step. An exception then generally follows the ruling, while an objection precedes it. It will be noted that the purpose of the objection is to guide the court in making a ruling, whereas an exception is primarily an indication to the appellate court that counsel is insisting upon review of a prior objection.

Generally an objection is necessary, either to the giving or the refusal to give an instruction, in order to preserve the alleged error for appellate review.[31] Whether or not an exception is necessary depends upon the statute or rule in a particular jurisdiction.[32] In some jurisdictions, a blanket exception may be taken to all adverse rulings; in others it is deemed that such an exception was made.[33] In the absence of such provision, an exception must also be taken.

Statutes or rules frequently provide when and how objections may be made or exceptions taken.[34] In some jurisdictions conferences with the court precede the actual giving of the instructions, and this then is the appropriate time to object or except. In others, these steps may be taken after the charge and before the jury retires, or before the jury returns the verdict, or within a specified period after the verdict is returned. These variations are present also in jurisdictions which have no governing statute or rule.

When there is no prior conference, which is usually conducted in an informal manner, exceptions are generally taken only after the court has concluded giving the entire charge.

Objections or exceptions should be made or taken out of the presence of the jury whenever possible. If not, then these steps should be taken as quietly as possible, making certain that the reporter is making a note of the exception. In some jurisdictions charges and refused requests are automatically part of the record;[35]

---

31 O'Connell v. Naess, 176 F. 2d 138; 4 C.J.S. Appeal and Error, § 305.
32 4 C.J.S. Appeal and Error, § 334.
33 Ind. Sup. Ct. Rule 1–5.
34 Fed. R. Civ. P. 51; 53 Am. Jur. Trial, §§ 827, 828.
35 Boggs v. Lumbar, 75 Colo. 212, 225 P. 266.

in others a bill of exceptions is necessary, as it was at common law.[36]

Objections or exceptions made during the trial may be made orally;[37] if after the jury has returned its verdict, where that is permitted, they are generally in writing.[38]

Objections and exceptions should always be specific, pointing out what part is deemed erroneous if not directed at the entire instruction; likewise, reasons should ordinarily be assigned for making an objection.[39] Fairness to the trial court and opposing counsel demand that. One exception to the above may occasionally develop, in that an exception is taken to the manner in which the entire charge is given. In such a situation, the exception could not be specific.

In determining whether to make an objection or take an exception, it is well to note that the action of the trial court generally will be deemed to constitute reversible error only if it is prejudicial to the appellant.[40] Thus, if the error is in favor of the appellant or if the result is such that it was not affected by the error, or if on the basis of the entire record the result is sound, no prejudice is present. In this connection, courts frequently hold that an erroneous instruction or failure to instruct is cured by a different and proper instruction, often given as an instruction of the court.[41] Also, under the doctrine of invited error, no complaint can be made of action which was requested by the appellant.[42] This latter doctrine is of course not applied where the trial court modifies a requested instruction so substantially that in fact a new and different instruction is given.

---

[36] McFadden v. A. B. Richards Medicine Co., 170 Ark. 1011, 282 S.W. 353; 4 C.J.S. Appeal and Error, § 768.

[37] Alcaro v. Jean Jordeau, Inc., 138 F. 2d 767.

[38] Mayer v. McLure, 36 Miss. 389, 72 Am. Dec. 190.

[39] Liverpool and London and Globe Ins. Co. v. McCree, 213 Ala. 534, 105 So. 901.

[40] Vaughan v. Jonas, 31 Cal. 2d 586, 191 P. 2d 432.

[41] Atlantic Coast Line R. Co. v. Wallace, 66 Fla. 321, 63 So. 583; 53 Am. Jur. Trial, § 554.

[42] Allen v. Quercus Lbr. Co., 171 Mo. App. 492, 157 S.W. 661.

Also, counsel would do well to use the same technique in making objections that were suggested with reference to requests, namely, that they be made only when supported by grounds and not in routine fashion. Frequently it is advisable to submit a substitute instruction when making an objection to one tendered by adverse counsel, as this suggests to the court a way in which your objection can be obviated.

SECTION 102. TAKING INSTRUCTIONS INTO JURY ROOM. Under the common-law practice, since instructions were oral and not a part of the record, no opportunity existed for the members of the jury to read instructions themselves in the jury room. But in approximately half the states today, either by statute, rule or decision this practice is required or permitted. In only one state is the practice expressly forbidden. In the remaining states apparently local rules govern.[43]

On the one hand, it may be argued that the jury may be more confused by a reading of the instructions. This result, however, need not follow if instructions are carefully worded, and couched in laymen's language. Again, it may be said that it is unwise to allow the jury to know who tendered the instruction. If this is a valid objection, which is doubtful, it too could be obviated. In favor of the practice it may be said that full understanding is more likely to be the result when the process of hearing the instruction read is supplemented by personal reading. Again, this practice would serve to avoid argument between members of the jury as to exactly what the court did say in a given instruction. Lastly, one of the few justifications for the requirement that instructions be in writing would seem to be the fact that this requirement permits the reading of the instructions by the jury.

In a few jurisdictions, experiments have been conducted, with consent of both parties, in which the jury is permitted to have played back instructions tape-recorded when given. On the whole,

---

[43] Supra, n. 28.

this innovation has been quite enthusiastically received by participating counsel.

SECTION 103. MUST STATE THE LAW CORRECTLY. In this and the following sections, attention is directed at some of the more common faults found in instructions.

It would seem at first glance, that any reference to the requirement that an instruction should correctly state the law would be unnecessary, perhaps even ridiculous. However, the fact is that many attorneys, in attempting to word an instruction so that it is as favorable as possible for their client's cause, do distort settled legal principles.[44] This practice takes many forms, depending upon the issues and the principles involved. It stems from the desire to obtain a favorable verdict, sometimes at any cost.

This practice of distortion should be avoided. In the first place, it is questionable whether it can be justified ethically. Secondly, it may have adverse practical effects. If the trial court is aware of the incorrectness, he will either refuse it, modify it, or give his own instruction which will be couched in less favorable terms. Thus any possible advantage is lost. If the trial court accepts the request as tendered and gives the instruction, the appellate court may rely upon it as grounds for reversal. It is possible that the higher tribunal will not consider the error as cured by the giving of other, and proper, instructions.[45]

The above comments assume that the law in a particular jurisdiction on a particular point is well settled. It does not envisage the situation where the law is unclear, or where it has not been previously settled by statute or decision. In this situation it is certainly proper and advisable to suggest what the law should be, and to couch the request in terms as favorable to your client as possible. Such request may be supported by citations from other jurisdictions.

---

44 Western Surety Co. v. Devils Lake, 58 F. 2d 161.
45 Fogarty v. Southern Pacific Co., 151 Cal. 785, 91 P. 650.

One advantage of standard instructions is that they are generally impartial, being compiled with no particular case in mind.

SECTION 104. COMMENT ON THE EVIDENCE. In the majority of jurisdictions the trial court is not permitted, by statute, to summarize or to comment on the evidence, contrary to the practice at common law.[46] This prohibition generally forbids an opinion as to where the weight of the evidence is, or what the probabilities are, or even as to the credibility of witnesses. It has been suggested that this restriction is a vestigial remnant from the time when judges, as officers of the crown, were held in disrepute, and that its continuation may be associated with the elective system for selection of judges. Whatever the reason, statutes in about half the states forbid summarizing, and in about three-fourths of the states comment is prohibited.[47] Such conduct on the part of the court is viewed as one type of encroachment upon the jury's function of deciding issues of fact.

In the federal courts, however, the judges have retained their traditional common-law powers.[48]

Where the court is permitted to summarize or comment upon the evidence, such instructions must be fair and accurate.[49] Frequently, an expression of opinion in jurisdictions permitting comment is phrased as a rule of law, and is hence considered to be erroneous. This point is considered again in Section 113 concerning cautionary instructions. Further, where the court is allowed to comment, he should not fail to inform the jury that what he has stated represents his own view of the evidence and is not binding upon the jury.

The responsibility of counsel in correctly instructing the jury is therefore greater in those jurisdictions which limit the power of the trial court. Requests accordingly should normally be in hypo-

---

[46] 53 Am. Jur. Trial, § 591.

[47] Vanderbilt, Minimum Standards of Judicial Administration, 226.

[48] Herron v. Southern Pacific Co., 283 U.S. 91; 53 Am. Jur. Trial, § 586.

[49] Hickory v. U.S., 160 U.S. 408; 53 Am. Jur. Trial, § 589.

thetical form, stating what the verdict should be, according to various, alternative, findings of fact. Any language should be avoided which suggests that a verdict is being directed.

SECTION 105. QUESTIONS OF LAW AND FACT. It is customary in legal circles to say that under our system of administration of justice questions of fact are to be decided by the jury and questions of law are for the court to decide. The difficulty which is experienced in attempting to apply this "maxim" stems from the fact that the terms "fact" and "law" are not defined.[50] Hence a question[51] which is decided by a *jury*[52] in one jurisdiction may be decided by a *court*[53] in another jurisdiction. The practice in even one jurisdiction may vary from case to case.[54]

Consequently counsel, in drafting requests, must consider how the question has been handled in his own jurisdiction in cases that are as similar to the one being tried as it is possible to find.

Where it is impossible to find "a case in point," it may be helpful to consider the following factors in the drafting of requests:

1. If a popular standard is desired then the question should be decided by the jury.[55] This approach is often used in submitting to the jury the question whether a party acted in accordance with the "reasonable man" standard.

2. If the given question is one that arises constantly in the same or similar circumstances or there is a definite policy involved, a fixed rather than a variable result may be desirable. In that event the question would normally be decided by the court. Thus, in

---

50 Scott, Fundamentals of Procedure, 81 ff.

51 E.g., Interpretation of statutes.

52 Daly v. New Staunton Coal Co., 280 Ill. 175, 117 N.E. 413.

53 Savannah, F. & W. Ry. Co. v. Daniels, 90 Ga. 608, 17 S.E. 647.

54 Penn Mutual Life Ins. Co. v. Crane, 134 Mass. 56 (whether a representation was material is for court); Fottler v. Mosely, 170 Mass. 295, 60 N.E. 788 (materiality a question for jury).

55 Pokora v. Wabash Ry. Co., 292 U.S. 98.

the area of commercial transactions, questions as to whether certain acts were done in a "reasonable time" are generally referred to the court for decision,[56] whereas similar questions in another context are decided by the jury.[57]

3. There is considerable confusion in the cases between two situations, namely: where the court decides the question (or, more accurately, decides there is no question for the jury) because of insufficiency of proof by the party who has the burden of coming forward with the evidence on the point; and where the court decides the question because that function is intrinsically that of the court, although both parties have satisfied their respective burdens. The latter situation is that to which the remarks in this section are directed.

4. If an objective standard is to be applied, the question is normally one for the court to determine; whereas, if a subjective standard is to be applied, it is left for the jury. By way of illustration: Where the objective intent of parties (as in contracts) or legislators (as in statutes) is desired, the court interprets the words of the contract[58] or statute; where the subjective (actual) intent is to govern, as in certain instances of false representations, the jury determines from the words and surrounding circumstances the actual state of mind of the speaker.[59]

An instruction whereby a question is decided by the court when it should have been decided by the jury is said to invade the province of the jury. The converse situation could perhaps be labeled as an instance of invading the province of the court, but more properly represents an abnegation of the judicial function.

SECTION 106. THE ABSTRACT CHARGE. When it is recalled that

---

[56] Leonard v. Olson, 99 Iowa 162, 68 N.W. 677 (presentment of demand note to maker, to hold indorser).

[57] Employers' Liability Assur. Corp. v. Roehm, 99 Ohio State 343, 124 N.E. 223 (notice of accident).

[58] Barcus v. Wayne Automobile Co., 162 Mich. 177, 127 N.W. 23.

[59] Fottler v. Mosely, supra, n. 54.

the primary purpose for instructing the jury as to the law which is to govern the case is to assist them in the process of applying that law, it is readily seen why an instruction, which merely states a legal proposition in the abstract without tying it down to the facts of the case, is so severely criticized by appellate courts.[60] Yet the abstract charge appears again and again.

This particular defect may be avoided by use of the hypothetical form previously referred to. In this form the rule of law is not expressly set out but is implicit in the statement of the result. The jury is merely informed what their verdict should be under various findings of fact.

SECTION 107. ASSUMING FACTS. There is no requirement that all issues of fact be presented to the jury in one instruction; it is generally sufficient if the entire charge, taken as a whole, touches upon every disputed fact.[61] It must be clear, however, to the jury, that they are to consider the charge in its entirety. If the charge is so set up, error in one instruction is frequently held not to be ground for reversal, providing other instructions correctly and adequately cover the point.

On the other hand, if the court gives a formula instruction, i.e., an instruction which purports to be complete within itself, it must cover all the issues of fact in the case.[62] Quite frequently this type of instruction is held to be erroneous because it assumes that a fact exists when this is very much disputed. For example, an instruction may proceed to set out the elements of damages for which recovery may be had, and by implication assumes that the plaintiff has suffered legal damages when that is one of the most hotly contested issues in the case.[63] Again, an instruction which informs the jury that they must determine whether the defendant has been

---

60 Stanich v. Western Union Tel. Co., 348 Mo. 188, 153 S.W. 2d 54; 53 Am. Jur. Trial, § 573.

61 State v. Newman, 91 Conn. 6, 98 A. 346; 53 Am. Jur. Trial, § 546.

62 Hansen v. Cline, 136 Iowa 101, 113 N.W. 504; 53 Am. Jur. Trial, § 581.

63 Purdy v. Waterloo, C.F. & N. Ry. Co., 172 Iowa 676, 154 N.W. 881.

guilty of a breach of legal duty may be held defective in that it assumes the existence of a duty, when that is in issue.[64] Or, the instruction may refer to all of the elements presented by one side and fail to include elements presented by the other side.[65] In this type of instruction the missing element may not be supplied in another part of the charge. It is obvious therefore that if this type of instruction is to be given, great care must be exercised in the drafting of it.

SECTION 108. FALSE ISSUES. In the preceding section instructions were discussed which omitted an essential element in the case. An instruction may also be faulty in that it injects a false issue into the case.[66] Thus far there is general agreement. But there is a difference of opinion as to what constitutes a false issue.

The strictest view holds that an instruction is improper if it leaves to the jury an issue that is not presented by *both* the pleadings and the proof.[67]

Under another view an issue is properly left to the jury, though it is not framed in the pleadings, if contradictory proof is presented by both sides. In this situation the pleadings may be amended to conform to the proof, or disregarded altogether as to the one issue.[68]

According to a third view, the matter depends upon the making of an objection to evidence on the grounds of variance. Under this view if an objection is made and overruled and the objecting party is thus compelled to introduce proof, an instruction on the issue involved is erroneous; but if no objection is made, and contradictory evidence is introduced, the objection is deemed waived and an instruction on the issue involved is proper.[69]

---

[64] Imhoff v. Chicago & Milwaukee Ry. Co., 20 Wis. 344.
[65] O'Hara v. Central Illinois Light Co., 319 Ill. App. 336, 49 N.E. 2d 274.
[66] 53 Am. Jur. Trial, § 574.
[67] Indiana Railway Co. v. Maurer, 160 Ind. 25, 66 N.E. 156.
[68] Fed. R. Civ. P. 15 (b).
[69] Howard v. Georgia Ry. & Power Co., 35 Ga. App. 273, 133 S.E. 57.

Under any view, it is error to instruct on an issue that is not raised by the proof in one of the ways outlined above; thus, if an issue is raised by the pleadings and the party having the burden of proof on that issue introduces no proof in support of the pleaded allegations, it is improper to leave that issue to the jury.

As stated earlier, one of the functions of the trial court is to state to the jury what the paper issues are. Hence it is improper for the court to merely refer the jury to the pleadings so that they may determine for themselves what the issues are.[70] Similarly, it is error to instruct the jury to find for the plaintiff if they find that he has proved all the material allegations of the complaint.[71] In view of the fact that pleadings are often drawn in a formal, legalistic style it is highly unrealistic to expect a lay body properly to interpret them. The above comments are applicable only where the jurisdiction permits the jury to take the pleadings into the jury room. In a number of jurisdictions this practice is prohibited.

Also, it is a function of the trial court to inform the jury when an issue of fact is presented by the proof. Under the more usual view, such an issue exists whenever the fact could be found either way. In making this determination, the court must determine in the first instance what inferences are warranted from the evidence which was introduced.

SECTION 109. UNDISPUTED FACTS. Certain allegations in pleadings are expressly admitted in the answering pleadings, or are tacitly admitted by a rule of pleading in some jurisdictions because of lack of denial. In either event, such allegations are, for purposes of the trial, assumed to be true. Hence it is improper to require or allow a finding thereon by the jury.[72]

More often, however, certain paper issues disappear because of failure of proof tending to negate allegations made in the plead-

---

70 Stevens v. Maxwell, 65 Kan. 835, 70 P. 873.

71 Baker v. Summers, 201 Ill. 52, 66 N.E. 302.

72 Long v. Booe, 106 Ala. 570, 17 So. 716; 53 Am. Jur. Trial, § 607.

ings and supported by proof, or because of admissions obtained by means of cross-examination.[73] Again, in either event, there is no true issue to leave to the jury, except such as may involve credibility.

The trial court may segregate the contested allegations from those admitted or assumed, in several ways. Both types of allegations may be pointed out to the jury, with directions to find only as to the disputed allegations, or only the disputed allegations may be presented for determination by the jury.

SECTION 110. IMPROPER EMPHASIS. Occasionally a charge, in its entirety, is held to be improper because of the undue prominence which it gives to one aspect of the case.[74] Such a charge is considered unfair to one party as it tends to overemphasize a claim at the expense of the defense, or conversely overemphasizes a defense at the expense of the claim. A series of instructions on the same point but in slightly different language is a rather common illustration of this error. Again, a charge may be considered lopsided if it brings out details shown by one side without including enough details brought out by the other side. If in a case in which liability is in issue there are numerous instructions on the issue of damages, there may be an implication that liability has been established.

SECTION 111. INCONSISTENCY. A charge, taken in its entirety, may have parts which are inconsistent with each other.[75] When this occurs, the jury is very apt to be confused instead of aided by the charge. Inconsistency may arise in several ways. In an effort to present both sides of the case, the court may give instructions tendered by opposing counsel, without making it clear that alternative propositions are thus being presented. Again, the inconsistency may arise from instructions tendered by only one side, if that

---

[73] Buyken v. Lewis Constr. Co., 51 Wash. 627, 99 P. 1007.

[74] Supra, n. 65; 53 Am. Jur. Trial, § 566.

[75] Deserant v. Cerillos Coal R. Co., 178 U.S. 409; 53 Am. Jur. Trial, § 557.

party's case is based upon several mutually inconsistent theories, and the jury is not clearly informed that only one or the other theory should ultimately govern the case.

The former difficulty may be avoided either in a conference with the court and opposing counsel held prior to the giving of the instructions, or by calling the court's attention to the matter when the charge is read. The latter difficulty need not arise if counsel is careful in the preparation of his requests for instructions.

SECTION 112. BURDEN OF PROOF, PREPONDERANCE OF THE EVIDENCE, CREDIBILITY OF WITNESSES. While there is some question as to the value of instructions attempting to define or explain to the jury such concepts as burden of proof and preponderance of the evidence,[76] in many jurisdictions it is considered proper for the charge to contain such definitions and explanations.[77] In other jurisdictions the court merely states that the burden of proof is on one side or the other, and that such burden must be satisfied by a preponderance of the evidence. This latter approach recognizes the difficulty of explaining complex legal concepts to laymen.

In the former group of states, courts frequently use either standard instructions or those given by the court in previous cases. Before submitting requests on these matters counsel should therefore check with the court to determine any preferences he may have.

Where an explanation of the term "burden of proof" is proper, it should refer to the use of that term in the sense of persuasion and not in the sense of going forward with the evidence. The question of allocation of the burden becomes important when the evidence is so evenly balanced that a determination as to its preponderance is impossible.[78] It should also be noted that this

---

76 McCormick, Evidence, §§ 306, 307, 319.
77 53 Am. Jur. Trial, §§ 676, 744.
78 McCormick, Evidence, § 307.

concept comes into play only when the mind of each juror is in equilibrium, not when six jurors are inclined in one direction and six in another. The jury may also be informed that to find for the plaintiff, they must find for him on all the elements of the cause of action, whereas they must find for the defendant if they find for him on only one of those elements.

Preponderance of the evidence is frequently defined as "the greater weight of the evidence."[79] The jury may be told that in determining where the greater weight lies, they may consider such matters as relevance and credibility. In some jurisdictions it is also proper to instruct the jury that they may view the evidence in the light of their common general experience, but that no special knowledge or experience of a particular juror is to be taken into consideration.[80]

Instructions concerning credibility must always be so phrased that the jury clearly understands that they are the final judges thereof, and any comments of the court are merely advisory.[81] Generally the court may point out certain factors which affect credibility, such as demeanor while testifying, interest, etc., as long as the jury understands that such factors are merely illustrative and not all-inclusive. In some jurisdictions the jury may be informed that they are free to disregard all of the testimony of a witness who testified falsely in some respect, or that they may draw unfavorable inferences from the failure to call an available witness.

SECTION 113. CAUTIONARY. Cautionary instructions are designed to assist the jury in properly carrying out their function. Many relate to credibility of witnesses and refer to factors considered by persons in everyday life when attempting to distinguish

---

[79] Id. § 319.

[80] State ex. rel. State Highway Comm. v. Stoddard Gin Co., 62 S.W. 2d 940 (Mo.); 88 C.J.S. Trial, § 389.

[81] Macon Ry. & Light Co. v. Barnes, 121 Ga. 443, 49 S.E. 282; 88 C.J.S. Trial, § 315.

truth from falsity. Other such instructions relate to the necessity of approaching their task in an impartial manner.

As stated earlier, there is a relation between the power of the court to comment and the power to give cautionary instructions, and frequently the two do overlap.[82] If a matter has solidified into a rule of law, a court has the power to instruct even though he does not have the power to comment on the evidence.[83] On the other hand, a cautionary instruction may be held erroneous even though the judge has the power to comment.[84] There is some confusion in the authorities on this point, in that some hold such instruction to be bad because there is no such rule of law, whereas in a jurisdiction allowing comment a cautionary instruction theoretically may be criticized also if it does not conform to human experience. Such an instruction would be as follows: One is presumed to remember what one once knew.

Generally cautionary instructions must be requested in order to assign as error the failure to give them.[85] Such an instruction should be requested only with reference to some matter already in the record or it will be denied as irrelevant.

In jurisdictions allowing cautionary instructions, the following have, where pertinent, frequently been held to be proper: that circumstantial evidence has the same weight as direct evidence;[86] that a party's economic, social or political position should not influence the jury's decision;[87] that the case should be decided solely on the law and the evidence.[88]

---

[82] 53 Am. Jur. Trial, § 619.

[83] Henry v. Wabash Western Ry. Co., 109 Mo. 488, 19 S.W. 239 (effect of false testimony).

[84] Quercia v. U.S., 289 U.S. 466 (witness wiping hands during testimony "almost always an indication of lying").

[85] Ideal Pure Milk Co. v. Whitaker, 243 S.W. 2d 479 (Ky.); 88 C.J.S. Trial, § 392 e.

[86] Hickory v. U.S., 151 U.S. 303.

[87] Wilson v. Singer Sewing Mach. Co., 184 N.C. 40, 113 S.E. 508.

[88] Chicago & E. I. Ry. Co. v. Burridge, 211 Ill. 9, 71 N.E. 838; 88 C.J.S. Trial, § 320.

The following instructions are much more doubtful: A witness who affirms is to be believed in preference to a witness who disaffirms;[89] verbal admissions made shortly after an accident by an injured person are to be received with caution;[90] expert testimony is similarly to be received;[91] statements against one's interest are to be considered more trustworthy than statements in favor of interest.[92]

Serving somewhat the same purposes as cautionary instructions are those generally termed "argumentative." Such instructions are to assist the jury in drawing inferences, and are frequently held to be erroneous in that they unduly restrict the jury in the process of reasoning and hence constitute a type of determinism.[93] Illustrative of such instructions are the following: Proof that something *may have* happened in a certain way is no proof that it *did* happen in that way; proof that a person was at one place at a particular time is proof that he was not at another place at that time. In the latter instance there may be a matter of credibility involved.

SECTION 114. AIDING THE JURY IN RECALLING THE EVIDENCE. If in the course of their deliberations the jury cannot recall the testimony of certain witnesses, such witnesses may, in some jurisdictions be again called to repeat their testimony;[94] in other jurisdictions the reporter may read his notes;[95] and in still others the court may summarize the testimony as he recalls it.[96] Even if the jury does not request such aid, counsel occasionally request that it be given. Such a request is appropriate if the jury has been out an unreasonably long time, and it is surmised that a reason

---

89 St. L. & S.F. Ry. Co. v. Rundell, 108 Okla. 132, 235 P. 491.

90 Blume v. C.M. & St. P. Ry. Co., 133 Minn. 348, 158 N.W. 418.

91 Gustafson v. Seattle Traction Co., 28 Wash. 227, 68 P. 721.

92 Valley Lbr. Co. v. Smith, 71 Wis. 304, 37 N.W. 412.

93 State Auto. Mut. Ins. Co. v. York, 104 F. 2d 730; 88 C.J.S. Trial, § 336.

94 Clark v. State, 28 Tex. App. 189, 12 S.W. 729; 53 Am. Jur. Trial, § 936.

95 Phillips v. Carlson, 178 Kan. 206, 284 P. 2d 604; 50 A.L.R. 2d 176; 53 Am. Jur. Trial, § 938.

96 Hrovat v. Cleveland R. Co., 125 Ohio St. 67, 180 N.E. 549; 84 A.L.R. 215; 53 Am. Jur. Trial, § 937.

therefor is disagreement as to certain evidence. Regardless of the method used to refresh the jury's recollection, the procedure should take place in open court in the presence of the judge and counsel. The whole matter is generally held to be within the trial court's discretion, and sometimes is specifically covered by statute.

The great majority of statutes do not allow depositions to be taken into the jury room, although a few expressly permit the practice.[97] Where the matter is not provided for by statute, the case law is conflicting, unless a substantial part of the testimony on both sides is in deposition form.[98] In the latter instance there is no undue advantage to one side. Where depositions are allowed to be taken into the jury room they must at least be admissible if not actually admitted into evidence.[99] If depositions are not in this category, it is generally deemed to be prejudicial error to allow the jury to examine them in the jury room.[100] If a deposition contains objectionable matter, such matter should be deleted before examination by the jury is allowed. It is generally held that a proper objection must be made before an examination by the jury can be grounds for a new trial or for a reversal on appeal.[101]

On the other hand, exhibits, especially writings, may be taken into the jury room with or without the authorization of a statute.[102] There seems to be a greater reluctance on the part of the courts to permit the same use to be made of physical objects.[103] The reason apparently concerns the fact that the jury may attach undue importance to such objects. Written exhibits should be examined by counsel before they are submitted to the jury, lest the

---

[97] 57 A.L.R. 2d 1014; 53 Am. Jur. Trial, § 931.

[98] Nat. Fire Ins. Co. v. Sayers, 16 Ohio App. 398; Gray v. Pennslyvania R. Co., 33 Del. 450, 139 A. 66; 57 A.L.R. 2d 1017.

[99] Moody v. Vickers, 79 Ohio App. 218, 72 N.E. 2d 280.

[100] Lurie v. Kegan-Grace Co., 209 Ala. 339, 96 So. 344.

[101] Skinner v. Neubauer, 246 Minn. 291, 74 N.W. 2d 656.

[102] Higgins v. Los Angeles Gas & E. Co., 159 Cal. 651, 115 P. 313; 53 Am. Jur. Trial, § 927.

[103] Jensen v. Dikel, 244 Minn. 71, 69 N.W. 2d 108.

jury's attention be unduly concentrated on portions of the exhibits because of notations made thereon. Also, counsel should make sure that the exhibits have been properly introduced into evidence.

Occasionally the jury may wish to consult a dictionary. The cases here are not in agreement; some courts presume prejudice to result from such action, and consider this as equivalent to a resort to incompetent evidence.[104] Others conclude that if there was error, it may be cured by proper instructions.[105]

---

[104] Palestroni v. Jacobs, 10 N.J. Super. 266, 77 A. 2d 183.
[105] Schreiner v. State, 155 Neb. 894, 54 N.W. 2d 224; 54 A.L.R. 2d 738.

Chapter 9

Verdicts

A. General Verdicts

SECTION 115. ORIGIN AND USE. In most jurisdictions a jury may be directed to return one of three verdicts: The general verdict, the special verdict, or the general verdict plus answers to special interrogatories.[1] The general verdict, though the oldest known type, is still the one most commonly used. The reasons for this phenomenon are discussed in subsequent sections.

The theory behind the general verdict is a simple one: The jury's function is to find the facts and to apply to the facts found the law as given to them by the court in the instructions. Where a general verdict is to be returned, the instructions should be complete as to all facets of the case, and should cover alternative findings of facts. In practice, however, the process of returning a general verdict may be an extremely complicated one, with the result that opportunities for error are numerous. Consequently this chapter will consider techniques designed to reduce the possibility of error when the general verdict is used, and also substitutes for such verdicts.

If no request is made for a special verdict, or for the jury to

---

[1] Blume, American Civil Procedure, § 5–01; First Nat. Bank, v. Peck 8 Kan. 660.

return answers to special interrogatories, the jury will, in most cases, be directed to return a general verdict.[2]

SECTION 116. REQUIREMENTS. The general verdict must meet the following requirements: 1. It must be responsive to the issues.[3] 2. It must be definite and certain as to result.[4] 3. It must be logically consistent internally.[5] 4. It must be agreed upon by all members of the jury (at common law and in many jurisdictions still today).[6] 5. It must conform to the law.[7] 6. It must be supported by evidence which would lead a reasonable man to arrive at the same conclusion.[8] The sixth requirement will be discussed in Chapter 11, which deals with new trials. The other requirements are considered in subsequent sections of this chapter.

SECTION 117. WHEN ADVISABLE. Assuming that in a given jurisdiction there exists a choice of verdicts, the following factors should be considered in determining whether a general verdict is appropriate in a particular case:

1. Whether the court or jury or both are known to be hostile to other than a general verdict. This hostility can manifest itself in any number of ways and may operate to the detriment of the party requesting a special verdict or that interrogatories be answered along with a general verdict.

2. Whether the case is a relatively simple one, involving one party on each side and one or two issues. If the fact issues are simple and the law applicable is relatively easy to understand, the chances of error are reduced to a minimum. The general verdict may then be safely used.

---

2 O'Neil v. Larkin-Carey Co., 106 Conn. 153, 137 A. 721; Busch, Trial Procedure Materials, § 420.

3 Hyndshaw v. Mills, 108 Neb. 250, 187 N.W. 780; 53 Am. Jur. Trial, § 1037.

4 Fries v. Mack, 33 Ohio St. 52; 53 Am. Jur. Trial, § 1050.

5 Pangburn v. Buick Motor Co., 211 N.Y. 228; 105 N.E. 423, 53 Am. Jur. Trial, § 1048.

6 State v. Bates, 14 Utah 293, 47 P. 78; 53 Am. Jur. Trial, § 1006; 93 A.L.R. 2d 410.

7 Stetson v. Stindt, 279 F. 209; Busch, Trial Procedure Materials, § 419.

8 Jones v. Pohl, 151 Kan. 92, 98 P. 2d 175; 89 C.J.S. Trial, § 501.

3. Whether one side legitimately feels that there is need for amelioration of harsh rules of law to reach a result that will be just. This is the area about which there is the greatest difference of opinion. The proponents of the general verdict contend that this is the point where law is properly molded to meet the standards of the common man. The opponents of the general verdict, on the other hand, view the general verdict as one of the chief obstacles to a proper administration of law. This conflict is a basic one, involving as it does the function of the jury.

A proper choice of verdicts can be made only after consideration of all three types and a weighing of the advantages and disadvantages of each with respect to the particular case to be tried.

SECTION 118. SUBMITTING FORMS OF VERDICTS. While oral verdicts, as at common law, are still permitted in some jurisdictions,[9] statutes or rules generally provide that the general verdict must be in writing, and must be signed by the foreman or all members of the jury.[10] In some jurisdictions the form is also prescribed. Where this is not the case, the verdict may take any form as long as it sufficiently manifests the intention of the jury so that a proper judgment may be entered thereon. The trial court is of course the arbiter in this matter, subject always to the review by the appellate court.

After a verdict has been reached, in most jurisdictions it is handed to the judge or clerk who reads the verdict aloud in the presence of the jury and the attorneys.[11] The jury is then asked if this is their verdict, and if they assent, normally the verdict is recorded and the jury is discharged. In some jurisdictions the verdict may be received by the clerk in the absence of the judge,[12] and generally by the judge or clerk in the absence of the parties.[13]

---

9 Griffin v. Larned, 111 Ill. 432.

10 McFarland v. Muscatine, 98 Iowa 199, 67 N.W. 233; 53 Am. Jur. Trial, § 1009.

11 Kneece v. Hall, 138 S.C. 157, 135 S.E. 881; Busch, Trial Procedure Materials, § 425.

12 Miller v. Young, 196 Mich. 276, 163 N.W. 27; 20 A.L.R. 2d 281.

13 Alusa v. Lehigh Valley R. Co., 26 F. 2d 950.

While it is customary to inform counsel when the jury is ready to return a verdict, there is generally no requirement that this be done. It is therefore advisable for counsel to have a representative present in the courtroom to inform him when this step is to be taken. For, as will be noted later, objections to the verdict must frequently be made at this time or they will be deemed to have been waived.

There are two ways in which counsel may assist the jury in returning a proper verdict: 1. By submitting correct forms of verdicts. 2. By calling the court's attention to the impropriety of a verdict when it is returned. The latter method is discussed in a subsequent section.

Even the simplest of cases generally requires the submission of several forms of verdicts, so that all the possible conclusions of the jury are provided for. The forms should be presented to the opposing counsel and to the court sufficiently early so that any needed corrections may be made before the case is finally submitted to the jury.[14]

If there is but one party on each side, the submitted forms may be: "We, the jury, find for P and assess his damages at $_____." "We, the jury, find for D."[15]

If the defendant has filed a counterclaim, the submitted forms may be: "We, the jury, find for P on his complaint and assess his damages at $_____, and for D on his counterclaim, and assess his damages at $_____." "We, the jury, find for P on his complaint and on D's counterclaim, and assess his damages at $_____." "We, the jury, find for D on P's complaint and on his counterclaim, and assess his damages at $_____." "We, the jury, find for D on P's complaint and for P on D's counterclaim."[16]

Similar forms may be drafted where there are other multiple parties or issues.

---

[14] McGrew Mach. Co. v. One Spring Alarm Clock Co., 124 Neb. 93, 245 N.W. 263; 53 Am. Jur. Trial, § 1035.

[15] Sheldon v. Imhoff, 198 Wash. 66, 87 P. 2d 103.

[16] Staples v. Dent, 220 S.W. 2d 791 (Mo.); 89 C.J.S. Trial, § 504.

SECTION 119. UNANIMITY—POLLING THE JURY—ALTERNATE JURORS. At common law a jury consisted of twelve persons and their verdict had to be unanimous. Since the Seventh Amendment to the Federal Constitution does not apply to the several states, the latter are free to modify these requirements.[17] In a few states the constitutions have been amended to allow a verdict agreed upon by a certain percentage of the jury, usually five-sixths.[18] In a number of other states, statutes or rules have been enacted or adopted providing that the parties may by agreement have their case tried by a jury of less than twelve or that they will accept a verdict that has been agreed upon by a percentage of the jury.[19] When the change has been affected by the constitution, agreement of the parties is not necessary.

Lack of unanimity may be shown: 1. By the length of the deliberations. 2. By express statement to that effect by the foreman during the trial. 3. By polling the jury. 4. By affidavits of the jurors after discharge.

In the first two situations above, it is uniformly held that the judge may make no statement which has a coercive effect upon the jury.[20] It is clear that threats of withholding food or of keeping the jury together until they agree constitutes coercion. On occasion the length of the deliberations has been considered in determining whether the verdict was induced by coercion.[21]

It has been held that the judge may inquire as to how much additional time will be needed;[22] he may restate the issues and repeat certain instructions requested;[23] he may admonish the jury to make every possible effort to reach agreement;[24] he may call

---

17 Walker v. Sauvinet, 92 U.S. 90.

18 N.Y. Const. Art. 1, § 2.

19 1958 Report of the Temporary Commission on the Courts 579 (N.Y. Legis. Doc. 13).

20 Armstrong v. James & Co., 155 Iowa 562, 136 N.W. 686; 53 Am. Jur. Trial, § 951; 19 A.L.R. 2d 1257.

21 Meadows v. State, 182 Ala. 51, 62 So. 137.

22 Central R. Co. v. Neighbors, 83 Ga. 444, 10 S.E. 115.

23 Benavides v. State, 3 Tex. Crim. Rep. 173, 20 S.W. 369.

24 Hutchins v. Haffner, 63 Colo. 365, 167 P. 966.

attention to the expense and time consumed by the trial,[25] and to the fact that another jury could do no better.[26] With these or similar admonitions, the court may send the jury out again to attempt to reach agreement. In general, the length of deliberations is a matter for the trial judge to determine and will depend upon the nature of the case. A few statutes limit the number of times a jury may be sent out for further deliberations, or provide for a five-sixths verdict after a certain period.[27]

If and when it becomes apparent to the court that agreement is impossible he should discharge the jury and declare a mistrial. The effect of a mistrial is considered in Section 138.

In some jurisdictions statutes or rules expressly or by implication authorize the entry of final judgment despite the failure of the jury to agree upon a verdict.[28] Generally, to warrant the entry of such judgment, a prior motion for a directed verdict must have been denied or a ruling on the motion must have been reserved. If the evidence is conflicting, judgment will usually not be entered.

As stated above, the failure to agree may be disclosed by polling the jury. Polling the jury has other purposes as well: To reduce the possibility of coercion of the minority by the majority, or the dominant faction; to ascertain whether the verdict correctly reflects the decision of the jury; to determine the degree of conviction. While these purposes would seem to justify the practice, it has been criticized as tending to destroy the independence of the jury. But, as will be noted below, whether this effect is likely depends upon the nature of the poll. In general, polling of the jury is advisable whenever counsel has reason to suspect irregularities or coercion in the jury room.

The practice of polling the jury, which existed at common

---

[25] Armstrong v. James & Co., supra. n. 20.
[26] Burton v. Neill, 140 Iowa 141, 118 N.W. 302.
[27] 53 Am. Jur. Trial, § 963; 164 A.L.R. 1265.
[28] Domarek v. Bates Motor Transport Lines, Inc., 93 F. 2d 522; 31 A.L.R. 2d 885.

law, is largely governed by statute or rule today.[29] In some jurisdictions, the right is absolute unless waived;[30] in others it is a matter of discretion with the court.[31] Where the right is absolute, all jurors must be present in open court at the time the verdict is read.[32] A failure by counsel to request that he be informed when the jury is ready to return the verdict, so that he may poll the jury, has been held to constitute waiver of the right to poll.[33] A failure to request, prior to the recording of the verdict, that the jury be polled, has also been held to constitute a waiver.[34] If there is an absolute right to have the jury polled, no reason need be assigned for the request.[35] Where a verdict is not in proper form, and the jury is sent out again for further deliberations, ordinarily a poll is not allowed.[36] If the court erroneously refuses to honor a request to poll the jury, the judgment is at most voidable and not void.

There is considerable variation among the jurisdictions as to the method of polling the jury and as to who may do so. Usually, however, this is done by the court, or the clerk or other official in the presence of the court; on occasion counsel have been requested to do so. While the clerk is sometimes authorized to receive a verdict, either because of a statute or by consent of the parties, he may not exercise the judicial functions of polling or sending the jury out again in the absence of the court.[37] Polling the jury should take place immediately after the verdict is read in open court, and before it is recorded.

The form to be used in polling the jury is sometimes pre-

---

29 53 Am. Jur. Trial, § 1016; 71 A.L.R. 2d 640.
30 In re Sugg's Will, 194 N.C. 638, 140 S.E. 604.
31 Tennessee Coal, I. & R. Co. v. George, 11 Ga. App. 221, 75 S.E. 567.
32 Rich v. Finley, 325 Mass. 99, 89 N.E. 2d 213.
33 Alusa v. Lehigh Valley R. Co., 26 F. 2d 950.
34 Rottmund v. Pennsylvania R. Co., 225 Pa. 410, 74 A. 341.
35 Watchtower Mut. L. Ins. Co. v. Davis, 99 S.W. 2d 693 (Tex).
36 Wightman v. C. & N.W. R. Co., 73 Wis. 169, 40 N.W. 689.
37 Folkner v. Hopkins, 100 N.J.L. 189, 126 A. 633.

scribed by statute.[38] One rather common form is to ask the jury collectively whether this is their verdict. If there is any indication of a disagreement, each juror may be asked whether "this was and is your verdict."[39] If the jurisdiction requires that the verdict be unanimous, the jury should be sent out again if one or more jurors dissents. This may be done even if the jury has been allowed to separate, and even if a sealed verdict has been returned, because a juror may dissent until a verdict has been recorded and the juror discharged.[40]

There is some conflict in the authorities as to whether a juror who states that he has agreed to the verdict only because the others did, or under protest, etc. has thereby dissented.[41] Similarly there is a difference of opinion as to the extent to which the court may probe into the reasons for the dissent.[42] A broader scope of questioning is allowed before separation than after separation. While unanimity may be required as to the verdict, this is not true with reference to the grounds on which the verdict was returned.[43]

Affidavits will generally not be received to show lack of unanimity if executed by members who presumptively participated in the deliberations and thus concurred in the verdict.[44] Such practice is obviously necessary to prevent a juror from changing his mind after discharge.

At common law, if a juror became incapacitated during the trial or was for any reason discharged, a new juror had to be sworn in and the trial had to proceed from the beginning, or the entire jury was discharged and a new jury impaneled. To avoid this occurrence, statutes or rules have been enacted or adopted in

---

[38] Leverette v. St. L.S.F. & T. R. Co., 266 S.W. 589; 89 C.J.S. Trial, § 490.

[39] Columbus Oil Co v. Moore, 202 N.C. 708, 163 S.E. 879.

[40] Coughlin v. Weeks, 75 Wash. 568, 135 P. 649.

[41] Weeks v. Hart, 24 Hun. 181 (N.Y.); Black v. Thornton, 31 Ga. 641.

[42] Columbus Oil Co. v. Moore, 202 N.C. 780, 163 S.E. 879; Walker v. Bailey, 65 Me. 354.

[43] Anderson v. Penn Hall Co., 47 F. Supp. 691.

[44] Egan v. First Nat. Bank, 67 Okla. 168, 169 P. 621.

many jurisdictions under which one or two more jurors than are needed to return a verdict are examined and sworn with the other members of the panel.[45] These are called alternate jurors, and they sit as regular members of the panel until the jury retires to deliberate. If after retirement a regular member of the panel becomes unable to serve, the common law procedure must be followed.[46] Because of the value of the alternate juror practice, counsel should request that it be followed in any case where it is permitted.

SECTION 120. PROCEDURE WHEN VERDICT IS IMPROPER. Improper verdicts have been the cause of much needless litigation. As will be pointed out, many defects may be corrected if detected soon enough. It is therefore important for counsel to examine carefully the verdict as it is returned. While it is true that often the judge, and sometimes a juror himself, will call attention to a defect, counsel should himself be alert to the possibility of error.

When error is discovered in the verdict, normally one of three, and sometimes two of three, procedures are available. These are: 1. Correction by the court (a) with or (b) without the aid of the jury. 2. Resubmission to the jury of (a) the whole or (b) part of the case. 3. Ordering a new trial. While there is considerable difference of opinion among the authorities as to the proper remedy in a given situation, those authorities approving a particular procedure are here relied upon.

Correction by the court without the aid of the jury seems to be proper where the intention of the jury can be gleaned from the record, and is usually limited to so-called defects of form. Such correction may take place even after discharge.[47] At times, the court has corrected a verdict on the basis of affidavits of the jurors as to their intention, and this too after discharge.[48] But this prac-

---

45 Fed. R. Civ. P. 47 (b); 71 A.L.R. 1385.
46 People v. Britton, 4 Cal. 2d 652, 52 P. 2d 217.
47 Beglinger v. Shield, 164 Wash. 147, 2 P. 2d 681; 53 Am. Jur. Trial, § 1097.
48 Gaither v. Wilmer, 71 Md. 361, 18 A. 590.

tice is questionable, as a verdict so entered is suspect, especially if the court labels the defect as one of form when in fact it is one of substance.

Resubmission of the entire case to the jury may result in a completely different verdict, e.g., for the party other than the one originally successful.[49] The second verdict should be received if the prior proceedings, including the resubmission, were proper. And it is generally proper to resubmit the whole case where the verdict is unintelligible or so contrary to law that no judgment can be entered upon it.[50] Resubmission of a part only of the case —to correct a relatively minor error—is similar to the correction by the court with the aid of the jury, except that the jury has not yet been discharged. No resubmission of either type is proper after a discharge.[51] On occasion a problem may arise as to whether a jury has *actually* been discharged.[52]

The awarding of a new trial should be a matter of last resort. However, it is often favored by appellate courts over either of the other methods, as resubmission is favored over correction by the court, if the error seems to be substantial.

Counsel desirous of having a judgment entered on the verdict corrected by one of the above methods should make certain that the verdict in its final form has been received, for otherwise the entry of judgment is improper.

Defects in verdicts here to be considered may be classified as follows: 1. Those not in accordance with law, sometimes also called inconsistent verdicts. 2. Those which are incomplete—that is, they do not supply enough information on which to base a judgment. 3. Those which are ambiguous. 4. Those which are the result of a mistake—a mistake which the jury would recognize as such were it called to their attention. Each type will be briefly discussed.

---

49 Blackley v. Sheldon, 7 Johns. 32 (N.Y.).

50 Ward v. Bailey, 23 Me. 316.

51 Abraham v. Superior Court, 50 R.I. 207, 146 A. 617.

52 Baird v. Ball, 204 N.C. 469, 168 S.E. 667.

1. Verdicts not in accordance with law may be illustrated by the attempt of the jury to apportion damages among joint tort-feasors, if not permitted by statute. The verdict may be in either of two forms: (a) Granting P a specific sum as the total damages to be awarded, followed by the apportionment. (b) Granting P the same or a different amount against each defendant. In the former case, some courts have merely disregarded the attempted apportionment, apparently with no regard to the fact that the jury was already discharged.[53] In the latter instance, some courts have awarded the plaintiff a judgment against both defendants for the highest amount,[54] or have allowed the plaintiff to choose one of the defendants from whom he will seek satisfaction, and dismiss as to the other.[55] There is other authority to the effect that apportionment is an essential element of the verdict, and hence the entire case must be resubmitted to the jury if they have not already been discharged.[56]

Other verdicts contrary to law are those in which the doctrine of respondeat superior is applicable. The jury may return a verdict in favor of the servant but against the master. In this situation some courts have taken it upon themselves to correct the verdict by a finding against the servant as well as the master.[57] However, the better practice would seem to be to require a resubmission of the whole case, if that is still possible.[58]

Similarly, the jury may return a verdict in favor of a principal and against the surety, where both are joined as co-defendants. Such a verdict would be proper if the principal had a defense not available to the surety.

---

53 Kinsey v. William Spencer & Son Corp., 255 App. Div. 995, 8 N.Y.S. 2d 529; 8 A.L.R. 2d 862.

54 Polsey v. Waldorf-Astoria, 216 App. Div. 86, 214 N.Y.S. 600.

55 Fort Worth v. Williams, 55 Tex. Civ. App. 289, 119 S.W. 137.

56 Kenney v. Habich, 137 Mass. 421.

57 Gable v. Bingler, 177 Va. 641, 15 S.E. 2d 33.

58 Pangburn v. Buick Motor Co., 211 N.Y. 228, 105 N.E. 423.

In cases where the defendant files a counterclaim, some courts have upheld a simple verdict for defendant on the theory that it showed an intention to find against both parties.[59] Here the difficulty could be avoided by requiring two separate verdicts, one on the claim and the other on the counterclaim. But where two verdicts *are* required, the jury may find for the defendant on the claim and for the plaintiff on the counterclaim, despite the fact that under the evidence the defendant is entitled to recover on his counterclaim when he is not liable on the claim.[60]

In personal injury actions improper verdicts may take several forms. A wife may be awarded damages for her own injuries, and yet the husband be awarded nothing for the wife's medical expenses paid by him.[61] Again, the plaintiff may be awarded damages for medical expenses and none for pain and suffering, though there was evidence of such injuries.[62] Such verdicts can usually be corrected only by resubmission or the awarding of a new trial.

The verdict may also be improper because of the apparent use by the jury of the wrong measure of damages. Thus, the verdict may be for a specific sum, plus "reasonable attorney's fees" or "all expenses." In these cases, resubmission is quite common;[63] or the nonallowable items may simply be stricken as surplusage;[64] or an allowable item, if known and fixed, may be added.[65] If the verdict is for the plaintiff, and damages are liquidated, an error in amount may often be corrected by a mathematical computation, with or without the aid of a jury.[66]

Finally, a verdict may be for a sum larger than that demanded

---

59 Phillips v. Lewis, 12 App. Div. 460, 42 N.Y.S. 707.
60 Ridenour v. Lile, 93 Ohio App. 435, 114 N.E. 2d 166.
61 36 A.L.R. 2d 1333.
62 20 A.L.R. 2d 276.
63 Prager v. Israel, 15 Cal. 2d 89, 98 P. 2d 729; 49 A.L.R. 2d 1328.
64 Colky v. Metropolitan Life Ins. Co., 320 Ill. App. 120, 49 N.E. 2d 830.
65 Income Guaranty Co. v. Zielinski, 107 Ind. App. 248, 21 N.E. 2d 87.
66 Davidson v. Turner, 191 Ga. 197, 12 S.E. 2d 308.

and for that reason subject to objection.[67] If no objection is made, however, the verdict may stand. If an objection is made, in some jurisdictions the plaintiff is allowed to increase the amount demanded by an amendment of the pleadings;[68] in other jurisdictions the court enters judgment for the amount demanded, disregarding the excess.[69] In the federal courts the pleadings are deemed amended to allow for a verdict larger than that originally requested.[70] As will be noted in Section 147, if the excess is deemed to be unwarranted by the evidence, the error may be corrected by a remittitur, and thus a new trial may be avoided.[71] However, if the excess is deemed to be the result of passion and prejudice, and not merely erroneous because beyond the amount demanded, a new trial is usually necessary.[72]

Verdicts of this nature are frequently due to a failure by the jury to understand the instructions. In a sense such verdicts also fall into the fourth class as they do not accurately portray the intentions of the jury. Thus, in cases where the defendant files a counterclaim, the jury may return a verdict for the defendant for a specific sum, when in fact they meant that the plaintiff's claim should be reduced by that amount. In such cases courts are reluctant to correct the verdict after discharge on the basis of affidavits of the jury.

2. A verdict should contain all the elements necessary for the

---

[67] This was said to be the view at common law. Stephen, Pleading (Tyler ed. 1898) 371. A distinction must be made between a statement of the damages incurred, and an "ad damnum clause" (or demand for judgment). Generally a verdict may not exceed the amount of damages allegedly incurred. Redwing v. Moncravie, 131 Cal. App. 569, 21 P. 2d 986. But a prayer for relief, after answer to the merits, becomes immaterial and the verdict may exceed the amount demanded. Losee, adm'r. v. Krieger, adm'r. 22 Ohio App. 395, 153 N.E. 857. Unfortunately, the cases often fail to make this distinction.

[68] Luddington v. Goodnow, 168 Mass. 223, 46 N.E. 627.

[69] Franke v. Reddan, 9 N.J. Misc. 396, 154 A. 201.

[70] Fed. R. Civ. P. 15 (b).

[71] Franke v. Reddan, supra, n. 69; 65 A.L.R. 2d 1331.

[72] Williams v. Cannon, 126 Fla. 441, 171 So. 308.

entry of a valid judgment.[73] These elements will vary from case to case. In general, however, the verdict should state who prevails, and what recovery, if any, is awarded. Thus, a verdict is incomplete which finds for the plaintiff but leaves the amount awarded blank;[74] so is a verdict which finds for or against some, but not all, of the parties;[75] or a verdict in which nothing is stated as to interest, where it is recoverable.[76]

In most of these instances the remedy is to resubmit the case to the jury. However, occasionally a court will interpret an omission as a finding against a party needing the finding to win. This approach is generally taken where it is too late to resubmit the case to the jury. In a few cases, such as the omission of a dollar sign, the judge may correct the verdict, with the concurrence of the jury if before discharge, or without their aid if after discharge.[77] However, there should be no change of circumstances between the time the verdict is returned and the time it is corrected.

Where the law requires the existence of damage, as in the usual negligence action, a verdict such as: "We, the jury, find the issues in favor of the plaintiff and assess his damages at no dollars" is defective and should be corrected before any judgment thereon is entered.[78] But if a cause of action exists without a showing of damages, as in an action to determine title to real property, such a verdict would probably be a sufficient basis for a judgment for the plaintiff.

3. A rather common type of ambiguity in verdicts consists of a discrepancy between the amount as stated in figures and that stated in words. Some courts simply apply the rule of construction

---

[73] 53 Am. Jur. Trial, § 1005.
[74] Misch v. Brockus, 97 Cal. App. 2d 770, 218 P. 2d 849.
[75] Goldbeck v. Cieslik, 5 Ill. App. 2d 529, 126 N.E. 2d 417.
[76] Gottesman v. Havana Importing Co., 72 N.Y.S. 2d 426.
[77] Re McLean, 84 Kan. 852, 115 P. 647.
[78] Ward v. Johnson, 72 Ariz. 213, 232 P. 2d 960.

whereby the written amount governs.[79] The use of such mechanical test is questionable, especially in the absence of some other indication of the jury's intention, such as is found in affidavits.

4. Occasionally the error in a verdict is due to mere inadvertence, where the verdict does not correspond to the intention of the jury. This may be illustrated by a case where the jury signs the wrong form of verdict. Or, property involved in litigation may be wrongly described. In the first example, the error should be discoverable by polling the jury; or, after discharge, by inquiry. The correction may be made by the jury upon resubmission, or by the court with or without affidavits of the jury. Affidavits are generally admissable to show that the wrong verdict form was signed,[80] unless there are cross-actions. In the second example the error may be discovered, and corrected, by a reference to the record.[81]

Again, the jury may erroneously report that they cannot agree, in a case involving multiple parties, when in fact there was a failure to agree only as to one party. If the jury has not been discharged, they may be recalled to enable the court to correct the entry in the minutes.[82] If the jury has been discharged, some courts make the correction on the basis of proper affidavits.

B. Special Verdict

SECTION 121. ORIGIN AND USE. The special verdict, like the general verdict, is of common-law origin. The special verdict device was used by juries who wished to escape the penalties attached to the writ of attaint which were assessed against juries returning "false" verdicts. In the special verdict the jury found the facts and requested the court to apply the law. This was done

---

79 Hays v. Hogan, 273 Mo. 1, 200 S.W. 286.
80 Paul v. Pye, 135 Minn. 13, 159 N.W. 1070.
81 Thacker v. Hicks, 215 Ark. 898, 224 S.W. 2d 1.
82 89 C.J.S. Trial, § 515.

because the law was frequently unsettled, and under a general verdict the jury would be required to correctly apply the law at their peril. Thus, the jury, after finding the facts would conclude in the alternative that if the law was for the plaintiff the jury found for him; if, however, upon the facts the law was for the defendant, the jury found for him.

The right of the jury to return a special verdict at its election was settled by the sixteenth century, and by the eighteenth century a jury could not be compelled to return a special verdict. In this country the matter is largely governed by statute today.[83] Some statutes, taking the position that the jury has no inherent right to return a general verdict, require the jury to return a special verdict when instructed to do so. In some states having such statutes the judge is required to so instruct when he is properly requested.[84] While in others it is discretionary with the judge even when properly requested.[85]

In a few jurisdictions, the judge is required to insist upon special verdicts in certain specified types of actions.[86] With this exception it is generally held that one may not complain of the failure of the court to demand a special verdict unless properly requested.[87] In a few jurisdictions a special verdict is not permitted even if the court and counsel are willing that such a verdict be returned.[88] In still others the jury may return a special verdict though instructed to return a general verdict, as at common law.[89]

No special form of request is required, but the request must be made in apt time. Generally this means that the request must be made no later than at the conclusion of the testimony and before

---

[83] 53 Am. Jur. Trial, § 1064.

[84] Wis. Stat. (1949) § 270.27.

[85] Fed. R. Civ. P. 49 (a).

[86] Vanderbilt, Minimum Standards of Judicial Administration, 241.

[87] O'Neil v. Larkin-Carey Co., 106 Conn. 153, 137 A. 721.

[88] Vanderbilt, supra, n. 86.

[89] Id.

argument has begun.[90] In this way the court and opposing counsel has time to consider the request and the forms submitted with the request, and counsel making the request may refer to certain findings in his closing argument.

SECTION 122. REQUIREMENTS. While some statutes prescribe certain qualities which must be found in special verdicts, case law more often must be examined to find the requirements. In a general way the requirements of the general verdict (with the possible exception of conformance to law) apply as well to the special verdict. Some of these requirements are more likely to be unsatisfied in the special verdict, due to its greater specificity; for example, indefiniteness and uncertainty are probably the most common defects of the special verdict, with internal inconsistency running a close second. Special verdicts which are inconsistent may be set aside on proper motion.[91]

But there are other requirements which are peculiar to special verdicts and in a more limited way to special findings returned with a general verdict. Some of the most common are noted below.

1. At common law a special verdict had to contain a finding on every fact necessary to support a judgment.[92] This meant that a finding on every factual issue as raised by the pleadings was imperative, including those where no issue was presented by the evidence. No finding was necessary on facts admitted by the pleadings, but if the admission was by an adverse witness, or if testimony was uncontroverted, a finding was required if the issue was raised by the pleadings.

Statutes or rules today may impose a like condition[93] or one of two other approaches may be taken: (a) That of the Federal Rules which, while still requiring a finding on all material issues of fact,

---

90 Sandford Tool & Fork Co. v. Mullen, 1 Ind. App. 204, 27 N.E. 448.
91 Ehlers v. Automobile Liability Co., 169 Wis. 494, 173 N.W. 325.
92 Pittsburgh, etc. Co. v. Adams, 105 Ind. 151.
93 53 Am. Jur. Trial, § 1076.

relies on the doctrine of waiver where a party fails to request a finding on a particular issue.[94] (b) That of certain statutes which simply provide that the jury may make a finding on only some of the issues.[95] The latter approach, however, has on occasion been stricken down by the courts on the theory that issues upon which there is no finding are thereby conceded to the opponent.[96] This attitude reflects the view of the common law that the special verdict, along with the pleadings, had to constitute a technically sufficient foundation of fact for a judgment; uncontroverted, as well as controverted matters had to appear in the formal record.[97]

The courts vary as to whether the state of the evidence may be looked to in determining whether all pleaded issues must be presented to the jury. In some jurisdictions if the evidence on a pleaded issue is such that a verdict would be directed on it, the court need not submit it to the jury for determination.[98] Again, if a finding on one issue makes a finding on another issue immaterial, the absence of a finding on the latter may be of no consequence, as long as the findings which are made are decisive of the action.[99]

2. Only material issues of fact should be submitted to the jury.[100] In a general way this conforms to the rules of pleading, and requires a thorough knowledge of the applicable substantive law. Occasionally counsel insert immaterial issues consciously at strategic places in order that the jury may not become aware of the legal consequences of certain findings. However, it is doubtful if this practice has the desired effect as most juries today are undoubtedly not as naive as many attorneys believe them to be; further, the attention of the jury should be directed to the genuinely important issues.

---

94 Fed. R. Civ. P. 49 (a).
95 First Nat. Bank v. Peck, 8 Kan. 660.
96 Noseda v. Delmue, 123 Ohio St. 647, 176 N.E. 571.
97 Standard Sewing Mach. Co. v. Royal Ins. Co., 201 Pa. 645, 51 A. 354.
98 Atchison, T. & S.F. R. Co. v. Wilkie, 77 Kan. 791, 90 P. 775.
99 Union Depot & R. Co. v. Londoner, 50 Colo. 22, 114 P. 316.
100 Drumm-Flato Commission Co. v. Edmission, 208 U.S. 534.

3. The number of issues should be kept to a minimum. This requirement precludes the framing of an issue a number of times in slightly different language. This requirement reduces the possibility of inconsistent findings due to confusion of the jury.

4. Consistent with the view taken by the standard codes with reference to pleadings, special verdicts should give facts and not state conclusions of law.[101] The interpretation of this requirement varies here as it does with reference to pleadings. Thus, in some instances terms such as "negligence" and "valid consideration" are classified as "facts" and in others as "conclusions of law."

5. Similarly, special verdicts should include ultimate or operative facts and not evidentiary facts.[102] By ultimate facts we generally mean those facts to which the substantive law attaches legal consequences. Evidentiary facts are those facts either circumstantial or testimonial, adduced as proof of the ultimate facts. Again, the line between ultimate and evidentiary facts is at times difficult to draw and the decisions are not uniform.

6. All questions should, whenever possible, be answerable by a simple "Yes" or "No."[103] This requirement necessitates the avoidance of questions in alternative or disjunctive form; or the use of double negatives, which requires a single affirmative to indicate a negative answer, and a single negative to indicate an affirmative answer.[104] It has also the effect of sanctioning the use of leading questions, although some authorities hold such questions to be improper. This requirement also forbids questions which call for an opinion, apparently on the premise that absolute certainty on the part of the jury is possible and hence is to be insisted upon.[105]

---

[101] C. St. L. & P. Ry. Co. v. Burger, 124 Ind. 275, 24 N.E. 981; 53 Am. Jur. Trial, § 1090.

[102] Seward v. Jackson, 8 Cow. 406 (N.Y.); 53 Am. Jur. Trial, § 1089.

[103] Fed. R. Civ. P. 49 (a).

[104] Martin v. Ebert, 245 Wis. 341, 13 N.W. 2d 907.

[105] Feldmann v. Conn. Mut. Life Ins. Co., 142 F. 2d 628.

7. Questions should respect the time-honored division of functions of the court and jury: Questions of law are for the court, questions of fact for the jury. This matter was considered earlier in Section 105 which deals with instructions. The application of the rule has not been uniform. Thus, the interpretation of a contract has usually been assigned to the court, in accordance with the doctrine that this process involves the ascertainment of the *objective* intent of the contracting parties; but at times this function has been assigned to the jury when the community standard is to be the criterion.

Whether a given term is used in its technical sense is generally determined by the court; but if it was used in a technical sense, and there is a conflict in the evidence as to the various technical uses of the term, the jury is frequently required to determine which meaning is to be used in interpreting a given contract. In this connection, it should also be noted that unless there is a waiver of a right to trial by jury a court cannot decide some of the fact issues himself and submit others to the jury.

SECTION 123. WHEN ADVISABLE. If the special verdict may be used under the statutes of a particular jurisdiction, the following factors should be considered in determining whether a request ought to be made to direct the jury to return such verdict:

1. The effect of a failure to meet the requirements of a special verdict in that jurisdiction. Thus, such verdict is more desirable if an omission to find on a particular issue is not fatal to such verdict, under some provision similar to the Federal Rule. Again, if the prohibition against conclusions of law and evidentiary facts is liberally construed, the chances of deriving benefits from a special verdict are increased.

2. The attitude of the court and jury towards a special verdict. If this attitude is hostile, the court may make his feelings known to the jury in the manner in which he gives his instructions. Again, the attitude becomes apparent in the approach used

to construe the verdict after it has been returned. If the attitude is favorable, the court is more likely to look at the entire verdict and attempt to harmonize various findings; or, the court may construe each finding most strongly against the party having the burden of proof.

3. The party having the burden of proof generally requires a finding in his favor on a number of issues, while the opponent needs a finding only on one issue. This factor must however be balanced with the state of the evidence, as stated below.

4. If the evidence is such that a general verdict in a party's favor is normally to be expected, there is less reason for him to request a special verdict. Thus, if the plaintiff's claim is fortified by an emotional appeal due to extensive injury, financial disparity between the parties, etc. the plaintiff generally will not request a special verdict. But, if a defendant relies on a technical defense, such as the statute of limitations, usually considered to be unpopular with the jury, a finding as to the date when the event involved in the lawsuit occurred would be in order.

5. Sometimes counsel who have no defense at all request a special verdict in the hopes that the verdict will be defective in some respect and thus subject to attack. This technique is similar to the use of a general denial and both practices have been condemned in recent years.

6. The possibility of an appeal should be considered. A special verdict places the facts into the record, and unless reference to the evidence is necessary to determine whether the findings are supported by proof, a bill of exceptions may not be necessary.

7. In some jurisdictions either the court or the jury has the right to modify submitted forms, and such modifications may be less favorable to the party requesting the special verdict than the form submitted by him.[106]

8. Quite frequently the side which does not request a special

---

[106] Hopkins v. Stanley, 43 Ind. 553.

verdict is permitted to submit forms of findings as alternatives to those submitted by the party requesting the special verdict, and such forms may highlight an otherwise obscure point.

9. Where a case is complicated both as to facts and law, so that there is some question as to the jury's ability to comprehend all of the facets thereof, both sides may request a special verdict. While a jury, in returning a general verdict may misunderstand the law or apply it erroneously, the errors are not always discernible. But with the use of the special verdict such mistakes are more easily detected and rectified. The entire verdict need not be discarded, but that part which is sound may be retained, whereas a general verdict must be accepted in toto or not at all.

Again, if the trial is lengthy, the jury may not recall all the testimony, and if a special verdict is used, attention is directed to all-important fact issues. The inability to recall is more likely to be made known, and the deficiency corrected by again hearing a part of the testimony. If a case contains multiple claims, upon some of which there may be recovery and not upon others, a special verdict is desirable. Likewise if the case involves a claim and a counterclaim, a special verdict indicates more clearly than does a general verdict whether the jury properly understood the issues.

SECTION 124. SUBMITTING QUESTIONS OR FINDINGS. A special verdict may be in at least two forms: 1. A series of findings on all material issues of fact. 2. A series of questions and answers on such issues. A question may properly begin as follows: "Do you find from a preponderance of the evidence . . . ?" If the first kind is used, alternative statements in narrative form covering all findings possible under the evidence must be submitted.[107] This can become a difficult task, especially where there are multiple issues or multiple parties, or both. This situation probably accounts for the fact that the second kind is much more common. Even this method

---

[107] Dowd-Feder Co. v. Schreyer, 124 Ohio St. 504, 179 N.E. 411.

can become complicated at times if a series of questions is needed to cover all possible answers to a previous question. The result may be very confusing to the jury.

In view of the requirements stated in Section 122, it is obvious that care must be exercised in the drafting of questions to be submitted to the jury. And because there is usually not much time available to do so during the trial, it is advisable to prepare at least rough drafts of most questions some time before submission.

In drafting questions, the pleadings should be carefully analyzed to determine what are the fact issues. If the pleadings themselves were drafted under the more modern practice acts or rules, in the form of single allegations in separate paragraphs and shorn of descriptive phrases and epithets, the questions can be quite easily drafted. But if the pleadings are lengthy and technical, as is common under the older systems of pleading, it becomes quite difficult at times to know what allegations are in issue.

If the jurisdiction demands that all paper issues must be covered by the special verdict, the pleadings alone should be consulted; but if the jurisdiction requires only that issues raised by the evidence be covered, it is necessary to examine a transcript of the evidence or to rely on one's notes taken during the trial. It should also be noted that any amendments to the pleadings made during the trial, to conform to the evidence, may alter the number and kind of issues to be submitted to the jury.

As stated earlier, when a special verdict is to be returned it is not necessary for the judge to give complete instructions as to the law to be applied to the various findings of fact possible under the evidence. But the jury should be informed as to their duties: what the basic issues are (but not what the legal effect is of specified findings on these issues); as to the rules for weighing and reconciling testimony; who has the burden of proof; the measure of damages to be applied; that a general verdict is not to be returned along with their answers to the questions; the definition of certain terms such as "negligence" which involve both fact and law.[108] It is therefore advisable for counsel to submit forms of instructions at the time that questions are submitted.

When the jury returns the verdict, either the clerk or the judge reads the written questions and answers. If all are in proper form, the verdict is recorded in the minutes and the party believing himself entitled thereto moves for judgment on the verdict. A subsequent section will discuss procedures to be followed where the verdict is defective.

SECTION 125. PROCEDURE WHEN VERDICT IS IMPROPER. Reference is made to Section 120, where the more general types of defects found in general verdicts and the proper procedures for the correction of such errors are discussed. Many of the same problems are presented in special verdicts. Reference is also made to Section 122 where the requirements of a special verdict are set out, and to Section 130, where the problem of inconsistency in answers to special interrogatories is considered. Portions of a special verdict may be inconsistent with the balance of such verdict. But reference may not be made to the evidence to determine whether there is an inconsistency. The present section will therefore consider only a few matters unique to special verdicts.

A verdict that does not find all necessary facts may be resubmitted, as is usually done if the jury has not yet been discharged.[109] If it is too late for a resubmission, unless the statute or rule allows for the indulgence in a presumption that the omitted facts have been found, a new trial is necessary.[110] Occasionally, however, a court may enter a judgment against the party who required a favorable answer.[111]

---

108 Udell v. Citizens' Street R. Co., 152 Ind. 507, 52 N.E. 799; 53 Am. Jur. Trial, § 638.
109 Guidry v. Morgan's L. & T.R.&S.S. Co., 140 La. 1007, 74 So. 534.
110 Maxwell v. Wright, 160 Ind. 515, 67 N.E. 267.
111 Noseda v. Delmul, supra, n. 96.

Findings on immaterial issues, repetitious findings, conclusions of law, evidentiary facts and ambiguous findings may all be stricken on motion, and judgment nevertheless entered on the verdict if the latter contains enough other proper findings to warrant the entry of judgment.[112]

If an answer shows that a question was not clear to the jury, the question may be amended and resubmitted to the jury. Resubmission is also proper if the jury answers some questions by stating "we do not know" or "unknown to us," instead of categorically stating "yes" or "no." If too late for resubmission, again a new trial should be granted.[113]

C. Special Interrogatories to Be Answered with General Verdict

SECTION 126. ORIGIN AND USE. At common law, a court occasionally interrogated the jury as to the grounds of a general verdict *after* the same had been returned, where the verdict was not as anticipated. It is not clear from the cases whether the jury could be compelled to answer the questions propounded. The practice was designed to enable the jury to correct its verdict. Also, where a special verdict had been returned, the court could interrogate the jury with a view of amplifying the findings of fact. This practice was followed in New England and in a few other states.

However, there was no precedent for the practice discussed in this and the immediately following sections, namely the submission of interrogatories, in writing, *before* the return of the verdict. Under this practice the interrogatories are to be answered in writing and returned with a general verdict. The purpose of this device is to check upon the responsibility of jury in the return of the general verdict.

---

112 24 L.R.A. (NS) 72.
113 Tourtelotte v. Brown, 1 Colo. App. 408, 29 P. 130.

Because of the lack of common-law precedent, this procedure required legislation authorizing it.[114] In New England, however, the practice developed apparently without the benefit of any legislation.[115] Over two-thirds of the states now have such legislation, patterned generally after the New York Code.[116] The statutes vary considerably.[117] In most states the submission of special interrogatories is discretionary with the court whether or not a request for such submission has been made. Sometimes this discretion is reviewable, at other times it is not reviewable. In a smaller number of states the court is required to accede to requests by counsel.

Regardless of the statute involved, a party cannot complain of the failure to submit interrogatories where no request to do so has been made. The time for the making of such request may be set by the court. Generally, the request must be made before argument to the jury.[118] This enables the court to examine the interrogatories during argument, and it also allows counsel to refer to the interrogatories in the argument. Questions may be withdrawn by the court after submission in those jurisdictions where the submission is discretionary with the court.[119]

Because of the fact that under this practice disputed questions of fact are left to the jury for determination, legislation authorizing the practice has been universally held constitutional.[120] It is not deemed to be an infringement upon the right of trial by jury.

SECTION 127. REQUIREMENTS. For the most part the requirements of special interrogatories are similar to the questions pro-

---

[114] While there were instances at common law in which special interrogatories, to be answered with the general verdict, were submitted to the jury, no judgment could be rendered on the answers thereto, but a resubmission or new trial was necessary. Walker v. New Mexico & S.P.R. Co., 165 U.S. 593.

[115] Freeman v. N.Y., N.H. & H. R. Co., 81 Conn. 601, 71 Atl. 901.

[116] Wicker, "Special Interrogatories to Juries in Civil Cases," 35 Yale L.J. 296.

[117] Clementson, Special Verdicts and Findings, 49.

[118] B. & O. R. Co. v. Cain, 81 Md. 87, 31 A. 801; 53 Am. Jur. Trial, § 1068.

[119] Robinson v. Silver Lake R. & Lbr. Co., 163 Wash. 31, 299 P. 356; 53 Am. Jur. Trial, § 1069; 91 A.L.R. 2d 776.

[120] Walker v. New Mexico & S.P.R. Co., supra, n. 114.

pounded to the jury when a special verdict is to be returned. For that reason attention is directed in this section only to a few exceptions to and qualifications of the requirements set out in Section 122.

1. Contrary to the rule in some jurisdictions with respect to a special verdict, it is not necessary that the special interrogatories cover every fact issue raised by the pleadings.[121] This is because the answers do not in themselves need to constitute the basis for the judgment, for a general verdict is returned along with the answers. However, the questions must, of course, relate to issues raised by the testimony as well as the pleadings.[122]

2. As in the case of special verdicts, special interrogatories must concern material issues.[123] However, this requirement is of greater significance with reference to special interrogatories. A special verdict may contain enough findings on material issues to support a valid judgment, though it also contains findings on immaterial issues. But if immaterial issues are included in special interrogatories and the answers thereon are contra to the general verdict, an attempt may be made to have the answers control; the result is an invalid judgment.

3. Controverted facts should not be assumed.[124] Thus, if one of the contested issues was whether a certain relationship had been created from which a duty of care allegedly arose, it is improper to ask the jury categorically to state whether the duty had been satisfied. The significance of this requirement again is greater with respect to special interrogatories because the entire case need not be covered by the interrogatories and hence the attention of the jury is not directed to the necessity of first finding the assumed fact.

---

121 Griffin v. United Services Life Ins. Co., 225 N.C. 684, 36 S.E. 2d 225.
122 Parkinson Sugar Co. v. Riley, 50 Kan. 401, 31 P. 1090.
123 Chicago Anderson Pressed Brick Co. v. Reinneiger, 140 Ill. 334, 29 N.E. 1106.
124 Runyan v. Kanawha Water & Light Co., 68 W. Va. 609, 71 S.E. 259.

4. Like special verdicts, answers to interrogatories, in order to support a general verdict must be consistent with each other.[125] This requirement too has greater significance with respect to special interrogatories because of the possibility, as will be discussed in subsequent sections, of entering a judgment on the answers contrary to the general verdict.

5. In some jurisdictions which provide for a three-fourths or five-sixths verdict, the same jurors who agreed to the general verdict must agree in those findings necessary to support the verdict.[126]

6. Statutes which require the signing of the verdict by the foreman or all members of the jury are generally held to apply also to answers to special interrogatories.[127]

7. The jury is not permitted to make findings on issues not submitted to them for determination.[128]

SECTION 128. WHEN ADVISABLE. The same factors which should be considered in determining whether a special verdict ought to be requested are also determinative as to the advisability of submitting special interrogatories. These factors are discussed in Section 123. It should be noted, however, that sometimes a special interrogatory may be used to cure an error that has occurred during the course of the trial; thus, it may be shown by a certain finding that a given instruction was not prejudicial.[129] Further, interrogatories may be appropriate where the opponent's argument has led the jury away from some controlling facts.

Some attorneys however follow the practice of submitting interrogatories on issues only when the answer must, under the evidence, be favorable to the party submitting them. This practice

---

125 Porter v. Western N.C.R. Co., 97 N.C. 66, 2 S.E. 581.
126 Biersach v. Wechselberg, 206 Wis. 113, 238 N.W. 905.
127 53 Am. Jur. Trial, § 1034.
128 Read v. Nichols, 118 N.Y. 224, 23 N.E. 468.
129 Marcott v. M., H. & O. Ry. Co., 49 Mich. 99, 13 N.W. 374.

is of doubtful validity, as an unfavorable (to the submitting party) response, coupled with an unfavorable verdict, is no more prejudicial than an unfavorable verdict standing alone.

SECTION 129. SUBMITTING SPECIAL INTERROGATORIES. The suggestions made in Section 122 with reference to the submission of questions leading to a special verdict are, for the most part, apropos the submission of special interrogatories. The discussion in this section is therefore limited to matters largely peculiar to the special interrogatories.

1. The number of interrogatories is usually very limited— sometimes only one key question is asked. Care must be exercised in the selection of such question or questions.

2. Since a general verdict is to be returned along with answers to interrogatories, general instructions covering all facets of the case will have to be submitted. In addition, it is advisable to submit instructions governing the special interrogatories. Reference is therefore made to the suggestions found in Section 122.

The jury should not be informed as to the effect of certain answers upon the general verdict, nor should they be instructed to harmonize their answers.[130] But they may be instructed that they need not answer a certain interrogatory if they answered a certain other interrogatory in a specified way.[131] Finally, care must be exercised not to let the jury know that their general verdict is not trusted, which impression they may easily get from the fact that the interrogatories are generally precise in nature. This may be done in much the same way that an explanation is made as to the reasons for the voir dire examination. Reference is therefore made to Section 30.

SECTION 130. PROCEDURE WHEN ANSWERS ARE INCONSISTENT. Answers to interrogatories may be: 1. Consistent with each other and with the general verdict. 2. Consistent with each other but

---

130 Thornton v. Franse, 135 Kan. 782, 12 P. 2d 728; 90 A.L.R. 2d 1040.
131 Tew v. Brewster, 103 Minn. 110, 114 N.W. 647.

one or more is inconsistent with the general verdict. 3. Inconsistent with each other and one or more is inconsistent with the general verdict. F. R. 49(b) provides that judgment may be entered in the first situation on both verdict and answers.

In the second situation the court may under the Rule (a) enter judgment on the answers to the interrogatories despite the general verdict, (b) direct that the jury reconsider the answers and verdict, or (c) order a new trial.[132] Alternative procedure (a) is based upon the assumption that the answers more nearly co-incide with the intention of the jury than does the general verdict. In such cases it is not necessary to set aside the verdict. When a motion is made to enter judgment in accordance with the answers, courts attempt to reconcile the verdict and answers and indulge in all reasonable presumptions in favor of the general verdict; the inconsistency must be apparent and not removable by any evidence admissible under the issues.

Alternative procedure (b) raises a number of problems other than the general one as to what constitutes an inconsistency. A resubmission may simply be with directions to correct the verdict to conform to the answers. If this procedure is followed, it is identical in result to procedure (a). But if the court resubmits the entire case, as seems to be contemplated by the language of F. R. 49(b), the question is presented: Can this be done without informing the jury as to the legal effect of their answers? This is a matter of concern to the court and counsel, for if a jury wishes to persist in the verdict, and is aware of the legal effect of their answers, they can alter their answers to make them consistent with the verdict. Perhaps the solution lies in merely informing the jury of the inconsistency, and if it appears that the answers were "rigged," to grant a new trial. This procedure seems to be most

---

[132] Crosse v. Supreme Lodge, Knights and Ladies of Honor, 254 Ill. 80, 98 N.E. 261; 53 Am. Jur. Trials, § 1084.

suitable where some of the answers are so ambiguous that it is impossible to determine what the findings of the jury were, or if some of the interrogatories were left unanswered or the answers were not properly signed by the foreman or jury. Here a new trial could very probably be avoided.

Alternative procedure (c) is appropriate especially where other errors occurred during the trial, but also as a "last resort" method of dealing with answers inconsistent with the general verdict. For example, if the verdict or answers are defective in some respect, and the defect is discovered too late for correction by the jury before discharge.

Situation three has evoked the greatest difference of opinion as to the appropriate procedure.[133] In many jurisdictions the general verdict stands and judgment may be entered upon it, contrary to Rule 49(b). That rule provides the court with but two alternatives: (a) to resubmit the verdict and answers for further consideration, or (b) to order a new trial. Resubmission here presents very much the same problems as are present in situation two.

As indicated earlier, the basic problem concerns the question of inconsistency. Since no generalizations can be furnished that will be of great assistance in solving the problem, counsel must check authorities in his own jurisdiction.[134] A few illustrations of answers that have been held to be *consistent:* 1. That plaintiff and defendant were both negligent. 2. That neither plaintiff or defendant were negligent. 3. That both parties were negligent, but damages were nevertheless awarded to the plaintiff. (The court said the awarding of damages was surplusage as not necessary for a disposition of the case.) 4. That the driver of a vehicle failed to

---

133 Drake v. Justice Gold Mining Co., 32 Colo. 259, 75 P. 912; McCoy v. Weber, 168 Kan. 241, 212 P. 2d 281; 53 Am. Jur. Trial, § 1083.

134 89 C.J.S. Trial, § 562.

see an object in the road, and that he was not negligent. 5. That the plaintiff crossed in front of a truck, and that he had crossed the path taken by the truck before he fell. Again, a verdict for the plaintiff may be upheld, though both parties were found to be negligent, on the theory that the plaintiff's negligence was not the proximate cause of the injury.

Further difficulty may be encountered where one or more of the interrogatories are not answered. As stated above, some courts view this simply as an omission and resubmit the question to the jury if the answer could affect the general verdict; on the other hand, if the answer would not affect the verdict, a resubmission is not required and judgment is entered on the verdict.[135] Other courts view the failure to answer an interrogatory as equivalent to a failure to agree.[136] But even among courts taking this position there is a conflict as to whether this vitiates a general verdict because of inconsistency.[137] Those courts taking the position that the general verdict is nullified contend that the failure to answer shows the verdict-winner has not sustained his burden of proof on vital issues. On the other hand, some courts take the position that if the losing party does not request answers, he cannot complain of entry of judgment on the verdict.

As a matter of fact, a distinction should be made between a case in which the jury answers that they cannot agree upon the answer to an interrogatory that would control the general verdict,[138] and a case in which they answer that they do not know what the fact is.[139] In the former case, if the jury has already been discharged, the remedy is a new trial, where in the latter case a

---

[135] Clawson v. Wichita Transp. Co., 148 Kan. 902, 84 P. 2d 878; 89 C.J.S. Trial, § 560.

[136] Welde v. Briar, 232 Iowa 972, 5 N.W. 2d 157; 89 C.J.S. Trial, § 559.

[137] 89 C.J.S. Trial, § 563.

[138] Tourtelotte v. Brown, supra, n. 113.

[139] A., T. & S.F. R. Co. v. Swarts, 58 Kan. 235, 48 P. 953.

judgment should be entered against the verdict-winner. It is only in the second case that the verdict-winner has not sustained his burden of proof. But some courts do not make the distinction and hold that in both cases there has been a failure of proof.

Other types of defects in answers to interrogatories have been considered in Section 127.

D. Sealed Verdicts

SECTION 131. ORIGIN AND USE. According to the common-law procedure a verdict could not be received and entered until it was returned in open court. The purpose of this requirement was three-fold: 1. To enable a nonsuit to be taken. 2. To enable the parties to poll the jury. 3. To enable the court to resubmit the case to the jury where the verdict was defective or lacked unanimity. Originally a jury was not allowed to separate during its deliberations until the verdict was returned. Statutes today generally provide for separation before deliberation and sometimes during deliberation.[140]

In order that the jury might separate where it reached agreement late in the evening, the practice developed of reporting a verdict privately to the judge. But it was still necessary for the jury to convene in open court and report its verdict. And this had to occur during the same term in which the trial was held, or the verdict was a nullity. Later, the jury was allowed to enclose its verdict in an envelope and deliver it, sealed, to the clerk to be opened, usually the following morning. This practice was followed for either type of verdict.

The procedure governing the use of the sealed verdict is today largely set out in a statute.[141] Consent of the parties is required in

---

140 Dulaney v. Burns, 218 Ala. 493, 119 So. 21; 53 Am. Jur. Trial, § 864.
141 53 Am. Jur. Trial, § 1010.

some states but not in others. In some approval of the court is necessary.

SECTION 132. SUGGESTED PROCEDURE. In jurisdictions which require consent of counsel for the use of a sealed verdict, counsel should determine the effect of such consent prior to giving the same. If the consent is deemed to be an assent to the discharge of the jury after it has delivered the sealed verdict to the clerk, the opportunity to poll the jury is lost and the verdict may not be corrected by resubmission to the jury. For once a jury is discharged it cannot be recalled.[142] Further, a discharge of one juror after the jury has agreed to a sealed verdict may be deemed to be a discharge of all jurors. As stated earlier, after discharge only such matters as clerical or typographical errors may be corrected. Also, it must be determined whether consent will be implied from a lack of objection to the use of the sealed verdict. On the other hand, if consent to the use of the sealed verdict does not involve assent to discharge there is no hazard in giving such consent, for mere separation after agreement is not the equivalent of discharge.

There is a difference of opinion as to the effectiveness of polling the jury when a sealed verdict is used. According to the one view, allowing a juror to change his mind after sealing of the verdict opens the door to corruption and is therefore prohibited;[143] according to the other view, the jurors must be accorded this privilege to prevent coercion by fellow jurors or the court.[144]

When a sealed verdict is to be returned, counsel should prepare cautionary instructions to be given to the jury, as this may be a factor in upholding a verdict. Whenever the jury is allowed to separate, they should be warned not to discuss the case with anyone until the verdict has been returned in open court.

Finally, counsel should be present in court when the envelope

---

142 Koon v. Phoenix Mut. L. Ins. Co., 104 U.S. 106; 53 Am. Jur. Trial, § 1018.
143 Dunbauld v. Thompson, 109 Iowa 199, 80 N.W. 324.
144 Kramer v. Kister, 187 Pa. 227, 40 A. 1008.

is opened and the verdict is read by the clerk. This is the time to object to the verdict and to poll the jury. In some jurisdictions a verdict is recorded when it is agreed to by a former dissenter;[145] in other jurisdictions a new trial will be granted.[146]

---

[145] Dunbauld v. Thompson, supra, n. 143.

[146] Sanders v. Charleston Consol. R. & L. Co., 154 S.C. 220, 151 S.E. 438.

Chapter 10

Trial by Court

SECTION 133. PROCEDURE IN TRIAL BY COURT. For the most part a trial to the court is conducted very much the same as a trial by jury. There is of course no voir dire examination and no challenge to the array or individual jurors. There may be an opening statement, providing the judge has not read the pleadings and is not acquainted with the issues. In any event, the opening statement may be much more succinct than in a jury trial. While a motion to dismiss is appropriate at the close of the plaintiff's case, there is no need for a motion to direct the verdict at the close of the entire case, for judgment may be rendered at this point. Objections to evidence may be made as in a jury trial, but the court is more likely to withhold ruling thereon until the proof is closed.[1]

In the final argument, unlike the situation in a jury trial, it is proper to urge that certain legal principles should be applied to the facts as proven. It is also proper to urge that certain inferences should be drawn from the evidence as introduced. Generally the final argument, like the opening statement, may be shortened considerably from the argument in a jury trial. Also, there is usually less emphasis placed upon an emotional appeal than where counsel is addressing the jury. Reference may be made to the conclusions

---

[1] Builders Steel Co. v. Comm'r., 179 F. 2d 377; McCormick, Evidence, § 60.

of law which counsel wishes the court to adopt, as discussed in subsequent sections.

Since there is no need for the court to instruct himself as to the law, this feature of the jury trial is omitted. The conclusions of law, however, serve much the same purpose. Also, while there is no verdict as in a jury trial, findings of fact, similar to a special verdict, may be made by the court.

The new trial procedure in a trial by court operates very much the same as in a trial by jury, but the grounds for the motion may vary considerably from those commonly relied upon in a trial by jury. In a trial by jury one of the common grounds for a new trial is that the verdict is contrary to the weight of the evidence. Such motion is sustained only where the verdict is so clearly wrong that no reasonable jury could have reached such result.[2]

In a trial to the court there is a conflict in the authorities as to whether this rule is to be applied to findings of fact in law cases.[3] Some courts give less weight to such findings than is given to the verdict of a jury, and some even hold that a trial de novo is necessary where the findings are not supported by the evidence, no weight at all being given to the findings.[4] In some jurisdictions findings, like verdicts, are aided by all reasonable intendments to support the judgment.[5] Part of the difference of opinion is due to varying views as to the significance of the trial court's opportunity to observe the demeanor of the witnesses on the stand.

The judgment should follow the findings of fact and conclusions of law and is similar in form to that used in a jury trial.

SECTION 134. NECESSITY OF FINDINGS OF FACT AND CON-

---

[2] Clark v. Great Northern Ry. Co., 37 Wash. 537, 79 P. 1108.

[3] 53 Am. Jur. Trials, § 1148.

[4] Kaeser & Blair v. Merchants' Ass'n., 64 F. 2d 575; 5 C.J.S. Appeal and Error, § 1660 (where evidence is documentary); Virginian Ry. Co. v. U.S., 272 U.S. 658; 5 C.J.S. Appeal and Error, § 1662 (equity).

[5] Skelly Oil Co. v. Holloway, 171 F. 2d 670; 5 C.J.S. Appeal and Error, § 1657.

CLUSIONS OF LAW. Although there was no analogous requirement in the early equity practice, the majority of jurisdictions today require the trial court, in cases tried without a jury, to make findings of fact and conclusions of law.[6] But there is a great variation in the statutes. Some require findings and conclusions, some only one or the other.[7] In some jurisdictions the court is not required to make findings or conclusions unless requested to do so, while in others the court is under duty to do so in the absence of a request.[8]

In some jurisdictions the findings may be either general or special, while in others they must be special.[9] A general finding merely states that the court finds the facts in favor of the winning party, while a special finding deals with only one fact issue. Some jurisdictions permit findings to be general unless special findings are requested. Other jurisdictions differ as to whether findings are necessary only in law cases or in both law and equity cases.

As suggested above, findings of fact are designed to serve much the same purposes as are special verdicts, and conclusions of law are the equivalent of instructions. They are to define the scope of the litigation for purposes of res adjudicata and to assist the appellate court in determining whether the trial court reached the proper conclusions on the facts and selected the proper principles of law as applicable to the facts. Conclusions of law also serve to direct the trial court's attention to the legal questions in the case. To serve this purpose they should be submitted early in the trial.

In the event that the findings and conclusions are not adequate for the purposes of review, sometimes an appellate court will examine the evidence and make its own findings,[10] or send

---

[6] Fed. R. Civ. P. 52 (a); 53 Am. Jur. Trial, § 1133.

[7] Id. §§ 1132, 1138.

[8] Id. § 1135.

[9] Id. § 1141.

[10] So. Pac. Co. v. Los Angeles, 5 Cal. 2d 545, 55 P. 2d 847; Inyo Chem. Co. v. Los Angeles, 5 Cal. 2d 525, 55 P. 2d 850; 5 C.J.S. Appeal and Error, § 1845.

the case back to the trial court to supply the deficiency.[11] In some jurisdictions the trial court is also empowered, upon request, to amend its findings, even after judgment, and within a specified period.[12] Occasionally the court will, however, as in the case of defective verdicts, assume that an omission is equivalent as a finding against the party requiring an affirmative finding.[13] Reversals because of lack of conclusions or wrong conclusions are quite rare. In practice there is a wide variation among appellate courts as to the importance attached to both findings and conclusions. It is not safe, however, for counsel to assume that an appellate court will be liberal in this respect.

SECTION 135. DRAFTING SPECIAL FINDINGS. Usually it is not necessary for counsel to submit to the court the form of general findings because of their simplicity. Where, however, special findings are desired and the court is not required to make them unless requested, the request usually takes the form of the findings desired to be made. This will be the case where counsel wants to establish a point in the record, particularly for purposes of appellate review. In the absence of a request for special findings, the appellate court may assume that all facts were found in favor of the judgment. But there may be other purposes. For example, if the validity of a mining claim is established, such fact may then be recorded in the mining records of the county.

Special findings should be drafted with care, for they are considered part of the record. They serve the same purpose, and are judged by the same standards as special verdicts. They, plus the conclusions of law, must be sufficient to sustain the judgment. Accordingly, the following requirements should be kept in mind when drafting special findings:

---

11 Dearborn Nat. Cas. Co. v. Consumers Petrol. Co., 164 F. 2d 332.

12 Fed. R. Civ. P. 52 (b); 53 Am. Jur. Trial, § 1146.

13 C.I. St. L. & C.R. Co. v. Gaines, 104 Ind. 526, 4 N.E. 34; 53 Am. Jur. Trial, § 1143.

1. Generally findings of fact must be stated separately from conclusions of law, and should be labeled properly.[14] However, the labels given by the trial court or by counsel will not necessarily govern as to the sufficiency of the labeled portion of the decision. It is true that on occasion it has been deemed sufficient to mingle findings with statements as to the evidence and the law, but this does not make for clarity.

2. There must be a finding on every material fact in issue under the pleadings, and under the evidence.[15] Such facts must be sufficient to substantiate a claim or defense. It should be noted in this connection that a fact may be material under one theory but immaterial under another, and may be different than that relied upon by the pleader. In general, it is the material facts upon which the conclusions of law are stated.

3. Findings must contain ultimate and not evidentiary facts.[16] This is the same requirement as in the pleading rules of many jurisdictions. Occasionally a court will relax this requirement where the evidential fact leads to but one conclusion.

4. Findings should contain facts and not conclusions of law.[17] This requirement also stems from a similar rule governing pleadings.

5. Findings must not be inconsistent with each other.[18] It is true that some courts will, on appeal, attempt to harmonize findings in order to sustain a judgment. But it is not advisable to assume that this approach will be taken, but rather to anticipate that that court will reverse and remand.

6. Facts should be stated in definite, precise, and unam-

---

14 53 Am. Jur. Trial, § 1132.
15 New Blue Point Min. Co. v. Weissbein, 198 Cal. 261, 244 P. 325; 53 Am. Jur. Trial, § 1134.
16 Wilson v. Merchants Loan & T. Co., 183 U.S. 121; 53 Am. Jur. Trial, § 1142.
17 Hailey v. Riley, 14 Idaho 481, 95 P. 686; 53 Am. Jur. Trial, § 1138.
18 U.S. v. Jefferson Elect. Mfg. Co., 291 U.S. 386; 53 Am. Jur. Trial, § 1140.

biguous terms.[19] How specific the statements must be will depend, of course, upon the nature of the case. Thus, where the priority of a lien is involved, the exact date when it arose, or was filed, as the case may be, must be stated. On the other hand, where liability depends upon the receipt of notice of a defect, it may be sufficient to state that the notice was received before the accident occurred.

There is some conflict in the authorities as to whether it is sufficient merely to refer to the allegations in pleadings and state that they are true, or are sufficient, or similarly to refer to the testimony of a witness.[20] The better practice is to avoid any such reference.

In some jurisdictions findings must be served upon all the parties a specified period before the court signs them. This enables the parties to object to the findings as proposed.

If the findings as submitted by counsel are not acceptable to the court, the latter may amend them or may require counsel to resubmit other findings which the court deems proper under the evidence. In any event another request for special findings may be necessary in order to predicate error on the refusal of the court to accept the findings as originally submitted.

SECTION 136. DRAFTING CONCLUSIONS OF LAW. Since conclusions of law take the place of instructions, the problems of draftmanship are quite similar. Although general conclusions, such as, "The law is with the plaintiff" have been approved as sufficient,[21] the better practice is to submit a series of specific conclusions whenever specific instructions on like points would be appropriate in a jury trial.

Like instructions, conclusions of law should not be in abstract

---

19 U.S. v. Jefferson Elect. Mfg. Co., supra, n. 18; 53 Am. Jur. Trial, § 1139.

20 Ferguson v. Koch, 204 Cal. 342, 268 P. 342; Sterrett v. Sweeney, 15 Idaho 416, 98 P. 418; 89 C.J.S. Trial, § 630.

21 Young v. Bunnell Cemetery Ass'n., 221 Ind. 173, 46 N.E. 2d 825; 89 C.J.S. Trial, § 631.

form, but should refer specifically to the facts as they have been proven.[22]

Nor should conclusions portray as a fact any material thing about which there is a conflict in the evidence.[23] All issues should be recognized as such.

Conversely, conclusions may not include points upon which there is no issue, either in the pleadings or in the evidence. However, if permission is given to amend the pleadings to conform to the evidence, a sufficient basis for a conclusion may be formed.

---

[22] Crerar v. Daniels, 209 Ill. 296, 70 N.E. 569.
[23] Seehorn v. Am. Nat. Bk., 148 Mo. 256, 49 S.W. 886.

Chapter 11

New Trials

SECTION 137. COMPARED WITH VENIRE DE NOVO. Common-law juries originally decided cases on the basis of their personal knowledge of the facts. No evidence was introduced at the trial, but the matter at issue was simply presented to the jury for decision. During this period a measure of control over the jury was exercised by means of the writ of attaint. This writ could be obtained by the unsuccessful litigant if he contended that the verdict was false, i.e., not in accordance with the fact. Such a verdict was considered to be the result of misconduct on the part of the jury. Hence, an attaint jury of twenty-four members was impaneled to determine the truth or falsity of the original verdict. If the latter was found to be false, the members of the original or trial jury were punished by fine or imprisonment.

In the course of time it became more and more difficult to obtain juries who were familiar with all the circumstances in a case, and consequently the juries were allowed to supplement their personal knowledge with evidence introduced in open court. This process continued until we have the situation existing today, namely that juries are not only permitted to decide questions of fact on the basis solely of evidence introduced in open court, but they are required to do so. When this last stage of development had been reached, obviously the writ of attaint was no longer an effective device to prevent irresponsibility on the part of the jury, and it fell into disuse.

During the period when the writ of attaint was losing its effectiveness as a control mechanism, several other procedures were in the process of development. The losing parties began to appeal to equity for relief, and those courts did, on occasion, direct that a new trial be granted. But, in accord with the general approach of equity, the granting of such relief was discretionary with the chancellor. Consequently, several other methods of control arose.

One of these methods was the venire de novo. There are instances of its use as early as the fourteenth century. These instances were usually ones in which the jury had returned a special verdict, and in which the error had appeared on the face of the record. The common-law record originally consisted of the writ, the return, the pleadings, the verdict and judgment, plus the rulings of the trial court thereon. Subsequently, by means of the bill of exceptions, the evidence and rulings concerning the admissibility thereof, plus the instructions to the jury, could be made a part of the record. Unlike the situation in equity, once an error in the record was shown, the decision on the motion for a venire de novo was not discretionary.

The new trial as we understand it today came into existence in the seventeenth century. By that time it was granted for matters outside the record as well as for errors apparent in the record. As to the former, like the rule in equity, the awarding of a new trial was discretionary; as to the latter, like the rule governing the venire de novo, it was not. New trials were generally awarded in cases where the jury had returned a general verdict.

It may be said, then, that as to matters appearing in the record, the new trial device was a substitute for the writ of error, under which there was appellate review of alleged errors of law; but as to matters de hors the record, the new trial represented a substitute for the writ of attaint. In the early cases the ground for new trial was always related to misconduct of the jury; thus, new trials were granted when the verdict was against the evidence, when it was excessive or inadequate, when it was contrary to law, and the like.

SECTION 138. COMPARED WITH MISTRIAL. A mistrial may be declared for many of the same reasons for which a new trial may be awarded. Such reasons include misconduct on the part of any of the participants in the trial.[1] Generally a mistrial is declared by the process of withdrawing a juror from the panel. The motion for a mistrial, unlike the motion for a new trial, must generally be made before the jury has returned its verdict.[2] Further, the mistrial should be requested as soon as the possible grounds therefore become apparent, or the court may conclude that the error has been waived.[3] It may thus be possible to obviate the effect of the misconduct by reprimanding the offending person or cautioning the jury not to be influenced by such misconduct.

It should also be noted that the court is empowered to take certain steps to prevent misconduct, such as instructing them not to discuss the case with each other until they retire to deliberate upon the verdict, nor to discuss the case with any other person before and during deliberations. It is proper for counsel to request that such instructions be given in the event the court overlooks doing so.

A motion for mistrial should preferably be in writing, and the argument thereon should take place outside of the presence of the jury. Counsel will not want the jury to draw unfavorable inferences in the event the motion is denied.

As is true also with reference to a new trial, counsel before

---

[1] Greenberg v. Shindel, 71 Misc. 465, 128 N.Y.S. 661; 53 Am. Jur. Trial, § 967.

[2] Cooper v. American Discount Co., 66 Ga. App. 6, 16 S.E. 2d 791; 88 C.J.S. Trial, § 36b.

[3] 86 A.L.R. 932.

moving for a mistrial must weigh the opportunity for success in the present trial as against the probable result in a new trial. He must be prepared to show that the misconduct is prejudicial—that his client cannot obtain a fair trial because of the misconduct.[4] Counsel must also bear in mind that the court may declare a mistrial on his own motion. In any event, a mistrial motion should not be used merely as a protest when there is good reason to believe it will be denied.

If a mistrial is granted, the effect is like that of a new trial, but unlike that of a voluntary nonsuit.[5] In the former, the case is retained on the docket and a new trial date is set either at that time or later; in the latter, the case is stricken from the docket and plaintiff, if he wishes to pursue his remedy, must start another action. If a mistrial is refused, counsel may make such refusal one of the grounds for a motion for new trial.

SECTION 139. WHEN ADVISABLE. The following factors, among others, should be considered when deciding whether to move for a new trial:

1. The probable existence of grounds, either those specified by statute or recognized by the precedents. This point is considered in Section 143.

2. The advisability of an appeal. In some jurisdictions if an error to be assigned in an appeal could have been specified as a ground for a new trial, a motion for a new trial is a condition to appellate review. See Section 151 for a discussion of this matter.

3. The probable outcome of a second trial, if one is granted.

4. The necessary expenditure of time and costs involved in a new trial.

5. The fact that a large percentage of new-trial motions are denied. This is due in part to the fact that generally today the motion is presented to, and ruled upon by, the judge who pre-

---

4 Gilbert v. Gulf Oil Corp., 175 F. 2d 705.
5 Osborne v. Stephenson, 36 Ore. 328, 58 P. 1103.

sided at the trial of the case. In the older English practice, on the other hand, the motion was heard by a court en banc, of whom the trial judge was merely one of several. Section 142 includes a consideration of this factor.

6. The possible effect that a motion for a new trial may have on any present or contemplated negotiations for a settlement.

7. The psychological effect upon one's own client. If the client is aware of the possibility of continuing the litigation, and is desirous of doing so regardless of cost, he may consider it to be the advocate's duty to move for a new trial.

SECTION 140. THE MOTION—HOW MADE. At common law, a motion for a new trial was made without any particular formality. Statutes and rules now generally provide that the motion must be in writing and that the grounds must be specified.[6] Often, it is required further that notice of the filing of the motion must be given to the adverse party in a specified time. Sometimes an oral motion is allowed if this is supplemented later by a written motion. If the grounds specified are not provable by a simple reference to the record, it is necessary to file supporting affidavits, usually at the time the motion is filed.[7] Copies of such affidavits are often served upon the adverse party at the time the notice of motion is served. See Section 144 for a further discussion of affidavits in support of the motion. If there are several parties on one side, a motion may be made by all or only some of those losing the verdict.[8] Each party should make a separate motion, as it may be upheld as to one and denied as to another.

If counsel has any choice with reference to setting the date for a hearing on the motion, the relative advantages and disadvantages of an early date should be kept in mind. Thus, it will usually be

---

6 Joiner, Trials and Appeals, § 906.

7 Reich v. Thompson, 346 Mo. 577, 142 S.W. 2d 486.

8 Young v. Woodward Iron Co., 216 Ala. 330, 113 So. 223; 39 Am. Jur. New Trial, § 25.

easier for court and counsel to refresh their recollection as to what occurred at the trial if the hearing is held close to the conclusion of the trial. On the other hand, if a settlement is possible, there may be some gain in delaying the hearing. Further, there may be more evidence available as to some grounds, such as misconduct in the jury room, after the lapse of time.

If possible, the motion should be argued by counsel who participated in the trial as he alone can recall what had occurred there. Argument on a motion for a new trial should be as carefully outlined and delivered as any other important argument. It should not be done in a perfunctory manner. Enough time should be asked to cover adequately all the points relied upon. Counsel should present his case with vigor but also with complete candor. There should be no distortion of the evidence. If possible, the persons whose affidavits were filed should be called as witnesses. In non-jury cases, it may be possible to introduce new evidence of a wider scope than is the case in trials with a jury. Authorities should be treated in the same way as they are treated in any argument involving cases, statutes and similar material; analogies should be drawn where they are in point, and distinguishing features should be emphasized where they are in opposition to one's position. Similarly, the universality or uniqueness of a rule can be indicated.

SECTION 141. THE MOTION—WHEN MADE. At common law the motion for a new trial was filed prior to the entry of judgment. This entry was made four or more days after the verdict was returned. The time for filing the motion is usually specified by statute or rule today.[9] In some jurisdictions, the motion may be filed at any time until the end of the term, and even this period may be extended by the trial court upon a proper showing.[10] At

---

9 39 Am. Jur. New Trial, § 183.
10 Gant v. Shelton, 3 B. Mon. 420 (Ky.).

the other extreme is that group of jurisdictions in which the motion is made as soon as the verdict is returned.[11]

If a judgment is entered immediately after the verdict is returned, it is considered provisional until the time for filing a motion for new trial has expired.[12] If the motion must be filed in a specified period after the judgment, the same test for determining whether the judgment is final is applied as is applied where appellate review is sought.[13] Usually the trial court's characterization of the judgment is not determinative. Quite generally a longer period is specified for matters which occurred since the trial and are not part of the record, such as newly discovered evidence.[14]

There is a conflict in the authorities as to whether the time limitation is jurisdictional.[15] Some courts have held that the limitation may be waived by assent of the parties, usually in the form of a stipulation.[16] There is a similar conflict as to whether new grounds may be specified after the expiration of the period for filing the motion but before argument thereof.[17] It is generally not too late to file a motion for a new trial after a judgment is set aside or reversed,[18] but the rule is otherwise if a motion for new trial is filed with a motion for judgment on special findings.[19]

As at common law, a trial court usually may award a new trial on its own motion.[20] There is a conflict in the cases as to whether

---

11 Cooper v. Omohundro, 19 Wall. 65 (U.S.); 39 Am. Jur. New Trial, § 181.

12 Middletown v. Finney, 214 Cal. 523, 6 P. 2d 938.

13 Gray v. Sawyer, 252 S.W. 2d 10 (Ky.); 34 A.L.R. 2d 1181.

14 Chambliss v. Hass, 125 Iowa 484, 101 N.W. 153; 39 Am. Jur. New Trial, § 182.

15 Wood v. Wood, 136 Iowa 128, 113 N.W. 492; Nichols v. Houghton Circuit Judge, 185 Mich. 654, 152 N.W. 482; 39 Am. Jur. New Trial, § 184.

16 11 Am. St. Rep. 404.

17 Walker Fertilizer Co. v. Cole, 144 Fla. 37, 197 So. 777; Kentucky, C.R. Co., v. River & Race Coal & Coke Co., 150 Ky. 489, 150 S.W. 641; 39 Am. Jur. New Trial, § 192.

18 Smale v. Mitchell, 143 U.S. 99; 39 Am. Jur. New Trial, § 185.

19 Dinneen v. American Ins. Co., 98 Neb. 97, 152 N.W. 307.

20 P., C. & St. L.R. Co. v. Heck, 102 U.S. 120; 39 Am. Jur. New Trial, § 9.

this must be done within the time provided for filing the motion.[21] Adequate notice should be given to the parties and the order should specify the grounds.[22]

The trial court similarly has power to vacate or modify an order granting a new trial at least during the term during which it was entered.[23] There is some authority to the contrary where the term has expired.[24] At the bottom of the conflict is the question whether the order constitutes a final judgment. There is also a difference of opinion as to whether a motion to vacate may be continued until a subsequent term.

In view of the above summary, it is suggested that counsel file his motion within the time provided if at all possible. In order that this may be done, it is well to note points during the course of the trial which may later be the grounds for a motion.

If the losing party does not move for a new trial within the specified period, the prevailing party should move for judgment on the verdict. As to this motion, see Section 154.

SECTION 142. THE MOTION—WHERE MADE. As stated earlier, the motion for a new trial at common law was heard by a court en banc. Modern statutes or rules generally specify that the motion is to be addressed to the judge who presided at the trial, or if he becomes incapacitated, certain alternatives are provided.[25] These statutes or rules generally permit the court to impose certain conditions or limitations upon the awarding of a new trial.[26] The additur and remittitur practice, considered in Section 147, illustrates one such condition.

If grounds for a new trial become known for the first time

---

21 De Vall v. De Vall, 60 Ore. 493, 118 P. 843; 39 Am. Jur. New Trial, § 12.
22 Hoppe v. St. L. Pub. Serv. Co., 361 Mo. 402, 235 S.W. 2d 347; 23 A.L.R. 2d 852.
23 Bateman v. Donovan, 131 F. 2d 759; 61 A.L.R. 2d 642.
24 Andrews v. Ackerman Coal Co., 59 Ohio App. 65, 17 N.E. 2d 274.
25 Adams v. Wallace, 94 Okla. 95, 221 P. 16; 39 Am. Jur. New Trial, § 178.
26 Y. & M.V.R. Co. v. Scott, 108 Miss. 871, 67 So. 491; 39 Am. Jur. New Trial, § 207.

after an appeal has been filed but before it has been acted upon, the motion may be presented to the court before which the case is pending.[27]

SECTION 143. THE MOTION—SPECIFICATION OF GROUNDS. The grounds upon which a new trial may be granted are often specified in statutes or rules.[28] As stated earlier, these grounds may be roughly classified into: 1. Those which occurred during the trial, and which are usually provable by a mere reference to the record. 2. Those which occurred subsequent to the trial, or more specifically, those which became known after the trial. The manner of proving such grounds is discussed in Section 144. As to the first class, normally these would be called to the attention of the trial court as they arose and would only be the subject of a new trial motion if the court ruled adversely to the party losing the verdict. As to the second class, no such opportunity for corrective action presents itself.

Specified grounds vary from jurisdiction to jurisdiction. Some of the most common are as follows: 1. Erroneous rulings of the court during the course of the trial. 2. Erroneous giving of or refusing to give instructions. 3. Verdicts that are contrary to the evidence or against the weight of the evidence. 4. Verdicts contrary to law. 5. Excessive or inadequate verdicts. 6. Misconduct of jury, counsel or the court. 7. Surprise. 8. Newly discovered evidence.

An illustration of each of the above is as follows: 1. The overruling of an objection to certain testimony which is clearly hearsay. 2. Refusing to allow recovery for a certain item of damages recoverable in that jurisdiction. 3. A verdict for the plaintiff in a personal injury action, though there is uncontradicted evidence of contributory negligence. 4. A verdict which is contrary to an instruction properly given. 5. A verdict in a personal injury action

---

[27] Nusser v. United Parcel Serv. of N.Y., 3 N.J. Super. 64, 65 A. 2d 549; 66 C.J.S. New Trial, § 225.

[28] 39 Am. Jur. New Trial, § 26.

is inadequate if it fails to compensate the plaintiff for medical expenses, normally recoverable in this type of action. 6. A chance verdict or one that is the result of compromise. 7. Calling an expert witness after stipulating at a pre-trial conference that no such witnesses would be called. 8. Becoming aware of the identity of an eyewitness to an accident, after the trial.

This is not to say that a new trial will necessarily be awarded whenever the above grounds exist. It must further usually be shown that the condition or occurrence prejudiced the losing party to the extent that he did not have a fair trial.[29] At common law prejudice was presumed to be present, but under many statutes or rules this must be proved, and the burden of proof is upon the complaining party.[30] Thus, it is generally held that the party against whom a verdict was rendered cannot raise the point that the verdict was inadequate on the theory that the verdict-winner should have recovered a larger amount or nothing, if the case is one of unliquidated damages.[31]

But where the case involves liquidated damages, the authorities are divided.[32] Where a new trial is granted in this situation the jury has usually returned a verdict that is contrary to law. Under this test there is obviously much room for a difference of opinion in a specific case. Thus, there is a conflict as to whether it is grounds for a new trial that counsel for the defendant, in his closing argument in a personal injury action calls attention to the fact that the plaintiff is entitled to workmen's compensation benefits.[33]

In the area of misconduct on the part of the jury, especially

---

29 A.C.L.R. Co. v. Taylor, 125 Ga. 454, 54 S.E. 622.

30 McLanahan v. Universal Ins. Co., 1 Pet. 170 (U.S.).

31 Ohio Boulevard Land Corp. v. Greggory, 46 F. 2d 263; 174 A.L.R. 765.

32 Daniel v. G. Ober & Sons Co., 52 Ga. App. 691, 184 S.E. 439; Metropolitan L. Ins. Co., 28 Ala. App. 357, 184 So. 282.

33 Altenbauer v. Lion Oil Co., 186 F. 2d 35; Black Gold Petroleum Co. v. Webb, 186 Okla. 584, 99 P. 2d 868; 77 A.L.R. 2d 1154.

that of communications between jurors and non-jurors about which there is much litigation, a diversity of opinion is noted in appellate reports.[34] The circumstances surrounding the communications, such as where they occurred, whether other persons were present, the state of the evidence, the nature of the communication, the knowledge on the part of the non-juror that the juror was such, the number of jurors involved, and the like, are all to be considered in determining whether grounds for a new trial exist. It should also be noted that in some instances it is possible to have non-jurors cited for contempt of court if they are guilty of tampering with the jury.

With reference to another type of misconduct, namely that of taking an unauthorized view of the premises, before such misconduct may be assigned as cause for a new trial, the information obtained must be material to some issue in the case upon which there is a deficiency in the evidence, and the complaining party must not have participated in the view.[35]

A further word concerning some of the above grounds. If the claimed surprise is the failure of one's own witness to appear, normally the moving party must show that the witness was served with a subpoena, and he must have requested, and have been denied, a continuance.[36] Further, it must be shown that his testimony was material. If the ground for new trial is that the jury returned a compromise verdict, the moving party must show that there was a prior agreement by the jurors to be bound by whatever figure resulted from the addition of the sums awarded by each juror and the division of that total by twelve.[37]

Certain disqualifications of jurors, such as bias or physical

34 52 A.L.R. 2d 182; 64 A.L.R. 2d 158; 62 A.L.R. 2d 298.

35 Roberts v. U.S., 60 F. 2d 871.

36 Cook v. Southwick, 9 Tex. 615, 60 Am. Dec. 181; 39 Am. Jur. New Trial, § 37.

37 Zook v. State Highway Comm., 156 Kan. 79, 131 P. 2d 652; 39 Am. Jur. New Trial, § 124.

incompetency, may be discovered or be discoverable during the voir dire examination. If so, it is usually too late to call the court's attention to the matter for the first time by way of a motion for a new trial.[38] If not discoverable on voir dire it must still be shown that the disqualification was of such a nature that the juror could not return an impartial or true verdict.[39]

One special problem should be mentioned: What to do when the court reporter dies or becomes disabled before he has completed his work. A distinction is frequently made between a case where this occurs during the course of the trial and a case where the evidence is all in but the transcript has not yet been finished. Frequently no relief is granted where there are other means for securing the record, or where the disability occurs after the time for taking an appeal has expired.[40] To provide for this contingency, as well as for other reasons, the practice of using tape or wire recorders during the trial, is growing in several jurisdictions.

There is a conflict in the authorities as to whether the specified grounds are exclusive.[41] For example, a statute may refer only to excessive damages, but the ground relied upon is inadequate damages, a ground recognized at common law.

The motion should not only state separately each ground that is to be relied upon, but it should do so specifically.[42] Thus, it is not sufficient to merely state: "Misconduct of the jury," although the statute so reads, but the motion must state further the nature of such misconduct, when it came to the counsel's (or party's) attention, and what, if anything, was done since that time. It is unfortunate that altogether too many groundless motions are filed because of the practice of listing all the grounds specified in hopes

[38] Drake v. State, 5 Tex. App. 649; 15 A.L.R. 2d 534.
[39] State v. Seiley, 197 La. 405, 1 So. 2d 675.
[40] White Pine Lbr. Co. v. Mfgr. Lbr. Co., 191 Mich. 390, 158 N.W. 124.
[41] Todd v. Bettingen, 102 Minn. 260, 113 N.W. 906; Toledo Rys. & Light Co. v. Mason, 81 Ohio State 463, 91 N.E. 292; 39 Am. Jur. New Trial, § 27.
[42] Garbutt v. Mayo, 128 Ga. 269, 57 S.E. 495; 39 Am. Jur. New Trial, § 190.

that one or two may apply. Such practice encourages the wholesale overruling of motions that may have some merit, with the result that appellate court dockets are crowded more than necessary.

The above suggestions and requirements are not only conducive to an orderly presentation, but they will preserve the points adequately in the record. While a court may, of course, grant a new trial for a ground not specified by counsel, ordinarily error cannot be predicated upon its refusal to do so.

SECTION 144. MATTERS OUTSIDE THE RECORD—HOW PROVEN. A prima facie showing of the existence of grounds for a new trial which are not provable by the record may be made by means of affidavits.[43] Such affidavits must be carefully prepared, generally by counsel, but are to be signed by the person having personal knowledge of the facts.

Affidavits should contain no statements which the affiant would not be permitted to testify to under the rules of evidence. The affidavits should be specific and contain only statements of fact. Legal terminology should be avoided as much as possible, although technical terms in other fields are of course permissible when they apply. Affidavits should contain the name of the affiant, and enough information about him and his relationship to the case that his statements will influence the court. At the hearing of the motion for a new trial, the affiants may be called to the stand so that they may be cross-examined. Hence they should be briefed as carefully as were the witnesses at the trial proper. As stated earlier, the affidavits are usually filed with the motion, and a copy is served upon the adverse party.

Affidavits involving alleged misconduct of jurors present a special problem. This is due to the fact that in the latter part of the eighteenth century it was held that a verdict could not be

---

[43] Reich v. Thompson, 346 Mo. 577, 142 S.W. 2d 486; 39 Am. Jur. New Trial, § 198.

impeached by affidavits of jurors as to their own misconduct in returning a chance verdict. Prior to this case such affidavits had been freely admitted. One of the chief reasons for this restriction was to prevent the jury from being besieged by unsuccessful litigants to the extent that freedom of discussion and action would be seriously hampered. Other reasons are (a) the desirability of concluding litigation as soon as possible, and (b) the policy against the upsetting of the result of a formal deliberative process by means of informal statements of questionable value, something equivalent to the reasons for the parol evidence rule.

Statutes and decisions today have grafted many so-called exceptions and qualifications upon the restriction, and counsel is urged therefore to consult the law of his own jurisdiction, before attempting to upset a verdict on the basis of jurors' affidavits.[44] Thus, in various jurisdictions the prohibition is deemed not to be applicable: 1. To criminal prosecutions of jurors for misconduct.[45] 2. To affidavits which are used to support rather than impeach a verdict.[46] 3. To affidavits of persons other than jurors.[47] 4. To cases involving misconduct of persons other than jurors.[48] 5. To cases of misconduct of jurors which occurred outside the jury room.[49] 6. To cases where the purpose of the affidavits is to get at the true intention of the jury when the verdict is in an unacceptable form or is unclear.[50] 7. To cases where the alleged misconduct is of a specified nature, as for instance, returning a chance verdict.[51] A chance verdict is one arrived at by some process such as flipping a coin. The objection to such a verdict is that it is not the product of deliberation.

---

[44] 53 Am. Jur. Trial, § 1105; 40 A.L.R. 2d 1119.
[45] Clark v. U.S., 289 U.S. 1.
[46] Morakes v. State, 201 Ga. 425, 40 S.E. 2d 120; 30 A.L.R. 2d 914.
[47] Wright v. Abbott, 160 Mass. 395, 36 N.E. 62.
[48] Welshire v. Bruaw, 331 Pa. 392, 200 A. 67.
[49] Pierce v. Brennan, 83 Minn. 422, 86 N.W. 417.
[50] Glennon v. Fisher, 51 Idaho 732, 10 P. 2d 294.
[51] Benjamin v. Helena Light and R. Co., 79 Mont. 144, 255 P. 20.

It will be noted that the difference of opinion is due to lack of agreement as to the fundamental reasons behind the prohibition. If the policy behind the prohibition is to protect the jurors from harassment, then the above numbered situations are not true exceptions to the rule. Further, some courts do not distinguish between the use of affidavits to support a motion for a new trial, and their use to warrant a correction of the verdict. Thus, affidavits have been admitted to show that the wrong form of verdict was signed by mistake;[52] but if there are cross-actions, some courts refuse to admit affidavits to the effect that the wrong form was signed on the theory that a misunderstanding of the law was involved.[53]

SECTION 145. NEWLY DISCOVERED EVIDENCE. It may safely be said that courts generally are not disposed to grant a new trial on the grounds of newly discovered evidence.[54] Some of the reasons are: A liberal attitude would encourage lack of diligence in preparation for trial; the use of perjured testimony once the state of the opponent's testimony is known would be invited; it would also tend to prolong litigation indefinitely. Hence the courts have, over a period of time, developed a series of conditions that must be satisfied before the motion will be granted. These conditions are as follows:

1. The new evidence must be such that it would probably change the result if a new trial were granted.[55] In some cases this may be readily apparent from the nature of the new evidence; in others it is more difficult to show such probability. It may be necessary to refer rather extensively to the evidence introduced at the trial.

Some courts have interpreted this requirement as forbidding

---

52 Paul v. Pye, 135 Minn. 13, 159 N.W. 1070.

53 Abraham v. Superior Court, 50 R.I. 207, 146 A. 617.

54 39 Am. Jur. New Trial, § 156.

55 Denver City Tramway Co. v. Brier, 60 Colo. 235, 152 P. 901; 39 Am. Jur. New Trial, § 165.

the grant of a new trial if the new evidence would change the damages allowed but would result in the same party receiving the verdict.[56] Other courts apply the remittitur and additur practice (discussed in Section 147) to this situation and grant a new trial conditioned upon the consent by the plaintiff to a reduction of the amount awarded or upon a consent by the defendant conditioned upon an increase of that amount.

2. The new evidence must have been discovered since the trial.[57] This is generally interpreted as meaning that *both* the party and his counsel were not aware of the existence of the evidence until after the trial. It is not sufficient to show that the evidence had been forgotten or that a known witness or document could not be found. In the latter situations the proper remedy is to move for a continuance when the case is called for trial. One of the reasons behind this requirement is the fact that it is almost impossible to disprove a want of recollection.

3. The new evidence must be such that it could not, by the use of due diligence, have been discovered prior to the trial.[58] This requirement in particular is designed to prevent the use of perjured testimony and to encourage adequate preparation for trial. The standard applied here is that of the reasonable man having before him the data known by both the client and his attorney.

4. The evidence must not be *merely* cumulative[59] or impeaching[60] in nature. As to the first of these requirements, this merely restates requirements 1 and 5 in another form. Evidence which merely contradicts that already in the record is deemed to be cumulative for this purpose. As to the second of the requirements, it should be noted that it does not preclude the grant of a

---

[56] Curtis v. Mann, 105 Ind. App. 601, 14 N.E. 2d 345; 66 C.J.S. New Trial, § 111.

[57] Ford Motor Co. v. Vanover, 303 Ky. 831, 198 S.W. 2d 660; 39 Am. Jur. New Trial, § 159.

[58] Birmingham v. Carle, 191 Ala. 539, 68 So. 22; 39 Am. Jur. New Trial, § 160.

[59] Ren v. Jones, 38 Ariz. 476, 1 P. 2d 110; 39 Am. Jur. New Trial, § 170.

[60] Foust v. State, 200 Ind. 76, 161 N.E. 371; 39 Am. Jur. New Trial, § 167.

new trial if the new evidence has substantive as well as impeachment value.[61] Thus, in negligence actions, where the plaintiff has testified that he is permanently injured as a result of the accident, new trials are frequently granted on the basis of new evidence which shows that subsequent to the trial the plaintiff engaged in activities which are inconsistent with the claimed nature of his injury.[62]

It will be noted that such evidence may result in a verdict for the defendant or merely in the reduction in the amount of damages awarded. Thus, the new evidence may show that the plaintiff never was permanently injured or it may show that he never in fact was injured. It should also be noted that a new trial may be denied if the plaintiff explains such activities as being prescribed by his physician.

Again, prior inconsistent statements may be grounds for a new trial although they serve to discredit a witness, if the statement is admissible for its substantive value and thus also satisfies requirement 5. Fraud on the part of the successful party in keeping the opponent's witnesses from testifying, or in procuring false testimony, has always been grounds for a new trial.[63] It is not sufficient, however, to show that a witness had been mistaken in his testimony given at the trial. The new evidence may also be offered by the plaintiff, to show that he in fact was more seriously injured than he was able to show at the time of the trial. But it may be difficult to convince the court that this proof could not have been given at the trial.

5. The evidence must be material to the issue.[64] In fact, this is no more than is required for admissibility of evidence generally and is related to requirement 1; that is, the evidence must prove

---

[61] Powell v. Com., 133 Va. 741, 112 S.E. 657.

[62] Anschutz v. Louisville R. Co., 152 Ky. 741, 154 S.W. 13; 31 A.L.R. 2d 1236.

[63] Block v. Szczukowski, 241 N.Y.S. 462, 229 App. Div. 394; 66 C.J.S. New Trial, § 114.

[64] Re Dolbeer, 153 Cal. 652, 96 P. 266; 39 Am. Jur. New Trial, § 164.

one of the ultimate points in issue under the pleadings and an element of claim or defense under the substantive law.

A motion for a new trial on the ground of newly discovered evidence must usually be supported by affidavits of individuals having personal knowledge of the facts attested to.[65] Such affidavits must contain a complete, detailed summary of the substance of the new testimony, so that the court may assess its probable effect in a new trial; they must explain in detail why such evidence was not introduced at the trial; they must state specifically what steps were taken in preparation for trial, so that the court may determine whether due diligence was used in obtaining the necessary evidence—it is not sufficient merely to use the language found in the statute, such as, "all reasonable diligence."[66]

The fact that there had been a prior unsuccessful appeal from the judgment does not generally prevent a new trial for newly discovered evidence.[67]

SECTION 146. VERDICT CONTRARY TO THE EVIDENCE. It will be recalled that in Chapter 6 reference was made to the various tests used in determining when a verdict should be directed against the party having the burden of proof. One of these tests was as follows: If a verdict for P would be set aside and a new trial granted because the verdict was contrary to the evidence, a verdict should be directed for D. It was noted that a court using that test would, of necessity, be required to examine the evidence produced by both sides. The function of the court is the same when a motion for a new trial is made on the ground that the verdict is contrary to the evidence. However, there is this difference: When a motion is made to set aside a verdict and to grant a new trial, the court does

---

65 Thompson v. State 58 Fla. 106, 50 So. 507; 39 Am. Jur. New Trial, § 162.

66 Fusselman v. Yellowstone Valley Land & Irrig. Co., 53 Mont. 254, 163 P. 473, 39 Am. Jur. New Trial, § 163.

67 State v. Hawkins, 121 S.C. 290, 114 S.E. 538; 3 Am. Jur. Appeal and Error, § 1239.

not make all reasonable inferences in favor of the verdict, nor will it assume the truth of all the evidence introduced by the verdict-winner.[68] Credibility will be determined by the court, as the jury has had the first opportunity to do likewise.[69] A verdict may thus be set aside though there is substantial evidence in support thereof, if the court, after weighing the evidence, concludes that it was unreasonable.

It will be noted that this ground does not involve any erroneous ruling or untoward occurrence, and is based solely on the desire of the court to prevent a miscarriage of justice. That is, cases are to be decided on the law and the facts, and not on the basis of possible bias or prejudice of the jury, or even on the basis of their well-meaning, but erroneous, sense of justice.

In drawing up and arguing a motion for a new trial on the ground that the verdict is contrary to the evidence, counsel must carefully analyze the evidence, pointing out the weaknesses of the opposition's evidence and the strength of his own. Generally the plaintiff has the more difficult task in this respect because he carries the burden of proof (normally) on all the issues and has to have a favorable finding on each issue, whereas the defendant need have a favorable finding on only one issue to retain his verdict.

The motion usually presents the court with a close question, as the verdict would otherwise have been directed against the one party or the other. As a consequence the decision of the trial court will not be the same as that of the reviewing court in as many instances as if a motion to direct the verdict were involved.

SECTION 147. EXCESSIVE OR INADEQUATE DAMAGES—REMITTITUR AND ADDITUR. When the defendant moves for a new trial because he believes the damages awarded to the plaintiff are excessive, in most jurisdictions the trial court may deny the motion on

---

[68] Iseman v. Hayes, 242 Ky. 302, 46 S.W. 2d 110.
[69] Bergh v. Spivakowski, 86 Conn. 98, 84 A. 329.

the condition that the plaintiff remit the excess.[70] This procedure is commonly referred to as remittitur. There is some variation in the state practice. In some jurisdictions it is used only if the excess if liquidated;[71] in others only where the court is satisfied that the excess was not the result of bias or prejudice;[72] in still others only if the plaintiff consents to accept the lowest amount the court would allow.[73] In no jurisdiction can the plaintiff be compelled to remit the excess, but if he does not do so, a new trial is granted. If he does consent he cannot thereafter object to the subtraction.

The converse practice, called additur, was unknown at common law and for that reason was held to be in violation of the Seventh Amendment which guarantees right of trial by jury.[74] As a result the practice is not followed in the federal courts. Although the Seventh Amendment is not a limitation upon the states, in very few states is the additur procedure utilized, unless both parties consent.[75] The courts may however, grant a new trial unless the parties settle upon an acceptable figure.

In both remittitur and additur, the court sets an amount which it believes is fair under the state of the evidence. There is obviously no rule of thumb applicable here, and counsel will have to use his best judgment in determining whether to give consent. The problem is very similar to that encountered in settlement negotiations, and in both the consent of the client must be obtained. Counsel must weigh the possibility of obtaining a different amount should there be a retrial; in a close case he should also consider the possibility of a contrary result. Further, he must note the possibility of appellate review if a new trial is ordered.

---

70 Dimick v. Schiedt, 293 U.S. 474; 39 Am. Jur. New Trial, § 210; 11 A.L.R. 2d 1217.

71 Tunnel Min. & Leasing Co. v. Cooper, 50 Colo. 390, 115 P. 901; 39 Am. Jur. New Trial, § 215.

72 International & G.N.R. Co. v. Wilkes, 68 Tex. 617, 5 S.W. 491.

73 Beach v. Bird & Wells Lbr. Co., 135 Wis. 550, 116 N.W. 245.

74 Dimick v. Schiedt, supra, n. 70.

75 Burdict v. Missouri P.R. Co., 123 Mo. 221, 27 S.W. 453, 3 Am. Jur. Appeal and Error, § 1180.

SECTION 148. PARTIAL NEW TRIAL. Closely related to the remittitur and additur practice is the practice of granting a partial new trial, limited either to the issue of liability or to the issue of damages. Although the practice was unknown at common law, a partial new trial is provided for by statutes or rules in a number of jurisdictions, especially if limited to the issue of damages.[76] It must be possible, however, to separate the two.[77] If the court believes the verdict was the result of compromise, a new trial on the whole case will be ordered.[78] Therefore, there is a greater willingness to order a new trial on the issue of damages alone where the verdict is excessive rather than where it is inadequate. Similarly there is less reluctance to grant a partial new trial where the error lies in the giving of faulty instructions as to damages.[79] If the court believes that the verdict was the result of passion or prejudice, it will order a new trial of the whole case.

Very rarely will a court grant a new trial on the issue of liability alone.[80] It may do so, however, where the damages are liquidated;[81] or the instructions as to liability were faulty;[82] or there is no objection to the amount of damages awarded;[83] or the court erroneously admitted evidence from which the jury drew an inference of negligence on the part of the defendant.[84]

Where several causes of action have been set out in the complaint and separate verdicts have been returned on each, it is frequently possible to request a new trial on only one or more of such causes of action.[85] And, as stated earlier, if there are multiple

---

[76] 39 Am. Jur. New Trial, § 21; 29 A.L.R. 2d 1199.

[77] Gasoline Prod. Co. v. Champlin Ref. Co., 283 U.S. 494; 39 Am. Jur. New Trial, § 24.

[78] Simmons v. Fish, 210 Mass. 563, 97 N.E. 102.

[79] Yazoo & M. Valley R. Co. v. Scott, 108 Miss. 871, 67 So. 491.

[80] Barnes v. Ashworth, 154 Va. 218, 153 S.E. 711; 34 A.L.R. 2d 988.

[81] Caldwell v. Modern Woodmen of America, 90 Kan. 175, 133 P. 843.

[82] Director General of Railroads v. Pence, 135 Va. 329, 116 S.E. 351.

[83] Griffin v. Boston & M.R. Co., 87 Vt. 278, 89 A. 220.

[84] Whitten v. McClelland, 137 Va. 726, 120 S.E. 146.

[85] Spawn v. So. Dak. C.R. Co., 26 S.D. 1, 127 N.W. 648.

parties involved, some may request a new trial while the others do not.

In determining whether to request a new trial limited to the issue of damages, counsel must consider the probable results of the new trial and whether he can submit any further evidence on that issue. He must also consider the factors of delay, added costs, and time involved in a new trial. He must determine whether a complete new trial would be a better solution of his problem.

In some jurisdictions a party desiring a partial new trial must still request a new trial of the whole case and the court may restrict the new trial to some of the issues.[86] In other jurisdictions the proper procedure is to specify the issues upon which the new trial is sought.[87]

SECTION 149. NECESSITY OF OBJECTIONS DURING THE TRIAL. It is a cardinal principle that a new trial will not be awarded if the attention of the trial court could have been but was not directed to some occurrence which is later to be set up as a ground for a new trial.[88] In the vernacular, "You cannot ambush the trial judge." More specifically, the trial court must be afforded every opportunity to cure any defect in the proceedings so that the trial may proceed properly and thus obviate the necessity for a new trial. Furthermore, it is considered contrary to sound policy to allow a party to gamble on the chance of receiving a favorable verdict. An impropriety remains just that, regardless of the outcome of the trial.

A few examples may serve to demonstrate this principle:

1. If one side offers evidence which the other side deems to be inadmissible, a proper, specific objection must be made at that time.[89] If the ruling is adverse to the objector, he must immedi-

---

86 Simmons v. Fish, supra, n. 78.

87 San Diego Land & Town Co. v. Neale, 78 Cal. 63, 20 P. 372.

88 Gielham v. State Bank, 3 Ill. 245, 35 Am. Dec. 105; 39 Am. Jur. New Trial, § 14.

89 Hastings v. Serieto, 61 Cal. App. 2d 672, 143 P. 2d 956; 39 Am. Jur. New Trial, § 115.

ately take exception to the ruling, unless there is in the jurisdiction a statute or rule under which it is assumed that every adverse ruling is excepted to. While the exception is necessary for appellate review, it also serves to call the attention of the trial court to the fact that counsel making the objection is not accepting the ruling as correct. The thought here is that this may cause the court to reflect further on the objection and possibly reverse himself.

2. The same procedure should normally be followed with reference to the giving or the refusal to give instructions.[90] The objection and exception must be taken as soon as possible or they will be considered as having been waived. Local procedures vary in this respect. If there is opportunity to confer in chambers prior to the giving of the instructions, this is the appropriate time and place to make one's point. It may also be necessary to do so formally in open court.

3. Objections to verdicts must normally be made within the time provided for the making of new trial motions. Here no prior objection is possible.[91]

4. Misconduct occurring during the course of the trial must be called to the court's attention when it occurs.[92] This has been discussed in Section 138, involving mistrials. If the knowledge of the misconduct does not come to the attention of counsel until after the trial has been concluded, he may of course raise the point at that time.

5. Surprise may occur at various stages of the proceedings— and must be claimed when it does so occur.[93]

6. Newly discovered evidence likewise must be acted upon promptly after its discovery.[94] In all of these instances what con-

---

[90] Cruze v. State, 114 Tex. Crim. App. 450, 25 S.W. 2d 875.

[91] Georgia R., etc., Co. v. Tompkins, 138 Ga. 596, 75 S.E. 664.

[92] McLaughlin v. Union Transp. Co., 177 Okla. 115, 57 P. 2d 868.

[93] Bayonne Knife Co. v. Umbenbauer, 107 Ala. 496, 18 So. 175; 39 Am. Jur. New Trial, § 151.

[94] Eclipse Mach. Co. v. Harley-Davidson Motor Co., 286 F. 68; 39 Am. Jur. New Trial, § 156.

stitutes promptness will depend upon all the circumstances in the case.

SECTION 150. NUMBER OF NEW TRIALS PERMITTED. The number of new trials that will be permitted depends in part upon the grounds assigned. Thus, for erroneous rulings, a new trial will be granted (perhaps by the appellate court if the trial court refuses to do so) whenever such rulings occur.[95] And so it is for many of the other grounds. But a special problem arises when the ground is that the verdict is against the weight of the evidence. At common law even here there was no limit, and the verdict-winner would be compelled to seek relief, if any, in a court of equity. This matter is today settled in some jurisdictions by statute or rule.[96] These statutes may simply adopt the common-law rule or they may provide that after a specified number of concurring verdicts a new trial may no longer be awarded. If the verdicts are contradictory, these statutory limitations do not apply.

If there is no statute preventing counsel from filing a succession of motions for a new trial on the grounds that the verdict is contrary to the weight of the evidence, it is questionable whether such a step is advisable in the face of several adverse verdicts. Certainly it would be difficult to justify to the client the added expense, in the event that the third verdict concurs with the first two. It may on occasion be justifiable to ask for a third new trial if it could affect settlement negotiations.

SECTION 151. PREREQUISITE TO AN APPEAL. Reference was made earlier to the fact that at common law a motion for a new trial was heard by a court en banc. There was therefore no need for appellate review of the decision on the motion, and this we find to be the rule. Where a motion is heard by the trial court, there is a natural tendency to overrule most motions. Hence we find stat-

---

[95] Louisville & N.R. Co. v. Woodson, 134 U.S. 614.
[96] 39 Am. Jur. New Trial, § 16.

utes in many jurisdictions providing for appellate review of the denial of the motion and in some instances of the granting thereof.[97] Some of the statutes provide review in a limited number of situations, as, for instance, when the motion is made on the ground of misconduct of the jury.

The factors determining such review are as follows: 1. If the action of the trial court is discretionary, then the decision of that court is subject to reversal only if there has been an abuse of discretion.[98] 2. If the determination of the court is deemed to be a final order, for example, where the motion is denied, review is much more likely than if it is considered interlocutory.[99] 3. In cases where a new trial on the ground of excessiveness of the verdict has been denied, some appellate courts refuse to review the order because of the difficulty of establishing an appropriate standard.[100] 4. The federal courts refuse to review an order either granting or denying a new trial requested because of excessiveness or inadequacy of the verdict because the Seventh Amendment is interpreted as a prohibition against reexamination of any fact tried by a jury.[101] However, if the evidence conclusively establishes the right to substantial damages and the jury awards only nominal damages the overruling of the motion may be considered as an error of law and hence subject to appellate review.[102]

Where a direct appeal lies from an order granting a new trial, many jurisdictions hold that the failure to so appeal precludes a review of such an order on an appeal from the final judgment rendered at the new trial.[103] The failure to take an appeal

---

97 4 C.J.S. Appeal and Error, § 123a.
98 Inland & S. Coasting Co. v. Hall, 124 U.S. 121.
99 Central of Ga. R. Co. v. Murphey, 113 Ga. 514, 38 S.E. 970.
100 Maroney v. Minneapolis & St. P.L.R. Co., 123 Minn. 480, 144 N.W. 149.
101 Miller v. Maryland Casualty Co., 40 F. 2d 463.
102 Carter v. Wells, F. & Co., 64 F. 1005.
103 Levy v. Joseph P. Day, Inc., 250 App. Div. 452, 294 N.Y.S. 583; 3 Am. Jur. Appeal and Error, § 849.

from the order is deemed to be a waiver of the right to raise the point later.

Where no such direct appeal from such order lies, but the appeal is permitted only from the judgment rendered at the conclusion of the second trial, there is a conflict in the authorities as to whether the participation in such new trial precludes such review.[104] But as to errors which were committed during the original trial, participation in the new trial generally will be treated as a waiver of the right to object on appeal.[105] There is a similar split as to whether review is precluded of issues raised at the original trial where the new trial is limited to other issues.[106]

Is a motion for a new trial ever a prerequisite to appellate review? It will be recalled that in Section 143 the grounds for a new trial were classified into those which were found in the record and those outside the record. At common law errors in the record could be the subject matter of a writ of error; errors not in the record could be presented to a court en banc by means of a motion for a new trial. Hence it was not necessary to present a motion for new trial, and have the same denied, before one could get appellate review.

The common-law rule has been changed by statute in a number of jurisdictions.[107] In some the statutes are interpreted as requiring a prior motion only for those grounds which do not appear in the record, such as insufficiency of the evidence to support the verdict.[108] In others it is possible to obtain appellate review of only those points which were raised by the motion, regardless of the fact that they are found in the record. If the statute

---

104 Atkinson v. Wiard, 153 Kan. 96, 109 P. 2d 160; Altrichter v. Shell Oil Co., 263 F. 2d 377.

105 Patton v. Minneapolis S.R. Co., 245 Minn. 563, 71 N.W. 2d 861.

106 Steinfeldt v. Pierce, 2 Wis. 2d 138, 85 N.W. 2d 754; Zywiec v. S. St. Paul, 234 Minn. 18, 47 N.W. 2d 465; 67 A.L.R. 2d 191.

107 3 Am. Jur. Appeal and Error, § 267.

108 Patapsco Ins. Co. v. Southgate, 5 Pet. 604 (U.S.); 3 Am. Jur. Appeal and Error, § 385.

specifies the point as a ground for a new trial, it has to be so raised.[109] Further, unless exceptions have been abolished, it is necessary to except to the overruling of the motion for a new trial.

In view of the varied statutes and their interpretations, counsel is advised to consult the authorities in his own jurisdiction when considering the possibility of an appeal.

SECTION 152. STAYING EXECUTION PENDING RULING ON THE MOTION. In some jurisdictions the filing of a motion for a new trial operates as an automatic stay as to the entry of judgment or the issuance of execution on the judgment.[110] But in other jurisdictions it is necessary for counsel filing the motion for a new trial to also move for such a stay.[111] In some jurisdictions the filing of the motion for a new trial also serves to extend the time within which an appeal may be taken,[112] and in others again it is necessary to make a supplementary motion to accomplish this result.[113]

---

[109] Hill v. Jamieson, 16 Ind. 125, 79 Am. Dec. 414.

[110] Thomas v. Darks, 127 Okla. 179, 260 P. 75.

[111] Winn & Lovett Groc. Co. v. Luke, 156 Fla. 638, 24 So. 2d 310; 66 C.J.S. § 128b.

[112] Morse v. U.S., 271 U.S. 151.

[113] Macartney v. Shipherd, 60 Ore. 133, 117 P. 814; 3 Am. Jur. Appeal and Error, § 435.

Chapter 12

Judgments

A. On Verdict or Findings

SECTION 153. APPROPRIATE FORM. After the jury returns a verdict or findings, or the court prepares findings of fact and conclusions of law, a specified period is allowed the defendant to make such motions as for a new trial[1] or in arrest of judgment.[2] If no such motions are made, or if made, are denied, the next step normally is the rendition of the judgment.

A judgment is an adjudication of the rights and obligations of the parties with specific reference to the fact-situation as it developed at the trial. Occasionally it will be in stages, in some jurisdictions; for example, a determination that the defendant is under obligation to account to the plaintiff, followed by an adjudication that defendant pay plaintiff the amount found due upon such accounting.[3] Again, there may be a preliminary injunction, followed by a dissolution thereof or the determination that the injunction be made permanent.[4]

In law actions, judgments are usually absolute,[5] whereas in

---

[1] 39 Am. Jur. New Trial, § 181.
[2] 30 A Am. Jur. Judgments, § 295.
[3] City of Eureka v. Kansas Elect. Power Co., 133 Kan. 708, 3 P. 2d 484.
[4] Richardson v. Kittlewell, 45 Fla. 551, 33 So. 984.
[5] Coiron v. Millaudon, 19 How. 113 (U.S.).

226

equity actions they may be conditional so as to allow for several possible contingencies.[6] In this way equity avoids piecemeal litigation. Such decrees are of course more difficult to draft than simple law judgments.

A memorandum decision,[7] or an opinion giving reasons for the decision[8] is not a judgment; nor is the minute entry[9] or order for judgment.[10] A mere recital is not sufficient.[11] Findings of fact and conclusions of law do not constitute a judgment.[12]

Unless the litigation culminates in a judgment, there can be no execution issued,[13] no lien exists,[14] and there is nothing from which an appeal may be taken.[15] Nor can the doctrines of res adjudicata[16] or stare decisis[17] be applied in future litigation between the same or other parties.

Forms of judgments in law actions are fairly well standardized, unless there are unusual circumstances.[18] In equity actions, however, there is more room for variation because of the greater flexibility of such actions. Decrees must state precisely what is directed or forbidden, in fairness to the defendant if questions of noncompliance should arise. But law judgments too must be certain, for purposes of enforcement and appeal.[19]

In general, the judgment must correspond to the verdict.[20] Some variation must exist depending upon whether the verdict was general or special, or whether it was general coupled with

---

6 Rutherford v. Haven & Co., 11 Iowa 587.

7 Fleming v. Vander Loo, 160 F. 2d 905.

8 G. Amsinck & Co. v. Springfield Grocer Co., 7 F. 2d 855.

9 Jackman v. North, 398 Ill. 90; 75 N.E. 2d 324.

10 Loper v. Hosier, 148 S.W. 2d 889 (Tex.).

11 Merchants' Southwest Fireproof Whse. Co., 113 Okla. 146, 243 P. 186.

12 G. Amsinck & Co. v. Springfield Grocer Co., supra, n. 8.

13 Barham v. Perry, 205 N.C. 428, 171 S.E. 614; 65 A.L.R. 2d 1162. The judgment may constitute color of title: 71 A.L.R. 2d 404.

14 Lawson v. Jordan, 19 Ark. 297, 70 Am. Dec. 596.

15 Merchants' Southwest Fireproof Whse. Co., supra, n. 11.

16 Arizona Grocery Co. v. Atchison, T. & S.F. R. Co., 284 U.S. 370.

17 Karlen, Primer of Procedure 116.

18 30 A Am. Jur. Judgments, § 56.

19 Barham v. Perry, supra, n. 13.

20 Slocum v. New York Life Ins. Co., 228 U.S. 364.

answers to interrogatories. Normally the parties should be named as in the process and pleadings, and the judgment must show which party prevailed.[21] If the plaintiff is given money damages, the amount must be specified, or the amount must be ascertainable by arithmetical computation.[22] There should be correspondence between figures and amounts written out.[23] The judgment should where necessary to make it understandable specify time, place and the matters in dispute.

A judgment must also be complete, that is, it must include all the issues in the case.[24] Thus, if the right to an injunction and damages are involved, the judgment should specify whether the plaintiff is entitled to both forms of relief, or only one, or neither. Ordinarily the issues must be raised both by the pleadings and the evidence, unless non-pleaded issues are litigated by consent.

Frequently judgments begin with a recital, in summary fashion, of the steps that have been taken, beginning with the service of process and continuing on to the verdict. A personal judgment can only be rendered after personal service or the defendant has appeared generally;[25] in attachment and garnishment, the judgment is limited to the property or funds seized.[26] A recital of service may be relied upon to uphold the judgment as against a collateral attack[27] (as to which, see Section 159) but not as against a direct attack.[28] Recitals may be contradicted by other portions of the record. If there has been a default, the recital should so state.[29] The recital normally indicates when judgment was rendered[30] and signed.[31]

---

21 Ferrell v. Simmons, 63 W. Va. 45, 59 S.E. 752.
22 Hutcheson v. Hutcheson, 197 Ga. 603, 30 S.E. 2d 107; 55 A.L.R. 2d 723.
23 Hays v. Hogan, 273 Mo. 1, 200 S.W. 286.
24 Tumulty v. State, 67 N.J.L. 509, 51 A. 466.
25 Beckman v. Beckman, 258 Mo. 1029, 218 S.W. 2d 566.
26 Pennoyer v. Neff. 95 U.S. 714.
27 Price v. Gunn, 114 Ark. 551, 170 S.W. 247.
28 American Cotton Oil Co. v. House, 153 Miss. 170, 118 So. 722.
29 Goodwater Whse. Co. v. Street, 137 Ala. 621, 34 So. 903.
30 Bevington v. Buck, 18 Ind. 414.
31 Faris v. Burroughs Adding Mach. Co., 48 Ida. 310, 282 P. 72.

It is customary for the successful party to move for judgment, as a reminder to the court.[32] It is not necessary that this motion be in writing. If the judgment is unusual, counsel may submit a form thereof at the time when the motion is made, and be certain that it is signed by the court if acceptable to him, or by the clerk, if that is in accordance with local practice.[33] Opposing counsel should have an opportunity to examine the judgment to enable him to make whatever objections he may have. Objections should be made when the judgment is submitted to the court, and modifications suggested at that time. If overruled, the objecting party may include this matter in his bill of exceptions.

Sometimes an objection may be obviated later by a nunc pro tunc order to make the judgment as written correspond to that actually rendered.[34] But this device may not be used to correct an erroneous ruling by the court.[35] A nunc pro tunc order may be entered only upon notice to the opposing attorney if the error is substantial and does not appear on the face of the record,[36] or if it is made after the term has expired.[37] Defects in judgments are also sometimes deemed inconsequential if other parts of the record supply the deficiencies.[38]

SECTION 154. MOTION FOR ENTRY. The entry of a judgment is important for purposes of proof, should it be necessary to refer back on some future occasion. Also, there may be difficulties in obtaining execution on a judgment which has not been recorded. Hence it is common to find statutes providing for the entry of judgments in certain specified books.[39] Subsequent docketing or indexing or both may be necessary to perfect a lien.[40]

---

[32] Carlson v. Benton, 66 Neb. 486, 92 N.W. 600.
[33] Fairbanks v. Beard, 247 Mass. 8, 141 N.E. 590.
[34] Webb v. Western Reserve Bond & Share Co., 115 Ohio St. 247, 153 N.E. 289.
[35] Hickman v. Ft. Scott, 141 U.S. 415.
[36] Re Reichel, 148 Minn. 433, 182 N.W. 517; 14 A.L.R. 2d 224.
[37] Tyler v. Aspinwall, 73 Conn. 493, 47 A. 755.
[38] Schwab v. Schwab, 255 Ala. 218, 50 So. 2d 435.
[39] 30 A. Am. Jur. Judgments, § 91.
[40] Vanstory v. Thornton. 112 N.C. 196, 17 S.E. 566.

Because of the significance of the entry to the successful party, it is customary in many jurisdictions for counsel of that party orally to move for entry. Ordinarily no notice of the motion need be served upon opposing counsel.[41] If the court refuses to enter judgment, mandamus will ordinarily lie.[42] Conversely, entry may be enjoined by appropriate proceedings, where it is contended that the judgment is erroneous.[43]

Statutes or rules generally specify that the clerk is authorized to enter judgment in certain cases without specific direction by the court, and that in other cases such direction is necessary.[44] Frequently the clerk is authorized to make the entry in cases where the damages are liquidated and the issues are simple.[45] In any event the clerk must be authorized to make the entry either by virtue of a statute or order of the court.[46] If the court makes an order, it may specify the terms under which the entry is made.

At common law, a judgment was entered four days after the return of the verdict. Today the judgment is usually entered as soon as it is rendered.[47] Entry, however, may be made at a subsequent time by means of a nunc pro tunc order, without notice to the parties, if no rights of third persons intervene and if no judicial finding is necessary.[48]

Until a judgment roll is prepared, the clerk's minutes serve as a record of the proceedings. The judgment roll, consisting of the summons, the pleadings, orders, verdict and judgment proper, is usually prepared by the clerk,[49] but in some jurisdictions this

---

41 Re Cook, 77 Cal. 220, 17 P. 923.
42 35 Am. Jur. Mandamus, § 285.
43 Houston, E. & W.T.R. Co. v. Skeeter Bros., 44 Tex. Civ. App. 105, 98 S.W. 1064.
44 30 A Am. Jur. Judgments, § 96.
45 Utah Asso. C.M. v. Bowman, 38 Utah 326, 113 P. 63.
46 Fed. R. Civ. P. 58.
47 30 A Am. Jur. Judgments, § 99.
48 Supra, n. 36.
49 Rockwood v. Davenport, 37 Minn. 533, 35 N.W. 377.

must be done by the attorney for the successful party.[50] The judgment roll should specify the date of the judgment.

SECTION 155. PROCEDURE FOR TAXING COSTS. The procedure for taxing costs, and the items to be included therein, are usually set out in statutes or rules.[51] A bill of costs may be submitted to the court, or to the opposing attorney, along with notice as to the time for settling thereof. Objections to the items may then be made at the hearing. A request is usually made to the clerk to fix costs. In some jurisdictions it is customary for a prayer for relief in the complaint to include the matter of costs.

Costs are usually assessed automatically against the losing party unless some allegedly unnecessary expenses have been incurred by the winning party.[52] If the verdict is only partially favorable, the court has discretion to divide the costs in an equitable manner.[53]

Common items of costs are filing fees, witness fees, expenses involved in printing the record and briefs for an appeal, the charge for certified copies of documents used at the trial, etc. Sometimes the statute specifies an amount which is a percentage of the judgment. Ordinarily, attorney's fees are not included unless by special provision of a statute.[54]

Costs must usually be settled before the judgment is entered.[55]

B. Default

SECTION 156. HOW OBTAINED. Under the early common law, a judgment could be rendered against a defendant only if he was present in court. Later the plaintiff was permitted to enter an appearance for the defendant. Today this formality has been

---

50 Dailey v. Northern New York Utilities, 129 Misc. 183, 221 N.Y.S. 52.
51 49 C.J.S. Judgments, § 78; 57 A.L.R. 2d 1243.
52 As to liability of state for costs, see 72 A.L.R. 2d 1379.
53 Kittredge v. Race, 92 U.S. 116.
54 Rude v. Buchhalter, 286 U.S. 451.
55 Burnham v. Hays, 3 Cal. 115, 58 Am. Dec. 389.

eliminated, and recognition is given to the proposition that jurisdiction of the court over the person of the defendant may be obtained by service of process or voluntary appearance, and that a
judgment may be rendered for either a failure to file an initial
appearance,[56] a failure to plead within a specified time,[57] or a
failure to appear at the trial.[58]

Occasionally a judgment for failure to plead is termed "nil
dicit," to distinguish it from the other types of default.[59] The time
within which to plead is either specified by statute or by an order
of the court in a particular case. A "nil dicit" judgment may be
entered if there has been proper service of process, and the defendant has filed an answer which is sham and false on its face, or where
the court has given the defendant leave to withdraw his answer
and appearance.[60] Such a judgment is not, however, proper where
the defendant has filed an answer which is legally insufficient.[61]

If the defendant has taken some step which in the opinion of
the court constitutes an attack upon the merits of the plaintiff's
claim, it will be deemed a general appearance.[62] In that event the
court has jurisdiction to render a judgment against the defendant
if he fails to appear at the trial.[63] An appearance may also be made
by counsel for the defendant filing a statement to that effect with
the clerk of the court, or in some jurisdictions, by delivering a
notice to the plaintiff's attorney.[64] When such a statement is filed,
defendant's attorney must be served with copies of any subsequent
papers filed by the plaintiff, as well as notice of any motions made

---

[56] N.Y.C.P.A. § 486; Rio Grande Irrig. & Colonization Co. v. Gildersleeve, 174
U.S. 603.
[57] Sporer v. Herlik, 158 Neb. 644, 64 N.W. 2d 342.
[58] N.Y.C.P.A. § 494a; Thomson v. Wooster, 114 U.S. 104.
[59] Clouts v. Spurway, 104 Fla. 340, 139 So. 896.
[60] Hutchinson v. Manchester St. Ry. Co., 173 N.H. 271, 60 A. 1011.
[61] Kansas City Ry. Co. v. Saunders, 98 Ala. 283.
[62] Elliott v. Lawhead, 43 Ohio St. 171, 1 N.E. 577.
[63] Hutchinson v. Manchester St. Ry. Co., supra, n. 60.
[64] Baldwin v. McClelland, 152 Ill. 42, 38 N.E. 143.

by the plaintiff.[65] Before filing such statement counsel should examine the process to determine whether it is proper with respect to content and service, for it would be unavailing to question the jurisdiction of the court over the person of the defendant after an appearance has been filed.

In chancery the analogous judgment was termed "pro confesso," which was properly entered after valid service where the defendant failed to answer the bill which stated a good equitable claim.

If it is the plaintiff who is in default with reference to appearance or pleading, generally the judgment against him is termed a dismissal or a nonsuit, although the defendant may be given a judgment of costs.[66]

There are two stages involved in the entry of a default judgment against the defendant:

1. A determination that the defendant is in default, which fact must appear in the record.[67] While the procedure here varies somewhat from jurisdiction to jurisdiction, it is quite common for the plaintiff to request the clerk to enter such default and to prepare the necessary order. The time when this may be done is usually specified by statute or rule, and generally reference is made therein to the return date.[68] In some instances the entry of default is made by the clerk, while in others it is made by the court. Local practice must therefore be consulted.

2. The determination of the plaintiff's claim. Here again procedure varies. In many jurisdictions a default judgment can be rendered against one who has appeared only after he has been notified of the plaintiff's intention.[69] In some jurisdictions the lack

---

65 Johnson v. Walsh, 65 F. Supp. 157.
66 Parr v. Chittim, 231 S.W. 1079.
67 Fed. R. Civ. P. 55(a); 158 A.L.R. 1104.
68 Murrell v. Rawlings, 170 Ark. 212, 279 S.W. 382.
69 Fed. R. Civ. P. 55(b) (2).

of such notice renders any default judgment void,[70] while in other jurisdictions the judgment is merely voidable.[71] If the defendant is a member of the armed forces, he may have to be represented by counsel under the Soldiers and Sailors Relief Act.[72]

In certain types of cases, particularly those involving liquidated damages, the clerk may be authorized to enter judgment without an order of court.[73] In others, this can be done only upon order, and in this event the plaintiff may be required to "prove-up" his claim.[74] This is usually required where the defendant has denied in his answer the allegations of the complaint, but is not required where the defendant has filed an affirmative defense. A "prove-up" may also be required in certain equity cases such as divorce, to prevent collusion. Since the defendant is in default, he will not be permitted to introduce contradictory evidence as to the merits of the case, and therefore it is usually not difficult for the plaintiff to prove a prima facie case. If the claim is for unliquidated damages, the damages are assessed either by the court or a jury, depending again upon local practice.[75]

While a defendant is not allowed to contest the merits of the plaintiff's claim after he is in default, he may introduce evidence on the issue of damages.[76] Where the defendant has failed to answer, a judgment cannot be entered for more than the plaintiff has demanded, nor can relief other than that requested be granted.[77] A judgment of that nature is invalid as to the excess or different relief. Sometimes the practice of remittitur is applied to this situation to save the judgment from attack. A default judg-

---

70 Bass v. Hoagland, 172 F. 2d 205.

71 U.S. ex rel. Knupfer v. Watkins, 159 F. 2d 675.

72 50 U.S.C.A. Appendix, § 501 et seq.

73 Providence Tool Co. v. Prader, 32 Cal. 634, 91 Am. Dec. 598.

74 Reilly v. Perekinys, 33 N.J. Super. 69, 109 A. 2d 449.

75 Electrolytic Chlorine Co. v. Wallace & T. Co., 328 Mo. 782, 41 S.W. 2d 1049; Pulaski Oil Co. v. Conner, 620 Okla. 211, 162 P. 464.

76 McClelland v. Climax Hosiery Mills, 252 N.Y. 347, 169 N.E. 605.

77 Russell v. Shurtleff, 28 Colo. 414, 65 P. 27.

ment, entered either by the clerk or the court in a proper case is final, and unless other steps are taken by the defendant, may be enforced in the usual manner.[78]

In some jurisdictions a default judgment may not be entered if any motions or demurrers are pending for decision,[79] but in other jurisdictions such a judgment may nevertheless be entered if the time within which to answer has expired.[80]

Although counsel for the plaintiff may be entitled to obtain a default judgment under the facts and the law, he may choose to refrain from doing so, at least for the present. Such action may be due to the fact that defendant has not as yet employed counsel, or because the chances for a satisfactory settlement may be enhanced by such restraint. If the defendant has employed counsel, it may be that it is he who is in default, and professional courtesy may suggest a somewhat lenient approach to the matter. In short, counsel for the plaintiff should explore all aspects of the case before proceeding with the default procedure.

SECTION 157. EFFECT OF. It is sometimes said that the effect of a default is similar to that of a demurrer, i.e., it admits as true all matters of fact well pleaded.[81] Hence, if the complaint does not state a cause of action a default judgment may be at least erroneous and in some cases void. If erroneous, the judgment may be reversed on appeal; if void, it is subject also to a collateral attack. If a complaint is merely defective in form, the default judgment is not subject to attack.

When a claim is for unliquidated damages, a default does not admit the damages alleged in the complaint, and the defendant may submit evidence to show that they are in fact less than claimed. And this is true despite a code provision that facts tend-

---

78 Ueland v. Johnson, 77 Minn. 543, 80 N.W. 700.
79 Johnson v. Sebring, 104 Fla. 584, 140 So. 672.
80 Ann. Cas. 1913 E 332.
81 International Harvester Co. v. Com., 170 Ky. 41, 185 S.W. 102.

ing to mitigate damages must be pleaded, as that provision is not relevant to the situation here discussed.[82] Where the claim is for liquidated damages, the default admits that allegation as well as those giving rise to the cause of action.

A valid default judgment usually has the same effect as a judgment rendered after a trial on the merits, with reference to future litigation between the same parties on the same claim.[83] The plaintiff cannot subsequently sue upon the same claim, for the doctrine of merger applies. The defendant cannot subsequently raise a question as to the merits of the claim, under the doctrine of res adjudicata. As stated in the previous section, a default judgment is final, and appellate remedies are available to the defendant. A judgment which is void or voidable may be attacked in the ways set out in the following section.

SECTION 158. HOW VACATED. In view of the wide variation among the various jurisdictions as to the proper procedure for vacating a default judgment, valid generalizations are difficult to formulate.[84] In this section therefore reference will be made only to a few factors which were of significance under the common-law and equity systems, upon which most of the present statutory procedures are based.

Before noting these factors it may be well to point out that a distinction must be made between setting aside an entry of default and setting aside a default judgment.[85] A motion may be used to set aside a default if it is filed before the entry of judgment. This motion is presented to the court in which the default was entered. Normally a notice thereof must be served upon the adverse party. If the default is set aside, leave may be given defendant to file an answer and the case proceeds to trial in the normal fashion. The

[82] McClelland v. Climax Hosiery Mills, supra, n. 76.
[83] Last Chance Min. Co. v. Tyler Min. Co., 157 U.S. 683; 77 A.L.R. 2d 1410.
[84] 30 A Am. Jur. Judgments, § 636.
[85] Fed. R. Civ. P. 55 (c); Booth v. Central States Mut. Ins. Ass'n, 235 Iowa 5, 15 N.W. 2d 893.

grounds of the motion must be such as to appeal to the discretion of the trial court—that is, some satisfactory explanation for the default must be presented. After a judgment has been entered, it is that which must be vacated.

The factors which determined the mode of vacating a default judgment under early systems were as follows:

1. The nature of the defect. It was common to classify defects into categories which either resulted in the judgment being void or voidable, or which did not affect the validity of the judgment. Those defects which rendered a judgment voidable were called substantive, while those which did not affect the judgment were called formal. The more serious a defect was, the more latitude was allowed in opening up the judgment.[86]

2. The time when the attempt to vacate was made—specifically whether the attack on the judgment was made during the term in which the judgment had been rendered or after the term had expired. It was said that after the term had expired the trial court lost jurisdiction over the subject matter.[87] There were some escapes from this doctrine. In some cases if a matter was presented during the term, the court could still rule thereon after the expiration.[88] Also, some cases recognized a power in the trial court to extend the term by an appropriate order.[89] In some jurisdictions terms of court are abolished and instead specified periods are allowed within which a particular step may be taken.[90] The concept of the term was not taken over by equity but instead that court applied the doctrine of laches, under which all the circumstances were taken into consideration.[91]

---

[86] Grayson v. Stith, 181 Okla. 131, 72 P. 2d 820; 20 A.L.R. 2d 1179; 16 A.L.R. 2d 1139.

[87] Keane v. Allen, 69 Idaho 53, 202 P. 2d 411.

[88] Ferguson v. Sabo, 115 Conn. 619, 162 A. 844; 168 A.L.R. 204.

[89] Zimmern v. U.S., 298 U.S. 167.

[90] Coulter v. Board of Commissioners, 22 N.M. 24, 158 P. 1086.

[91] Williamson v. Hartman, 92 N.C. 236.

3. Whether the defect appeared on the face of the record or de hors the record.[92] This factor also was of particular significance to a law court but not to an equity court.

The most common methods whereby a default judgment could be vacated were: A motion addressed to the trial court, with or without supporting affidavits;[93] a writ of error coram nobis addressed to the same court;[94] a bill of review similarly addressed;[95] a suit in equity, either to enjoin the enforcement of the judgment[96] or to vacate the same,[97] brought either in the same court which rendered the judgment or any other of competent jurisdiction. Many of the statutory procedures are virtually modern counterparts of these earlier remedies.

Where the alleged defect was so serious as to render the judgment void, and was apparent on the face of the record, in law cases the judgment could be set aside on motion during the term, and it would be necessary only to point out the defect. After the term, either a writ of error or a collateral attack (as to which, see the following section) could be employed.

Where the alleged error was not apparent on the face of the record, the trial court could still set aside the judgment during the term, on motion either supported by affidavits or other proof of the defect. After the term a writ of error coram nobis was available, or a separate suit in equity could be brought, setting out the defect.

In equity cases a petition for rehearing could be employed during the term, and a bill of review after the term. Both were addressed to the trial court. The petition for rehearing was analogous to a motion for a new trial. The bill for review could be

---

[92] Magin v. Lamb, 43 Minn. 80, 44 N.W. 675.
[93] Williamson v. Hartman, supra, n. 91.
[94] U.S. v. Mayer, 235 U.S. 55.
[95] Putnam v. Day, 22 Wall. 60 (U.S.).
[96] Fawcett v. Atherton, 298 Mich. 362, 299 N.W. 108.
[97] Magin v. Lamb, supra, n. 92.

used for errors of law that were apparent on the face of the record and for newly discovered evidence. The latter had to be brought in a reasonable time after the trial.

Where the alleged error was such that it would render the judgment voidable, the available devices were the same as those outlined in the preceding paragraph, with these exceptions: A collateral attack was not available; further in the suit in equity, the bill had to set out facts that ordinarily were the basis of equitable relief, such as fraud surprise, mistake, accident, excusable neglect, etc. In some jurisdictions fraud could be set up only if it was extrinsic—such fraud as would deprive the party of a fair trial. There is some difference of opinion as to the facts which would fall into that category. Also, the bill would have to show that there was a good defense to the action. While a technical defense was not tolerated, a defense was recognized though it was only to a part of the cause of action.

The statutory variations of this basic pattern are considerable. In some jurisdictions a judgment void on its face may be vacated, after the term in which it is rendered, by a simple motion;[98] in others, there are special procedures for setting aside judgments based upon constructive notice;[99] sometimes an action to set aside a default judgment may be maintained upon a mere showing of some equitable ground,[100] and sometimes a showing of meritorious defense is alone sufficient;[101] statutes frequently provide that the court may impose conditions, such as the payment of costs, witness fees, etc.[102]

There is general agreement that a court may vacate a judg-

---

[98] Crabtree v. Aetna Life Ins. Co., 341 Mo. 1173, 111 S.W. 2d 103.

[99] Padol v. Home Bank & Trust Co., 108 Ind. App. 401, 27 N.E. 2d 917.

[100] Loew v. Krauspe, 320 Ill. 244, 150 N.E. 683.

[101] Atlantic Dredging & Construction Co. v. Nashville Bridge Co., 57 F. 2d 519; 174 A.L.R. 2d 10.

[102] Gray v. Lawlor, 151 Cal. 352, 90 P. 691; 21 A.L.R. 2d 863.

ment as to some but not all of the parties, providing that the interests of all the parties can be protected.[103]

Some special problems are created when an effort is made to set aside a judgment after the term of office of the judge who entered the judgment has expired. In some jurisdictions the successor judge is deemed to be without authority to vacate the judgment.[104] Likewise, counsel who represent a party after former counsel have withdrawn from a case, with or without notice to the defendant, may encounter difficulties if a judgment was entered because of neglect of the prior attorney of record.[105] Cases involving corporations whose officers were not in fact informed by a statutory agent of litigation in which the corporations are defendants present special difficulties.[106]

Occasionally a party in whose favor a default judgment had been entered will be permitted to have it set aside, unless rights of third parties intervene, if the party seeking relief has been prejudiced by such judgment.[107] As an illustration of prejudice, a case may be cited in which the plaintiff discovered after the judgment had been entered that there was in fact no service of process upon the defendant.[108]

SECTION 159. WHEN COLLATERAL ATTACK IS APPROPRIATE. Attacks upon judgments are usually classified as either direct or collateral. A direct attack has been defined as one provided by law for one specific purpose, such as a motion to vacate, an appeal, an action to set aside, or an action to enjoin enforcement. A collateral attack is conversely one whose chief purpose is not that of vacating a judgment, and is not provided by law for that purpose. If in an action by a purchaser at a judicial sale to recover posses-

---

103 Durre v. Brown, 7 Ind. App. 127, 34 N.E. 577; 42 A.L.R. 2d 1030.
104 Bolton v. State, 223 Ind. 308, 60 N.E. 2d 742; 11 A.L.R. 2d 1117.
105 Heinsius v. Poehlmann, 282 Ill. App. 472.
106 Rollins v. North River Ins. Co., 107 W. Va. 602, 149 S.E. 838.
107 Meyer v. Lemley, 86 Mont. 83, 282 P. 268; 40 A.L.R. 2d 1127.
108 State v. Fishing Appliances, 170 Wash. 426, 16 P. 2d 822.

sion of land, the former owner sets up the invalidity of the sale, because of the invalidity of the judgment under which the sale took place, the action of the former owner would be termed a collateral attack.

A collateral attack may be made on a default judgment only if the court which rendered it lacked jurisdiction over the subject matter of the action[109] or of the person of the defendant[110] or the res involved in the litigation,[111] depending upon the nature of the judgment. If the judgment purportedly was a personal one, jurisdiction over the person of the defendant must have been acquired; whereas if the judgment was purportedly in rem, jurisdiction over the res is sufficient.

Furthermore, for the judgment to be subject to collateral attack, the lack of jurisdiction must be apparent from the face of the record.[112] If both of these requirements are not present, the judgment is said to be void on its face. A judgment void on its face may be set aside at any time,[113] whereas a judgment whose invalidity is not apparent may be set aside only by a direct attack and in a prescribed period.[114] In neither instance is it necessary to rely on surprise, mistake, etc. nor is it necessary to show that there is a meritorious defense.[115] The fact that a complaint does not state a cause of action does not permit a collateral attack as the significant question concerns jurisdiction of the court.[116] Also, the fact that the wrong venue was employed does not affect the validity of the judgment.[117]

The above comments are made particularly with reference to

---

109 Tooley v. Comm'r. of Internal Revenue, 121 F. 2d 350.
110 Warmsprings Irr. Dist. v. May, 117 F. 2d 802.
111 Fall v. Eastin, 215 U.S. 1.
112 Jelliffe v. Thaw, 67 F. 2d 880.
113 New Jersey Cash Credit Corp. v. Zaccaria, 126 N.J. Law 334, 19 A. 2d 448.
114 Guyan Machinery Co. v. Premier Coal Co., 291 Ky. 84, 163 S.W. 2d 284.
115 Dewell v. Suddick, 211 Iowa 1312, 232 N.W. 118.
116 In re Keet's Estate, 15 Cal. 2d 328, 100 P. 2d 1045.
117 Gilbert v. Nantucket Bank, 5 Mass. 97.

domestic judgments and are not applicable to foreign judgments. Judgments of sister states are placed substantially in the same category as domestic judgments by virtue of the Full Faith and Credit Clause of the Federal Constitution. This matter is considered further in Section 164.

C. Miscellaneous

SECTION 160. JUDGMENT BY CONFESSION—HOW OBTAINED. In certain situations such as the loan of a sum of money, it may be advisable for the lender to require the borrower to execute a special type of instrument popularly referred to as a cognovit note. In this instrument the borrower executes a power of attorney to any member of the bar to enter judgment against him without service of process and confesses the existence of the claim against him.

Before attempting to use such an instrument in a particular transaction, counsel should consult the statutory and case law of the jurisdiction where the transaction takes place, and also where the borrower is domiciled. Some jurisdictions have held such instruments to be invalid as against public policy.[118] And in those jurisdictions which sanction the use of such instruments, such use is generally minutely regulated.[119] Hence the statutory requirements must be scrupulously followed in the execution of the instrument. The instrument must be clear and not subject to misunderstanding, and must contain a complete statement of all details of the transaction.[120] If the instrument is executed by a partner or an officer of a corporation, the usual authorization should be obtained.[121]

Similarly, the statutory procedure for entering judgment

---

[118] Farquhar v. De Haven, 70 W. Va. 738, 75 S.E. 65.
[119] 30 A Am. Jur. Judgments, § 171.
[120] Spence v. Emerine, 46 Ohio St. 433, 21 N.E. 866.
[121] Dahlstrom v. Walker, 33 Idaho 374, 194 P. 847.

should be followed very carefully. The statute may require the filing of a complaint and an affidavit of genuineness of the defendant's signature, as well as the filing of the cognovit note itself.[122] In some jurisdictions the entire procedure is supervised by the clerk, while in others the court has to examine the documents and approve the entry of judgment.[123]

The statute may provide the manner in which such a judgment may be vacated and the time within which this may be done.[124] In the absence of such provisions, such judgment is subject to the usual methods of attack, such as a motion to vacate or requesting a stay of execution. Obviously in this type of judgment, the grounds of attack are much more limited than in one requiring service of process.[125] In a sense any judgment entered is interlocutory until the time to vacate has expired. Generally this is no great hardship upon the creditor as the judgment is entered largely for security purposes and not with a view to immediate collection.

SECTION 161. DECLARATORY JUDGMENT PROCEDURE. Relief analogous to that afforded by declaratory judgment procedure was available in the early equity system. Suits to remove a cloud from title, to quiet title, quia timet, to cancel an instrument, or to interpret a will are some of the more common types of relief which are illustrative of this general category. Equity, however, did not provide relief in many other similar situations, and hence legislation was needed to supply the deficiency. Today over half the states have adopted the Uniform Declaratory Judgment Act,[126] and a federal statute provides for similar relief.[127] A number of

---

122 Rogers v. Cherrier, 75 Wis. 54, 43 N.W. 828.
123 Deibert v. Rhodes, 291 Pa. 550, 140 A. 515.
124 State Bank of Blue Island v. Kott, 323 Ill. App. 27, 54 N.E. 2d 897.
125 Knoettner v. Integrity Corp. of N.J., 109 N.J. Law 186, 160 A. 527.
126 62 Harv. L. Rev. 782, 791.
127 28 U.S.C.A. § 2201.

other states have legislation which is somewhat more restrictive than the Uniform Act, as will be noted below.

Declaratory judgment actions are advisable where the immediate problem can be solved by a judicial declaration of rights and obligations, where there is some dispute as to such rights and obligations, and where further relief is either not available or not necessary. Thus, the action may be used to test the validity of legislation[128] or an administrative ruling[129] *prior* to embarking on a course of conduct. Also, the legal effect of a contract may be determined if there is a difference of opinion concerning it.[130] In such instances the parties are often willing to abide by a decision of the court and they can do so safely because the decision is final and res adjudicata as to the issues involved.[131]

It is obvious that such procedure is often of more practical value than the procedure involved in usual litigation, as it is not necessary to wait until harm is caused or even threatened. The courts in the exercise of their discretion have generally refused to grant declaratory relief in negligence cases, although even in those cases there would seem to be instances where such relief would be desirable and appropriate.[132]

Before declaratory relief will be afforded, it is generally required that there be a genuine controversy.[133] But there is some difference of opinion as to how far one must go in pressing or resisting a claim in order to present a controversy. The Uniform Act does not require, however, that the plaintiff be entitled to coercive relief;[134] there need be no showing that there has been an actual invasion of the plaintiff's rights, nor that there is a lawsuit

128 United Public Workers of America v. Mitchell, 330 U.S. 75.

129 New York Foreign Trade Zone Operators, Inc. v. State Liquor Authority, 285 N.Y. 272, 34 N.E. 2d 316.

130 Aetna Life Ins. Co. v. Haworth, 300 U.S. 227.

131 De Charette v. St. Matthews Bank & T. Co., 214 Ky. 400, 283 S.W. 410.

132 16 Am. Jur. Declaratory Judgments, § 17.

133 Ashwander v. T.V.A., 297 U.S. 288.

134 Woollard v. Schaffer Stores Co., 273 N.Y. 527, 5 N.E. 2d 829.

pending. Under the Uniform Act the plaintiff may however demand coercive relief as well as a declaration of his rights,[135] or a declaratory action may be followed up with an action in which coercive relief is demanded. In other words, under the Uniform Act it is of no significance that the plaintiff could or could not maintain an action for coercive relief. Under some other statutes the plaintiff must show that he could not sue for damages, or for an injunction, or some similar relief.[136]

The requirement of an existing controversy precludes the use of the declaratory judgment procedure merely to obtain an advisory opinion,[137] or where the question is moot or academic.[138] Because of this requirement, declaratory judgment legislation is now held valid, presenting as it does questions proper for judicial determination.[139]

Some courts require, in addition to a genuine controversy, that the declaratory judgment action may not be maintained unless the action will result in a termination of the controversy.[140] This requirement also has been variously interpreted.

The procedure in a declaratory judgment action is usually similar to any other civil action.[141] In his complaint the plaintiff should clearly state the nature of his claim. If the case involves, for example, a contract between the parties, the pertinent part thereof should be set out verbatim, along with the plaintiff's interpretation. The answer should set out how the defendant construes the contract. If the plaintiff desires relief in addition to a declaration as to his rights, the complaint should state specifically the nature of such relief. This may include the extraordinary legal remedies

---

135 87 A.L.R. 1247; 101 A.L.R. 691.
136 Brindley v. Meara, 209 Ind. 144, 198 N.E. 301
137 Coffman v. Breeze Corp., 323 U.S. 316.
138 Pub. Serv. Comm. v. Wycoff Co., 344 U.S. 237.
139 Washington-Detroit Theater Co. v. Moore, 249 Mich. 673, 229 N.W. 618.
140 Pitzer v. City of East Chicago, 222 Ind. 93, 51 N.E. 2d 479.
141 16 Am. Jur. Declaratory Judgments, § 51.

or equitable remedies. If the defendant desires affirmative relief, he may so state in a counterclaim.

Under the terms of the Uniform Act, the plaintiff must join as parties all persons who have or claim an interest that would be affected by the litigation, and the usual distinction between proper and necessary parties is made by the courts.[142] In a proper case the action may be maintained as a class action.[143]

Statutes usually provide for jury trials if there are disputed questions of fact, the same as if coercive relief were sought.[144] In some jurisdictions, however, declaratory relief will be denied under those circumstances.[145] Further, if equitable relief is also sought, in some jurisdictions no jury trial may be had as a matter of right.[146]

Generally, for purposes of venue, a distinction is made between in rem and in personam actions, with the former considered as local in nature,[147] whereas the latter are deemed to be transitory.[148] Actions involving title to land are usually classified as local, and must be brought in the county where the land is situated.

The usual statute of limitations obviously is not applicable to a situation where the defendant has committed no act which would give rise to an action for coercive relief. But if coercive relief is available, the action, though for declaratory relief only, must be brought within the statutory period.[149]

Appellate procedure is normally the same as in cases where coercive relief only is requested.[150]

---

[142] Uniform Declaratory Judgments Act, § 11.
[143] Wilson v. Beebe, 99 F. Supp. 418.
[144] Uniform Declaratory Judgments Act, § 9.
[145] Transport Oil Co. v. Bush, 114 Cal. App. 152, 1 P. 2d 1060.
[146] State Farm Mut. Auto. Ins. Co. v. Massey, 195 F. 2d 56.
[147] De Charette v. St. Matthews Bk. & Trust Co., supra, n. 131.
[148] State ex rel. Toberman v. Cook, 281 S.W. 2d 777 (Mo.)
[149] Maguire v. Hibernia Savings & Loan Soc., 29 Cal. 2d 719, 146 P. 2d 673.
[150] Uniform Declaratory Judgments Act, § 7.

SECTION 162. SUMMARY JUDGMENT PROCEDURE. Statutes or rules in about half of the states and in the federal system now provide for a summary judgment.[151] This procedure is designed to relieve court dockets of congestion by eliminating cases wherein there is clearly no valid claim or no valid defense. Although originally designed as a substitute for a motion to strike sham defenses, it has served other purposes as well. By sifting out cases where the facts are not in issue, the procedure provides an opportunity to settle disputed issues of law without the necessity of a full dress trial. The procedure also serves as a discovery device, for the adverse party is required to disclose the true basis of his claim or defense, and what evidence will be relied upon to support the same. The objection aganist a fishing expedition is met by the fact that the moving party also has to disclose much the same information as does the adverse party.

Summary judgment procedure has been upheld against the charge that the practice is unconstitutional in that it deprives a party of a right of trial by jury.[152] The rationale of such a position is that the trial court is not deciding disputed issues of fact, but is merely determining whether such issues exist. But the courts go beyond the paper issues, and it is no longer sufficient to withstand a summary judgment that such issues are presented by the pleadings.[153] If a true issue of fact is present, the summary judgment is denied and the case is tried with a jury.

There is considerable variation among the jurisdictions as to the type of case in which the summary judgment procedure may be used.[154] Originally, it was limited to cases of collection of monies due on commercial paper. In many jurisdictions it is per-

---

[151] Vanderbilt, Minimum Standards for Judicial Administration 219.

[152] General Insurance Co. v. Interborough Rapid Transit Co., 235 N.Y. 216, 139 N.E. 216.

[153] Dwvan v. Massarene, 199 App. Div. 872, 192 N.Y.S. 577.

[154] 49 C.J.S. Judgments, § 220.

mitted in any case.[155] Jurisdictions specify types of cases falling between these two extremes, but in any event the procedure is limited to civil cases. There is a similar difference of opinion as to the use of summary judgment procedure where counterclaims are filed.[156]

A like difference exists among the various jurisdictions as to the party who may move for a summary judgment. As stated above, originally this device was available only to the plaintiff, but present statutes or rules generally provide that the motion may also be made by the defendant.[157] Some jurisdictions allow a defendant to move on the basis of a counterclaim just as a plaintiff may on the basis of a claim. The court may grant the motion as to the excess or it may reserve its decision until after a trial of the issues.

In most jurisdictions providing for a summary judgment procedure, a judgment may be entered against the movant without the necessity of a countermotion by the adverse party.[158] Hence it is advisable to move only if counsel is satisfied that his claim or defense cannot, on the facts, be repudiated.

Jurisdictions vary as to the time when the motion for summary judgment may be made. In some, a plaintiff may move at any time after the defendant has appeared,[159] in others, any time after a defendant has answered,[160] and in still others at any time after the issues have been joined.[161] A defendant may usually move as soon as the complaint is filed.[162]

---

155 Fed. R. Civ. P. 56.

156 Smith v. Cranleigh, Inc., 224 App. Div. 376, 231 N.Y.S. 201; Dell 'Osso v. Everett, 119 Misc. 502, 197 N.Y.S. 423.

157 Banco de Espana v. Federal Reserve Bank of N.Y., 28 F. Supp. 958.

158 Bd. of Education of Union Free School District No. 3, Town of Huntington, Suffolk County, to Use and Benefit of Stickley Mfg. Co. v. American Bonding Co. of Baltimore, 177 Misc. 341, 30 N.Y.S. 2d 428.

159 Conn. Prac. Bk. 1934, p. 34, § 53.

160 N.Y.C.P. Rule 113.

161 Mich. Stat. Ann. Henderson, 1936, § 27. 989.

162 Fed. R. Civ. p. 56 (b).

According to the statutes or rules in some jurisdictions a summary judgment may be entered as to some but not all of the paper issues.[163] Thus, if in an action to recover for personal injuries there is in fact no dispute as to damages, the case may proceed to trial on the issue of liability alone.

Counsel wishing to move for a summary judgment should support the motion with affidavits to be executed by persons having personal knowledge of the facts. Evidential facts must be set out.[164] Conclusions of law are to be avoided.[165] If any of the evidence is of a documentary nature, certified copies thereof should also be filed.[166]

It is a common practice today to precede the filing of a motion for summary judgment with the employment of whatever discovery devices are available in the jurisdiction and appropriate to the particular case. Information thus derived, as, for example, in depositions or answers to interrogatories may be used to further support the motion. Counsel opposing the motion may attack the motion or affidavits as not complying with the requirements, or he may file counter-affidavits stating his client's version of the facts. Discovery devices may also be available to the defendant.

The court then, on the basis of the papers presented, makes a determination as to whether an issue of fact exists. If no counter-affidavit is filed, this may be considered as an admission of the truth of the averments in the affidavits of the moving party, unless the absence of such counter-affidavit is satisfactorily explained.[167] On the other hand, a counter-affidavit which simply denies the allegations in the original affidavit may be deemed insufficient.[168]

---

163 Reid v. Reid, 170 Misc. 719, 10 N.Y.S. 2d 916.

164 Jameson v. Jameson, 176 F. 2d 58.

165 Schau v. Morgan, 241 Wis. 334, 6 N.W. 2d 212.

166 Otis Elevator Co. v. American Surety Co. of N.Y., 314 Ill. App. 479, 41 N.E. 2d 987.

167 Wilkinson v. Powell, 149 F. 2d 335.

168 Frick Co. v. Rubel Corp., 62 F. 2d 768.

There is some question also whether a denial of information sufficient to form a belief is adequate to defeat the motion.[169] There is a wide difference of opinion among courts as to what data is or is not sufficient to grant the motion, and counsel must act in accordance with the trend of the decisions in his own jurisdiction.

Generally appeals are provided for by statute or rule, but these are normally granted only if the motion is sustained.[170] Overruling the motion is not usually considered as a final order and hence is not appealable at that time. But counsel may, upon being overruled, usually renew the motion after furnishing additional data.

Section 163. Procedure for obtaining an injunction. In cases where threatened action by the defendant is likely to cause irreparable harm to the plaintiff, the latter may obtain a temporary restraining order.[171] The hearing may be ex parte, that is, without notice to the defendant, but the order will be in effect only long enough to give notice to the defendant so that a full hearing may be had.[172] The restraining order may usually be obtained by filing a petition and supporting affidavits.[173] At the second hearing, the court may grant a temporary injunction, usually upon filing by the plaintiff of a bond indemnifying the defendant, upon facts which warrant such an order.[174] The temporary injunction is also for a specified period, and will continue in effect during that period unless dissolved by the court on motion of the defendant.[175] If the plaintiff wishes to have the injunction made permanent, a petition to that effect is filed, notice served upon

---

[169] Doniger v. Lasoff, 125 Misc. 838, 211 N.Y.S. 486.

[170] Fisher v. Sun Underwriters Ins. Co. of N.Y., 55 R.I. 175, 179 A. 702.

[171] Fort v. Co-operative Farmers Exchange, 81 Colo. 431, 256 P. 319.

[172] State ex rel. Cook v. District Court of Ninth Judicial District in and for Glacier County, 105 Mont. 72, 69 P. 2d 746.

[173] Giordano v. Asbury Park & Ocean Grove Bank, 102 N.J. Eq. 64, 139 A. 881.

[174] Utah Radio Products Co. v. Boudette, 69 F. 2d 973.

[175] Boatmen's Nat. Bk. of St. Louis v. Cantwell, 161 S.W. 2d 431 (Mo.).

the defendant and a hearing held on petition and answer, if one has been filed.[176] At the third hearing the injunction is either dissolved or is made permanent.

D. Enforcement

SECTION 164. IN STATE OTHER THAN WHERE OBTAINED. A judgment obtained in a state court may not be directly enforced against the defendant in another state.[177] The traditional method of enforcement therefore involved bringing an action in the second state based upon the judgment, proceeding to judgment and then using procedures available in the second state to enforce the judgment there obtained.[178] Unless changed by statute, this is still the only method available.

To the action on the judgment the defendant may set up as defenses only lack of jurisdiction of the subject matter or of the person of the defendant on the part of the court that rendered the judgment,[179] or fraud in the procurement of the judgment.[180] In either case this constitutes a collateral attack as that term was defined in Section 159. It is not at all clear as to what constitutes fraud in the procurement of the judgment, and whether it constitutes a defense or grounds for affirmative relief only in the state which rendered the judgment. Generally speaking the fraud must go to the acquisition of jurisdiction or it must have been such as to prevent the defendant from setting up available defenses to the original action.[181] In many code states combining legal and equitable procedural rules this type of fraud may be set up as a defense.

If the judgment debtor has assets in another state, the attach-

---

176 Pilcher v. Stadler, 276 Ky. 450, 124 S.W. 2d 475; People v. Henriques & Co. 267 N.Y. 398, 196 N.E. 304.

177 Cole v. Cunningham, 133 U.S. 107.

178 Boston India Rubber Factory v. Hoit, 14 Vt. 92.

179 Thompson v. Whitman, 18 Wall. 457 (U.S.).

180 Levin v. Gladstein, 142 N.C. 482, 55 S.E. 371.

181 Britton v. Gannon, 285 P. 2d 407 (Okla.).

ment and garnishment procedures may be employed to collect the judgment. Normally attachment is limited to situations where the assets are tangibles, and garnishment is available where assets are intangibles. It is not necessary to obtain service of process upon the judgment debtor in the state where he has assets, but enforcement is limited to the assets found in the second state.[182] If the judgment debtor is likely to transfer his assets outside the state in which the judgment was originally obtained, the transfer may be enjoined or a receiver may be appointed.[183] After transfer, if it can be shown that it was executed for the purposes of avoiding payment of the judgment, a creditor's bill is probably the most effective remedy.[184]

A somewhat more expeditious procedure for enforcement of a judgment in a state other than that in which it was obtained is found in the Uniform Enforcement of Foreign Judgments Act. This act, or one similar to it, has been adopted in about eight states. Under this act, a judgment may be "registered" by means of petition and service of process must be had personally or by registered mail at the last known address if personal service cannot be had. The only real advance from the traditional feature is the speeding up of the procedure for obtaining the second judgment.

The simplest procedure of all is that found in the federal system. An Act of Congress[185] provides, in brief, that a judgment rendered in one district may be registered in any other district, and enforcement may then be had directly in the second district. Registration of a judgment in a district has the same effect as a judgment originally rendered in that district.

In any procedure, it is important to designate the parties in

---

182 Harris v. Balk, 198 U.S. 215.
183 Boston Sheridan Co. v. Sheridan Motor Car Co., 244 Mass. 425, 138 N.E. 806.
184 Fed. R. Civ. P. 18 (b).
185 28 U.S.C.A. § 1963.

the same way so as to show identity. Identity of names gives rise to a presumption of identity of parties.

SECTION 165. ENJOINING ENFORCEMENT. A judgment debtor against whose property an execution is about to be levied may, under statutory procedure claim his exemptions.[186] This usually involves an appraisement of the debtor's property[187] and selection by him of those items, up to the maximums exemption allowed, which he claims are exempt.[188] Also, in most jurisdictions the judgment debtor is allowed to retain possession of property otherwise subject to execution by executing a bond which meets the requirements of the statute.[189]

In addition to the above, the judgment debtor has, in certain circumstances, two other procedures available to him. These are: 1. Staying execution;[190] 2. an independent action to enjoin the enforcement of the judgment.[191] Execution may be stayed for such grounds as fraud, lack of jurisdiction,[192] or irregularity in the issuance of the writ of execution.[193] Ordinarily the lack of jurisdiction must appear on the face of the record. It must be shown that other grounds could not have been raised prior to the rendition of the judgment. It is generally a matter of discretion whether a stay should be granted,[194] and the court may require the judgment debtor to execute a bond in favor of the plaintiff[195] before such stay will be granted. If no bond is required, the plaintiff may obtain an order prohibiting the defendant from transferring his property during the period the stay is in effect.

---

[186] 35 C.J.S. Exemptions, § 119.
[187] Ibid. § 137.
[188] Ibid. § 136.
[189] Gordon v. Johnston 4 La. 304.
[190] Augustine v. Augustine, 291 Pa. 15, 139 A. 585.
[191] State v. Gaudet, 108 La. 601, 32 So. 328.
[192] Gravette v. Malone, 54 Ala. 19.
[193] Lewis v. Linton, 207 Pa. 320, 56 A. 874.
[194] Lineker v. Dillon, 275 F. 460.
[195] Sweigard v. Consumer's Ice Mfg. & Coal Co., 198 Pa. 253, 48 A. 495.

An independent action to enjoin enforcement of a judgment may be maintained if there has been extrinsic or collateral fraud in the case.[196] The fraud must have been such as to prevent the defendant from making a full and fair defense, as for example, inducing defendant not to testify by a false promise to compromise. In some jurisdictions even intrinsic fraud has been held to be sufficient grounds to enjoin enforcement, if the result probably would have been different absent the fraud.[197] The most common illustration of intrinsic fraud is that of perjury on the part of witnesses.

SECTION 166. ENTERING SATISFACTION OF JUDGMENT ON THE RECORD. After a judgment has been satisfied, the judgment debtor should obtain a receipt for the payment, either from the judgment creditor, his attorney, or a court officer, depending upon local practice. In addition, the satisfaction should be entered in the judgment record in accordance with statutory procedure. This step is very important as it serves to release the judgment lien on property of the defendant. If the defendant is engaged in a business enterprise, his credit rating may be adversely affected by a judgment not satisfied, and in any event transfer of the property is well nigh impossible as long as the judgment remains a lien against it. Further, entering satisfaction prevents the possibility, admittedly remote, of attempts to again enforce the judgment.

---

196 Cohen v. Randall 137 F. 2d 441.
197 Fiske v. Buder, 125 F.2d 841.

Chapter 13

Trends in Litigation

SECTION 167. CRITICISM OF TRIAL PROCEDURE. The traditional mode of conducting trials has been subject to attack for many years. The attack has been directed principally at three features, which, while they are not present in all lawsuits, occur with sufficient frequency to be a cause for concern.

First, there is dissatisfaction with the fact that in many instances too much time is consumed in coming to issue; that many cases that have reached the trial stage are not tried until several years thereafter; that many cases, particularly those tried to the jury, require an inordinate length of time to try.

Attorneys report a considerable number of instances where one or both parties die before the case is tried; where witnesses move and their whereabouts cannot be ascertained; and, where witnesses, when found, are reluctant to testify to an occurrence far in the past; where medical or business records are destroyed after a period of years. The result may be that a litigant, after waiting many years, may be ultimately deprived of his day in court, or compensation may be made too late to serve the purpose for which it has been designed.

Second, the cost of litigation is often prohibitive if it is to be chiefly borne by the litigants. The investigative process, employ-

255

ing, as it frequently does, modern scientific techniques and discovery devices, can be both time consuming and costly. Fees paid to experts are often quite substantial. Since many of these expenses are relatively stable and do not vary with the amount in controversy, many small claims are never pressed.

Third, there are reported cases where a judgment is not in accord with the merits. This may result because of the ineptness of counsel, because of archaic rules of evidence or trial procedure, because of a judge who is prejudiced or unskilled, or because of a jury whose verdict is dictated by passion rather than the evidence. In addition, some attorneys apparently interpret the adversary system as an authorization to use any tactic that will result in ultimate victory for their clients.

In the following sections attention is directed to some of the recent developments directed at the objectionable aspects of litigation.

SECTION 168. COMPULSORY ARBITRATION. Probably the most drastic "remedy" for the deficiencies in the judicial process is that embodied in a rule found in a few jurisdictions, requiring parties in certain types of cases, to submit their disputes to a board of arbitrators.[1] An appeal to the courts is provided for. If this procedure proves to be successful, its use will undoubtedly spread in the immediate future.

SECTION 169. SEPARATE TRIALS FOR ISSUES OF LIABILITY AND DAMAGES. A few jurisdictions have recently introduced another innovation in trial practice, namely, the separation for trial of the issues of liability and damages.[2] Where this practice prevails, the damage issue is seldom litigated once the liability issue is decided in favor of the plaintiff. Some plaintiff's lawyers favor the practice, being of the opinion that settlements are higher where liability is established; others are opposed to the separation as it

---

[1] Application of Smith, 381 Pa. 223, 112 A. 2d 625.
[2] 85 A.L.R. 2d 9.

reduces the chances of a favorable verdict where the proof of liability is weak and the proof of damages is strong.

SECTION 170. WAIVER OF JURY TRIAL. Under traditional practice, if a case was properly triable by jury, it was tried by a jury unless counsel expressly agreed to a trial to the court. Under modern procedure, the situation is reversed; parties are not entitled to a trial by jury unless a proper and timely demand for a jury trial is made.[3] Furthermore, the tendency is to shorten the time within which the demand may be made.

SECTION 171. UNANIMITY. At common law all twelve jurors had to concur in a verdict or it would not be received. In a growing number of jurisdictions, constitutions have been amended to allow reception of a verdict concurred in by a given fraction of the jury.[4]

SECTION 172. ALTERNATE JURORS. At common law it was necessary to declare a mistrial if one of the twelve jurors, due to health or other reasons, was released from jury duty prior to the rendition of a verdict. In many jurisdictions this result is avoided by the use of one or two alternate jurors who sit through the entire proceedings and take the place of a juror who has been dismissed.[5]

SECTION 173. SELECTION OF JURORS. Where the process of selecting a jury is solely in the control of counsel, almost as much time may be spent in that process as is spent in all the other stages of the trial combined. Further, many attorneys have converted this process into a vehicle for conditioning the jury or for suggesting that the case be pre-judged on the basis of counsels' statements. For these and other reasons, in some jurisdictions the control of the process has now been placed in the judge who alone conducts the voir dire examination.[6]

---

[3] Fed. R. Civ. P. 38 (d).
[4] N.Y. Const. Art. 1, Sec. 2.
[5] Fed. R. Civ. P. 47 (b); 84 A.L.R. 2d 1288.
[6] Fed. R. Civ. P. 47 (a).

SECTION 174. STANDARDIZED INSTRUCTIONS. Where the traditional form of conducting trials obtains, it is not uncommon for counsel to submit fifty or more instructions to the court. Not only does this practice require much time of counsel in the preparation of the instructions, but also the time of the court in determining their correctness. In addition, the jury is more likely confused than aided by great numbers of instructions. At the same time the giving or refusing of tendered instructions constitutes one of the principal sources of reversible error. Hence a number of jurisdictions have adopted the use of pattern or standardized instructions.[7]

Under the revised practice, general instructions referring to frequently recurring subjects, as definitions of negligence, proximate cause, burden of proof and the like, are prepared by committees of the bar or bench, and approved by the highest appellate tribunal in the jurisdiction. After publication, such instructions are merely referred to by number.

SECTION 175. USE OF RECORDING DEVICES. If the court reporter takes shorthand notes, and dies or becomes incapacitated before he has transcribed his notes there is no record upon which to base an appeal. A new trial is the only solution to the problem. In some jurisdictions electronic recording devices have been used effectively under such circumstances. Normally such devices simply supplement, rather than supplant the time-honored method of recording trial proceedings.

Such recording devices have also been used, with consent of counsel, to play back instructions where requested by the jury during the period they are deliberating upon a verdict. The manner in which the instructions are given, which may be a significant factor in the jury's deliberations, is thus faithfully reproduced.

SECTION 176. PLEADINGS AND DISCOVERY TECHNIQUES. Under

---

7 "Standard Jury Instructions," 98 U. Pa. L. Rev. 223.

common-law, equity and code systems, pleadings were relied upon rather heavily to apprise the opposing party of the nature of the claim or defense. In some actions, as for defamation, much detail had to be supplied; in others, as the common counts, generalities were sufficient. Where modern discovery techniques have been adopted, a greater degree of generalization in pleadings in all types of actions is usually permitted.[8]

Since the discovery techniques enable counsel not only to know the nature of the claim or defense in advance of trial, but also how opposing counsel intends to prove his contentions, the element of surprise does not play the important role in trials it once did. For example, it is quite uncommon today to observe the sudden and dramatic appearance, at the close of the trial, of the "star witness," whose testimony completely demolishes the case of the opposition.

SECTION 177. PARTIAL NEW TRIAL AND JUDGMENT NOTWITHSTANDING THE VERDICT. Traditional practice rules required a new trial on all the issues, if a new trial was to be had. In some jurisdictions, a new trial may be had on only some of the issues, if the court determines that a reconsideration of the entire case is not necessary.[9]

Furthermore, rules in a number of jurisdictions allow an appellate court, where it determines that a verdict should have been directed for the party against whom the verdict was returned, to enter a judgment contrary to the verdict.[10] This pracice is designed to reduce the number of new trials and thus speed up the process of litigation.

---

[8] Fed. R. Civ. P. 8 (a).
[9] Coll v. Sherry, 29 N.J. 166, 148 A. 2d 481.
[10] Fed. R. Civ. P. 50 (b).

Index